ITALY AND ENGLISH LITERATURE 1764-1930

ITALY AND ENGLISH LITERATURE 1764–1930

Kenneth Churchill

BARNES & NOBLE BOOKS
TOTOWA, NEW JERSEY

First Published in the U.S.A. 1980 by
BARNES & NOBLE BOOKS
81, Adams Drive, Totowa,
New Jersey, 07512
ISBN 0 – 06 – 491130 – 6
LCN 79 – 55524

Printed in Hong Kong

British Library Cataloguing in Publication Data

Churchill, Kenneth
   Italy and English literature, 1764–1930
   1. English literature – Italian influences
   I. Title
   820'.9   PR408.I/

   ISBN 0-333-26444-4

Contents

Preface

This book began one morning in Rome in front of the statute of Byron in the Villa Borghese gardens. A sympathy with Byron's description of Rome as 'my country! city of the soul!' led to thinking of what other English writers had made of Italy; to pondering particularly on the total reversal of attitudes to ancient Rome between Gibbon and Lawrence and wondering whether there was an organic development of English literary attitudes to Italy between these two extremes. If one traced the appearance of Italy in English literature chronologically through two centuries, would one be able to examine in detail the working of a literary tradition; and see how each writer develops out of, and contributes to, the available picture of Italy? Would the study of literary change in this local case offer suggestive perspectives onto the overall movement of English literature in the period? Would it offer a means of arguing the quality of writers who seem commonly underrated (Byron, Ruskin) and many of whose strengths were particularly associated with Italy; or a new way of looking at the work of others, notably Lawrence? And would an historical examination of the growth of some of the assumptions about Italy that we normally assimilate synchronically from our literature help analyse one's own feelings for the endless fascination of Italy and its perennial imaginative necessity to the northerner?

In doing this work my own answers to all these questions have been positive, and I hope that the reader who bears the questions in mind while reading the book may share the feeling that just as so many English writers found sources of vitality in Italy so we can find stimulating patterns in their work by exploring in it part of our inherited creative debt to Italy.

In seeking to establish these patterns the main emphasis is naturally on those English writers who have written most interestingly about Italy. The works of lesser writers have been mentioned when they serve to illustrate conventional attitudes from (or against) which more important work developed; a great many works do not merit even this degree of attention, and are listed in the bibliography for the reader who wishes to explore further these particular byways of literature. Foreign writers, and workers in the other arts, are included only when their work contributed so significantly to the English literary apprehension of Italy that the picture would be incomplete without them.

In its first form this book was a Ph.D. thesis in the University of Cambridge, and I am most grateful to Professor Graham Hough for his clear yet kindly supervision of its progress. An earlier version of the chapter on Byron appeared in *The Literary Half-Yearly* (Mysore) and I am grateful to the editor, Professor H. H. Anniah Gowda for his permission to reprint it here.

The author and publishers wish to thank the following who have kindly given permission for the use of copyright material: Edward Arnold (Publishers) Ltd for the extracts from *A Room with a View* and *Where Angels Fear to Tread* by E. M. Forster; Oxford University Press for the extracts from *Browning's Major Poetry* by Ian Jack; and Laurence Pollinger Ltd and Viking Penguin Inc, on behalf of the Estate of the late Mrs Frieda Lawrence Ravagli, for extracts from *The Rainbow, Sea and Sardinia, Aaron's Rod, The Lost Girl, Twilight in Italy, Etruscan Places, Phoenix, The Complete Poems of D. H. Lawrence* and *The Collected Letters of D. H. Lawrence*.

April 1979   K. G. CHURCHILL

1 From Addison to Gibbon

Could Nature's bounty satisfy the breast,
The sons of Italy were surely blest . . .
But small the bliss that sense alone bestows,
And sensual bliss is all the nation knows.
In florid beauty groves and fields appear,
Man seems the only growth that dwindles here.
Contrasted faults through all his manners reign,
Though poor, luxurious, though submissive, vain,
Though grave, yet trifling, zealous, yet untrue,
And even in penance planning sins anew.
All evils here contaminate the mind,
That opulence departed leaves behind.

These lines are from Goldsmith's *The Traveller*, published in 1764, a convenient focal year for the commencement of our study. Quoted thus in isolation, the passage epitomises the contemptuous attitude of the English Grand Tourists to what they supposed to be the modern Italian character. From Chaucer to Milton contemporary Italy had been a recurrent stimulus to English poetic achievement, whether it was the stimulus of Dante, Petrarch and Boccaccio, of the sensationally 'Machiavellian' Italy of the dramatists, or of the exciting intellectual activity which Milton found in Italy in 1638–9.[1] But in the century following the Restoration Italian influence, supplanted by the French, was at its nadir.[2] The Grand Tourists followed each other over their well-trodden paths from year to year with a disappointing monotony and lack of inspiration. Recoiling from contact with contemporary Italian life, they contemned its apparent poverty and squalor as a pitiful contrast with the former greatness of Rome, a greatness to which they felt themselves, the British ruling classes, to be the rightful and magnificent heirs. The master-works of Italian art and architecture were at best little more than curiosities, with the pregnant exception of Palladio, who seemed to be a direct link with the domestic architecture of the classical age[3]; for what really interested them in Italy was the constant sense of contact with the Latin authors and Roman politicians in whom they saw their models and their fellows.

The representative work of the Grand Tour is Addison's. His *Letter From Italy* (1701) is redolent of the complacency of the age. The attraction of Italy, he declares, is that there 'Poetick fields encompass me around' and 'Immortal glories in my mind revive'; and for those less intimate with these glories than himself his *Remarks On Several Parts Of Italy In The Years 1701, 1702, 1703* (1705) provided a prodigious repertoire of Latin quotations associated with every place along the route. His preface, indeed, acknowledges that there is more to Italy than this, but the stress of the book is significant: what mattered in Italy was the grandeur it had lost, and not the artistic and natural wealth it still possessed. These latter Addison felt to be superficial, and insidiously enervating, in comparison with the intellectual glory of Rome, which had now descended to England; and in the most accomplished Augustan fashion he embodies in his verse this transfer of intellectual pre-eminence by adapting to modern England Virgil's tributes to Italy:

> We envy not the warmer Clime that lies
> In ten Degrees of more indulgent Skies;
> Nor at the Courseness of our Heav'n repine,
> Tho' o'er our Heads the frozen *Pilads* shine:
> 'Tis *Liberty* that Crowns *Britannia's* Isle,
> And makes her barren Rocks, and her bleak
>   Mountains smile.[4]

The link between Rome and England via the wretchedness of modern Italy was taken up by Lord Lyttleton in his *Epistle To Mr Pope From Rome* (1730). Lyttleton dutifully adores the 'hallow'd ruins' and, quite ignoring the entire Italian Renaissance, associates the loss of Roman liberty with the decline of art in Italy:

> From tyrants, and from priests the muses fly,
> Daughters of reason and of liberty.

Again, the point is made by adopting a classical argument, from the *Appendix On The Causes Of The Decline Of Literature* where Longinus argues that the moderns, of his day, did not produce great art because they were not free, and that their not being free was a result of their devotion to luxury. In the eighteenth century context liberty has flown to England, and the muses have naturally followed. At the tomb of Virgil the poet's spirit appears to Lyttleton and delivers a message for Pope: if he wishes to rank near Virgil and Homer the Englishman must write an epic poem

> To sing the land, which yet alone can boast
> The liberty corrupted Rome has lost.

Pope did not take up the challenge, but Thomson adopted the theme for his massive poem *Liberty* (1734–6). Thomson is visited not by the spirit of Virgil but by the goddess of Liberty herself as he muses among the ruins at Rome. The goddess attacks the 'mean and sordid' life of contemporary Italy and, predictably, praises her favourite, England; while the poet chronicles at unreadable length Liberty's journey through history from Greece to Rome and thence via the Italian republics to England.

But such self-confidence and pride could not be sustained for ever; and, indeed, by 1764, Goldsmith, while sharing the conventional scorn for the debased condition of Italy, begins to throw doubts on the health of the state of England and to suggest that even liberty is not without its ill effects:

> That independence Britons prize too high,
> Keeps man from man, and breaks the social tie;
> The self dependent lordlings stand alone,
> All claims that bind and sweeten life unknown;
> Here by the bonds of nature feebly held,
> Minds combat minds, repelling and repell'd;
> Ferments arise, imprison'd factions roar,
> Represt ambition struggles round her shore,
> Till, over-wrought, the general system feels
> Its motions stopt, or phrenzy fire the wheels.[5]

In tracing the subsequent history of literary attitudes to Italy we shall repeatedly meet the pattern of aspirations to establish fruitful contact between English life and one aspect or another of the rich stimulus of Italy rising into magnificent hopes only to crash into disappointing failure: the first appearance of the syndrome is here in the eighteenth century, as literature came gradually to realise that it had to face a situation of greater complexity than was involved in the chimerical, if attractive, equation of modern British with ancient Roman grandeur.

Suggestions of an incipient change of mood had begun to appear in the English poetry of the Grand Tour some time before Goldsmith's *The Traveller*, and notably in its treatment of the ruins of Rome. To the classical Grand Tourist the ruins were the emblems of the greatness of Roman civilisation, and contemplating them the traveller would reconstruct in his mind's eye their days of former glory. Addison is their spokesman, in his *Letter From Italy* (1701):

> Immortal Glories in my mind revive,
> And in my Soul a thousand Passions strive,
> When *Rome's* exalted Beauties I descry
> Magnificent in Piles of Ruin lye:
> An Amphitheater's amazing height
> Here fills my Eye with Terror and Delight,
> That on its publick Shows unpeopled *Rome*,
> And held uncrouded Nations in its Womb.

As the self-confidence began to wane, however, poets began to contemplate the phenomenon of ruin itself, to see the Colosseum as testifying not simply to the power of the civilisation which built it but, more importantly, to the destructive power of time which makes even the greatest of man's achievements pathetically ephemeral. John Dyer, in *The Ruins of Rome* (1740), takes up the theme of Longinus noted earlier and stresses not the achievement of the Romans but the significance of 'luxury' as a cause of their decline; and when he meditates among the physical remnants of their world, it is not with the exhilaration of Addison but in 'a kindly Mood of Melancholy', as he contemplates

> The Solitary, Silent, Solemn Scene,
> Where Caesars, Heroes, Peasants, Hermits lie
> Blended in dust together.

George Keate, contemplating the Colosseum in 1755, develops more explicitly the theme of the 'pleasing Pensiveness' and 'meditating Mood' of the ruins in his *Ancient and Modern Rome* (published 1760):

> Here DESOLATION, mocking the vain Farce
> Of human Labours, and the low Conceits
> Of human Pride, thron'd on a craggy Pile,

Smiles pleas'd with his own Work; amid the Spoils,
Of Time's fell Hand, where nought is seen to move,
Save, the green Lizard sporting in the Sun
Sole Tenant of the solitary Waste.

By thus fundamentally changing the attitude to ruin in their verse these two minor poets are introducing the first elements of the Gothic and Romantic images of Italy, which were to become much more vivid and creatively fruitful than that of the Grand Tourists. But at the same time a more stimulating and significant change of attitude along similar lines was being effected in the work of Piranesi. The nightmare images of his *Capricci di Carceri* (1745) and the bleak decay of the Roman ruins in *Vedute di Roma* (1743) turn the technique of the Baroque against the ethos of the Baroque: Piranesi exploits all the Baroque techniques for the manipulation of vast spaces, but uses them to create not the exuberant self-confidence of the grandiose interior, but prisons and ruins, claustrophobia and decay. The potent and obsessive images of his etchings seized the imagination in such a way that whereas the English tourists of the early eighteenth century went to Rome in search of inspiration from the glories of its classical age, their successors at the end of the century went there with very different expectations 'formed', as one of them wrote, 'on the sketches of Piranesi.'[6]

The influence of this strikingly new vision of Rome first appears in English literature in the second of those events which make 1764 a convenient focal year for the commencement of our study: the creation of Gothic Italy with the publication on Christmas Eve of Walpole's *The Castle of Otranto*. Walpole's library contained the *Antichità Romane* etchings of 1756 and his admiration of Piranesi's 'sublime dream' is avowed in the *Advertisement* to the fourth volume of *Anecdotes of Painting in England* (1771); while in *The Castle of Otranto* itself the monstrous helmet which falls from the sky to kill Conrad clearly recalls the similar helmets which appear in the eighth plate of the *Carceri* series. More deeply, the whole conception of the scenic effects in the novel is redolent of Piranesi; and it was doubtless to some extent the association of the Italian artist with the sensational and the terrific which led Walpole to lay his story in Italy. For, indeed, there is no inherent reason in the story why it should be set there; nor does its southern setting bear very much relation to the realities of Italy.

Gothic Italy was essentially an imaginary Italy. Few of the

Gothic novelists ever visited Italy, and their picture of the country was very much third-hand, each writer tending, as we shall see, to draw heavily on the work of his or her predecessors. Walpole, of course, had travelled in Italy, with Gray, in 1739–41, but the Italy they actually saw left scarcely a trace in the creative work of either man, although Walpole's lifelong fascination with Italy was a major inspiration for his books on art. For his fantastic novel, Walpole preferred a location in the far south of Italy, an area which he had not been to and which was scarcely visited by eighteenth century travellers: a region, that is, which had the ideal qualities for his spine-chilling purposes of being mysterious and unknown, yet only just beyond the familiar horizon, sufficiently far from everyday life not to be incredible, yet sufficiently close to be threatening. More generally, any Italian setting suited Walpole's purpose because of the inevitable association of Italy with Roman Catholicism. In his story he makes much of the apparatus of Catholicism, intrinsically mysterious and suspicious to post-Reformation Englishmen, and, although the events of the story, in the medieval period in which it is set, could equally well have taken place in the then Catholic England, it was evidently convenient for Walpole to be able to count on his readers' ready association of such things with Italy. Shakespeare, too, contributed towards this pattern of associations. Walpole's awareness of a debt to Shakespeare is explicit in the *Preface* to the second edition, and in connecting the first Gothic novel with Shakespeare Walpole forged a link which was to be central to the genre. It was, indeed, a natural link, since for the gothic novelists the most recent model both of response to more modern rather than merely classical Italy and of the exploitation of excitement in literature was to be found in the English Renaissance tragedy which, from Marlowe to Otway, had habitually associated sensation and horror with an Italian setting and had created a most potent image of a country of incest and intrigue, violence and hypocrisy, whose Church was Anti-Christ, whose Jews pursued the evil trade of usury, and whose intellectuals were typified by the fiendish Machiavelli.

By combining the stimulus of this sensational view of Italy with that of the graphic vision of Piranesi, Walpole is indicating the direction of the next wave of literary interest in Italian material: seeking release from the constraints of the classical impulse whose ultimate aspirations had been shown, by the stress on the inevitable phenomena of ruin and decay, to be chimerical, future generations of writers would find in Italy not a model for their imperial aspirations but an imaginary atmosphere of violence and suspense in which they could seek illusory escape from the comparative monotony of life in a more rationally ordered society. *The Castle of Otranto* founded the genre of the Gothic novel, but grossly under-exploited its potential, and is thus more interesting historically than intrinsically. A quarter of a century elapsed before its example was taken up more vigorously by novelists whose work we shall consider later. In the meantime another, very different, contribution had been made to the developing literary apprehension of Italy, a contribution which also had its origin in the *annus mirabilis* of 1764. For this was the year of Gibbon's visit to Italy. As a tourist Gibbon was almost a personification of the principles expounded in Bacon's essay *Of Travel*, which had helped to establish the pattern of the Grand Tour. When he toured Switzerland, 'in every place we visited the Churches, arsenals, libraries and all the most eminent persons'[7] – Gibbon's list is effectively a synopsis of the more detailed list given by Bacon. When he visited Florence, Gibbon made a thorough study of the Uffizi gallery, going there fourteen times and filling his journal with long, detailed notes on its collections, notes which were mostly copied straight from the guide-books; and he compiled a list of classical references to each significant place in Italy.[8] Gibbon shared the feelings towards modern Italy expressed by Addison and Goldsmith; on his return to England, for example, he wrote to a relative in Spain in terms absolutely representative of the attitudes of the Grand Tourist:

> You will be glad to hear that I have found great amusement in my tour of France and Italy, and perhaps still more pleased to hear that I am come back a better Englishman than I went out. Tho' I have seen more elegant manners and more refined arts I have perceived so many real evils mixed with these tinsel advantages, that they have only served to make the plain honesty and blunt freedom of my own country appear still more valuable to me. What a mixture of pride vice, slavery and poverty have I seen in the short time I passed at Naples. I do not know any place where one is so sorry for it. The favors which nature has lavished upon that delicious country make one desire to see it the seat of an industrious a virtuous and a happy people. I am sure it is not so at present, and the distant prospect seems but indifferent. I am told great pains are taken to extinguish every ray of sense in the mind

of their prince and to leave it as meer a blank as possible. I make no doubt of their success in so laudable a design.[9]

But from this very conventional tour quite exceptional results emerged. No previous English traveller to Italy had been so deeply affected by his experiences there. Gibbon spent only thirteen months in Italy in 1764–5 and he never returned south of the Alps; but the rest of his life was to be built around his experience of Rome. Everyone knows, but it is irresistible to quote again, his almost mystical description of the conception of *The Decline and Fall*:

> It was at Rome on the fifteenth of October 1764, as I sat musing amidst the ruins of the Capitol while the barefooted fryars were singing Vespers in the temple of Jupiter, that the idea of writing the decline and fall of the City first started to my mind.[10]

The book was to dominate Gibbon's thoughts for the next quarter of a century, and must have been a major formative element in the anticipations of all subsequent English literary visitors to Rome. The significance of the work, from the point of view of our present study, is implicit in its title: Gibbon's chosen subject is the decline and fall, not the greatness, of Rome.

Gibbon was at least as fully aware of the nature and value of Roman civilisation as the poets whose enthusiasm for it we have noted: from time to time he explicitly evokes the attractiveness of its finest age:

> If a man were called to fix the period in the history of the world, during which the condition of the human race was most happy and prosperous, he would, without hesitation, name that which elapsed from the death of Domitian to the accession of Commodus.[11]

Like the poets, Gibbon feels that this great social achievement of the Romans provides a model to be emulated in contemporary Britain, and his work is a deliberate contribution to the process of attempting to create a civilisation in the modern world worthy of comparison with the most noble glories of the ancients. The qualities of Gibbon's prose – its rational lucidity and authoritative lack of insistence, with their implied respect for the intelligence of the reader – are models of some of the qualities which will be essential to the attainment of such a society. But in *The Decline and Fall* they are applied not to the optimistic assertion of the greatness of modern Britain, but to the narrative analysis of the process and causes of the decay and destruction of the great historical example of social happiness (at least for the ruling classes), and so serve the purpose of warning against the type of danger which must threaten any such success of civilisation. The life of the book is in the tension between the civilised poise of its style and the barbarous violence of its history. As well as providing the vital force whose intellectual excitement and perennial significance give his work an enduring relevance and greatness which normally lie beyond the range of straightforward historical narrative, this tension makes Gibbon the crucial figure at the turning point between classical and Romantic attitudes to Italy. The finest monument of Enlightenment culture, *The Decline and Fall*, in its emphasis on decay and devastation, foreshadows and influences the Romantic stress on the same phenomena, and most notably that of Byron, whose work abounds in references to Gibbon.

The difference was that, whereas Gibbon's book had grown out of a solid base in the rational values of eighteenth century culture and had analysed the specific forces which had destroyed the Roman Empire as the type of those forces which perennially threaten any attempt at achieving a sophisticated civilised order such as that to which Gibbon himself aspired, the Romantics who went to Italy with a knowledge of his work were involved in trying to come to terms with a world in which the political and intellectual events associated with the French Revolution and the expansion of industry appeared to have shattered all possibility of attaining any such calmly and rationally ordered society. The phenomenon of ruin which to Gibbon had been a threat was to them the image of the reality in which they lived. The bulk of our study will concern the attempts of the nineteenth century to effect a creative re-direction of the energy of society in order to build a more vital future out of this sense of loss. Repeatedly, we shall find such efforts coming to grief as one after another of the apparent ways forward turns out to be an impasse. Gibbon's work, growing from his meditations among the Roman ruins to contemplate the massive process of the destruction of the classical achievement, with its evident implication, all too soon to be rendered explicit by events, of the fragility of the eighteenth century's effort at civilisation, is the first of such disillusionments, and our natural point of departure.

2 Between Gibbon and Byron

In the period between the publication of *The Decline and Fall* and Byron's adoption of Italy as the country of his exile the major growth point in the development of literary attitudes to Italy was in the novel, and it was the novelistic image of Italy which provided the immediate literary background to Byron's own poetic exploration of the country. Little advance, indeed, was made in the poetic treatment of Italy between the mid eighteenth century and the height of the Romantic period; but the work of one small group of minor poets, and particularly the one remarkable volume in which they collaborated, does demand attention.

The Florence Miscellany, which was printed privately at Florence in 1785, is important as the first collection of poetry to concern itself with what were to become some of the characteristic themes of nineteenth century writers. Its verse is generally attractive, without ever being particularly distinguished; in style it is very much in the manner of Gray and Collins, while in feeling it often looks forward towards Byron and Keats. All of the Romantic poets were probably familiar, if not with the book itself, which was rather rare, at least with some of the poems, many of which appeared in widely circulated English magazines. The volume grew out of the friendship in Florence between Mrs Piozzi – Dr Johnson's Mrs Thrale, now married to an Italian music master – and three young English residents and aspiring poets, Robert Merry, William Parsons and Bertie Greatheed. Merry, who was the guiding spirit behind the volume, and who had also contributed to the insignificant *Arno Miscellany* of the previous year, was known familiarly to the others as Della Crusca, whence the group came to call themselves the Della Cruscans, a name commemorating the suppression of the liberal Accademia della Crusca by Duke Leopold of Tuscany in 1783, and thus symbolising the opposition of the poets to the repressive Tuscan government of their day.[1]

The political opposition represented by the name was, in fact, a major, and most significant, theme of their poetry. Gibbon's work, with its emphasis on the vulnerability of civilisation, had destroyed for ever the possibility of a complacent attitude towards liberty similar to that of the earlier part of the century, and in this volume one finds for the first time the insistence, which was to become so characteristic of English interest in Italian affairs in the next century, on freedom as a cause requiring constantly to be fought for.

Dilettante and minor though the poetry of the Della Cruscans is, it has the distinction of turning attention towards a positive engagement with the living reality of Italy. Greatheed's *Ode to Apathy*, exclaiming 'O! would the sons of Italy arise . . .', introduces a new attitude of sympathetic concern towards the same phenomena of poverty and oppression which had aroused Goldsmith's and Gibbon's contempt only twenty years before.

The extent to which the poets felt themselves to be involved in the political situation is interestingly suggested by a bibliographical curiosity of their volume, in which the Florentine printer left blank spaces in some of the poems, where the more extreme attacks on the government were omitted in order to evade the attention of the censor. The missing passages were then printed on slips of paper and circulated privately among trusted friends, who could paste them into the appropriate spaces. Thus some extant copies contain, while others do not, a passage on page 27, where William Parsons attacks 'the fierce Austrian eagle' and its grip on Florence. Elsewhere, Parsons bids Duke Leopold tremble, 'lest soon th' impatient throng/ Tear the vain crown from thy too impious head', although this was perhaps too extreme in its forthright opposition to be risked in the Florentine volume, and was reserved for subsequent publication in London.[2] Merry, too, launched his major attack on Austrian tyranny in Italy from the safer distance of London. In his celebration of the French revolution of 1789, *The Laurel of Liberty* (1790) he digresses for a 38-line lamentation on the state of Florence:

> O SWEET FIRENZE! what are all thy stores,
> Thy PARIAN VENUS, which the world adores,
> What are thy treasur'd gems, thy tow'ry domes,
> Whilst in thy halls the spectre Slav'ry roams?

The preface to the poem, which is dedicated to the National

Assembly of France, proclaims that 'THE CAUSE OF FREEDOM IS THE CAUSE OF ALL MANKIND', and the Della Cruscans have the honour of being the first in England to treat this great Romantic theme.

Nor was this the only advance towards Romantic feeling marked by the poetry of *The Florence Miscellany*. Merry's *Ode On A Distant Prospect Of Rome* opens with an address to the ruins:

> Ye awful wrecks of ancient days,
> Proud monuments of ages past,
> Now mould'ring in decay!
> Vainly ye glitter in the parting rays!

With this scornful insistence on vanity we are distinctly nearer to the feeling of Shelley's *Ozymandias* than of the eighteenth century poetry of ruins quoted earlier. The significant detail is the introduction of the setting sun. Earlier poets, conceiving the ruins more as emblems than as actual objects, had not concerned themselves with the texture or appearance of the stones. Merry, however, introduces the typically Romantic effect of the sunset: the sun's light ironically bringing the decaying stones most fully to life at just that moment when it is itself dying away on the horizon. A few years later Parsons took a step further, introducing moonlight and horror to establish the pattern for the obligatory Romantic visit to the Colosseum by moonlight:

> Hail awful scenes! congenial darkness hail!
>   For times there are when man's wide-grasping soul
> Flies Nature's sweets, clear stream or painted vale,
>   And willing yields to Horror's mad control.[3]

The light of the setting sun, the mystery of night-time, the shiver of horror: the two poets between them are beginning to build up the atmosphere of pathos which hung thickly over Romantic Italy. Another of Parsons' contributions to *The Florence Miscellany* was his translation of the Francesca da Rimini episode from the fifth Canto of Dante's *Inferno*, the first appearance of what, a few years later, would become a conventional piece for translation: the Francesca episode, together with Dante's accounts of Ugolino and of Pia dei Tolomei[4] and the pathetic tales from Boccaccio were constantly being reread and retranslated by post-Napoleonic visitors to Italy;

whilst another of their interests in Italy, the pathos of the ceremony of a novice taking the veil, was treated by Robert Merry in *The Pains of Memory* (1796), in a passage whose heroine is a beautiful blue-eyed nun cursed with the memory of the delicious days of freedom before she became 'a mournful wreck/In the oblivious gulph of bigotry'. (George Keate had also mentioned this ceremony in his *Ancient and Modern Rome* (1760).) Although the the theme of commitment to Italian revolutionary politics had to wait in abeyance until it found major champions in Byron and Shelley, these other developments in the Della Cruscan poetry were immediately and strikingly taken up by the novelists of the turn of the century.

William Beckford's travel diaries provide a suggestive indication of the change that was taking place. Although not published until 1834, when the Romantic re-appraisal of Italy was complete, the North Italian sections of the diaries were written in 1780, and privately anticipate something of the essence of Gothic and Romantic Italy. For Beckford went to Italy with an imagination deeply impressed by Piranesi. He describes, for example, his reaction after crossing the Bridge of Sighs and visiting the State Prisons within the Ducal Palace at Venice:

> Horrors and dismal prospects haunted my fancy upon my return. I could not dine in peace, so strongly was my imagination affected; but snatching my pencil, I drew chasms and subterraneous hollows, the domain of fear and torture, with chains, racks, wheels, and dreadful engines in the style of Piranesi.[5]

This is quite a new kind of English response to the imaginative stimulus of Italy: Beckford cultivates and describes the excited feelings which the Italian environment arouses in him, feelings which are personal and violent, rather than conventional and composed. This contrast with his classically minded predecessors on the tour of Italy is particularly evident in his account of Verona.

The gradual broadening of interest in Verona is one of the clearest markers of the development of English attitudes towards Italy. The Victorians first introduced an admiration for the Gothic and Romanesque architectural glories of a city that for the Romantics had been predominantly the city of Romeo and Juliet. But the eighteenth century was interested neither in the Gothic nor in the Shakespearean associations of the place. Of all the eighteenth century guide-book writers, only John Breval seems to have mentioned Romeo and Juliet, in his *Remarks on Several Parts of Europe* (1726). The standard guide-books of the time, such as Thomas Nugent's *The Grand Tour* (1747) or John Northall's *Travels Through Italy* (1766), give little space to Verona, merely quoting historical and topographical details about its Roman amphitheatre, taken from Scipio Maffei's massively erudite *Verona Illustrata* (Verona, 1731–2). To visit, and often to take measurements of, the amphitheatre was the major interest of the eighteenth century tourist in Verona. Beckford, however, has quite a different attitude. He gets rid of his antiquarian guide, goes into the amphitheatre alone, and records not objective facts about the building but his own immediate feelings in its presence:

> When I paced slowly across it, silence reigned undisturbed among the awful ruins, and nothing moved, save the weeds and grasses which skirt the walls and temble with the faintest breeze. I liked the idea of being thus shut in on every side by endless gradines, abandoned to a stillness and solitude I was so peculiarly disposed to taste. Throwing myself upon the grass in the middle of the arena, I enjoyed the freedom of my situation, and pursued the last tracks of light, as they faded behind the solitary arches, which rise above the rest. Red and fatal were the tints of the western sky; the wind blew chill and hollow, and something more than common seemed to issue from the withering herbage on the walls. I started up, fled through a dark arcade, where water falls drop by drop; and arrived, panting, in the great square before the ruins.[6]

The emphasis on the emotional apprehension of decay, the eeriness of the scene, the Piranesian image of endless gradines, the evocation of the phenomenality of the passing moment, with its reddening sky and chill wind, the violence of Beckford's flight from the pressure of feelings in the arena, all make the passage radically different from the kinds of response to the Italian ruins associated with Addison or Gibbon. On the contrary, passages like this anticipate the great Romantic discovery of Italy as the country whose richly textured environment offered an incomparably powerful catalyst to creative release of the deepest personal feelings. The diaries remained, however, an unpublished private anticipation. The published English literary exploitation of Italian material between Beckford's visit to Venice in 1780 and Byron's arrival there in 1816 also associated Italy with emotional excitement, but in a different and more superficial way than Beckford had done in an isolated passage of his diary or than Byron was to do as part of the central development of his work.

The superficiality of the treatment of Italy in the Gothic novel is an index of a fundamental flaw in the unresolved conflict between the novelists' desire both to escape from what appeared to be a world of mundane and monotonous reality into a rapidly pulsing world of excitement and suspense, and yet to retain within that violent escape world precisely those comfortable assumptions of an unshakeable equation of good with ultimate reward and evil with inescapable misery which were the basis of that very monotony and which would have to be sacrificed if life were really to be lived more spontaneously and more sensationally. Unconvincing on this moral level, their works are also shockingly unrealistic – though powerfully vivid and historically important – in their treatment of Italy, where, for reasons such as those we have already noted in connection with *The Castle of Otranto* and largely through its example, they frequently – indeed, characteristically – laid their scene.

Dr John Moore, who first took up the novelistic presentation of Italy after Walpole, is an interesting case in point. Moore had travelled in Italy, and produced an attractive *View of Society and Manners in Italy* (1781). He is one of the earliest English admirers of the contemporary Italian character. An Italian exile in England, Giuseppe Baretti, in *An Account of The Manners and Customs of Italy; With Observations on The Mistakes of Some Travellers, With Regard to That Country* (1768) had defended the probity of Italian morals and the congeniality of Italian life against the contemptuously dismissive attitude we have noted earlier, and particularly against the scurrilous attacks of Smollett's *Travels Through France and Italy* (1766) and Samuel Sharp's *Letters From Italy* (1766), and Moore's book develops the good work of Baretti. Moore felt the Italians to be the most sensitive people in Europe and looked forward to the independence of their country; and he appears to be the first Briton to have appreciated the Italian genius for self-sufficient lounging, admiration for which, in contrast to puritanical British guilt feelings about work, has been perhaps the most consistent hallmark of subsequent British Italophiles:

The Italians are the greatest loungers in the world, and while walking in the fields, or stretched in the shade, seem to enjoy the serenity and genial warmth of their climate with a degree of luxurious indulgence peculiar to themselves. Without ever running into the daring excesses of the English, or displaying the frisky vivacity of the French, or the invincible phlegm of the Germans, the Italian populace discover a species of sedate sensibility to every source of enjoyment, from which, perhaps, they derive a greater degree of happiness than any of the other.[7]

When, however, Moore comes a few years later to write a novel set in contemporary Italy, he unhesitatingly abandons this sympathetic knowledge of the Italian character and reverts to the 'Machiavellian' image of the Jacobean drama to create the fiendish Sicilian hero of *Zeluco* (1789). The novel follows Zeluco's career from his early killing of a pet sparrow, through a series of gratuitous cruelties to his mother, his mistresses, and his various wives, his soldiers in the Spanish army, and his slaves in Cuba, until, back in Naples, he strangles his baby son as a result of his mistress's malicious insinuation that the child is the product of an incestuous affair between his wife and her half-brother. Then, going to his mistress, he finds her in bed with a servant, at whose hands Zeluco dies, repenting all his evil ways, and enforcing Moore's pathetically simple moral point that misery is inseparable from vice and that happiness can only result from conscious integrity.

The novel achieved some success in its day, and has continued to attract attention as a result of Byron's reference to Childe Harold as 'a poetical Zeluco'. (The reference, however, seems somewhat misleading, since Zeluco has none of the introspective melancholy of Byron's Romantic hero.) *Zeluco*'s popularity doubtless contributed to the establishment of the stock Italian properties of the Gothic novel and the general belief among novelists that nowhere was so suited to tales of villainy and horror as a setting in Italy; and if a man who knew Italy and admired its inhabitants could produce such a fictional travesty as *Zeluco*, it is scarcely surprising that subsequent novelists, entirely dependent upon second-hand information and attitudes, should have continued to exploit the supposed sensationalism of an imaginary Italy which bore only a minimal relation to reality.

Of all the sensational pictures of Italy, none was so impressive or so influential as Mrs Radcliffe's. She herself, however, never visited

Italy, and her impressions of the country were utterly eclectic – a secondhandness profoundly characteristic of the Gothic novel. Her general notions of Italian character were derived principally from Shakespeare, and of Italian landscape from Salvator Rosa (to whom she occasionally refers in her novels), while information on the different parts of Italy was culled from a wide reading in contemporary guide-books. For her picture of the south she relied heavily on one of the most popular of such books, Patrick Brydone's *Tour Through Sicily and Malta* (1773), which Dr Moore, who had not been south of Naples, also used, while for Venice she relied on Mrs. Piozzi, to whom we shall return later.

This lack of direct contact with the country inevitably shows in the novels, where Mrs Radcliffe is frequently inaccurate. She thinks, for example, of monasteries as institutions housing both men and women in the same building, and she post-dates the operations of the Italian inquisition. She has remarkably little sense of geography and regularly makes her characters travel at ludicrously incredible speeds, while in *The Mysteries of Udolpho* (1794) she at one point moves the Mediterranean coast to the foot of the Apennines on the Venetian-Tuscan border and then later moves it back to Livorno when she wants to stage a flight across Tuscany. More seriously, she often fails, through lack of familiarity with it, to realise the full potential of her material. In *A Sicilian Romance* (1790), for instance, the superstitious servants are patently modelled on English servants, and there is no hint of any awareness of the deep pagan-Catholic superstition of the southern Italian peasant; nor is there in the novel any suggestion of the oppressive heat of the Sicilian summer, which is so memorable a feature of the genuinely Sicilian novels of Verga and Lampedusa.

Yet, unreal as it is, Mrs Radcliffe's picture of Italy was of major importance to the Romantic apprehension of the country. Byron mentions her in *Childe Harold* (IV.18) as one of the writers who had formed his image of Venice, and tourists in Naples began first to look for the scenery of *The Italian* (1797) and only afterwards for the sites traditionally associated with Virgil, which had previously been a major attraction of the area.[9] Mrs Radcliffe herself, however, was certainly no Romantic. She has nothing of the Romantic questioning of the established moral order. On the contrary, it is the weakness of her books that all the chilling horrors she is capable of evoking are never allowed seriously to threaten an exceedingly simple moral pattern of reward and retribution. Her basic plot is always the same: the course of true love is thwarted by some act of villainy which separates boy from girl, and subjects both of them, but especially the girl, to a series of mental horrors, from which they eventually escape to be happily married. Incredibly, their sufferings leave no scar upon their minds: and, moreover, their fundamental invulnerability is the moral of the story. The final paragraph of *A Sicilian Romance* is representative:

> In reviewing this story, we perceive a singular and striking instance of moral retribution. We learn also, that those who do only THAT WHICH IS RIGHT, endure nothing in misfortune but a trial of their virtue, and from trials well endured, derive the surest claim to the protection of heaven.

There is no Romantic anguish about this. The cosy reassurance that the good will always come out all right in the end vitiates the terrific element of the novels, by depriving it of any force to threaten the stability of the moral order. The role of the ghosts in Mrs Radcliffe's novels is symptomatic. Unlike the ghost in *Hamlet*, on which they are largely modelled, they are always eventually explained by natural, mundane phenomena, and always have an ultimately beneficial effect on the situation of the principal characters; by comparison with the disturbing force and violent consequences which Shakespeare's ghost unleashes, they are a cheap literary confidence trick. In its day, however, the trick was received with great applause, and vividly impressed upon its readers' minds an horrific vision of Italy. The villains – Mazzini, Montoni, Schedoni – re-invigorated the 'Machiavellian' figure of the Jacobean drama- tists and suggested malice and mystery in every hooded figure in the Italian streets. The Salvator Rosa landscapes of Italy became peopled by malignant marquisses scheming in gloomy castles, while the traveller in the Italian mountains or on the wide plains felt himself to be on roads where heroes had fled or been led prisoner, and nervously looked out for banditti in the forests and passes. Monasteries appeared as subtle and sadistic prisons, while in the churches each confessional box seemed to shade the progress of some wicked machination.

It was an image of Italy which spawned a whole series of minor but vigorous novels in the early years of the nineteenth century, novels which attempt to reproduce the commercially successful formula of Mrs Radcliffe, and which rely for their effects of 'local colour' on her and on her sources. A curious index of their artificiality and lack of originality is the constant recurrence in almost every 'Italian' novel or story of the name Rosalia (or Rosalie, Rosolie, Rosaline); apparently taken from the account of the feast of Santa Rosalia at Palermo in Brydone's *Tour Through Sicily and Malta*, the name seems to have struck the novelists as peculiarly Italian and an essential part of the creation of an Italian atmosphere: when it is not the name of the heroine, Rosalia is the name of the servant girl, or even, on one occasion, of a horse.

Almost all the novels set in this artificial Italy follow the same broad pattern; they are stories of violence and passion, whether it is the violence of bravi and banditti, the sexual passion of the Latin lover, or the sadism of nuns and inquisitioners, in which the reader is intended to enjoy the vicarious excitement while thankfully assenting to the usually explicit moral that Providence will always take care of the good. The stock reliance on an Italian setting for this kind of story is scathingly portrayed by a contemporary Italophile:

> Is a scene of lewdness or debauchery to be introduced into a Romance? It is placed in an Italian convent. Is an assassin wanted to frighten ladies in the country, or to terrify a London mob on the stage? An Italian appears; a monk or a friar probably, with a dose of poison in one hand and a dagger in the other. Is a crime too great for utterance to be presented dimly to the imagination? It is half disclosed in an Italian *confessional*. In short, is some inhuman plot to be executed, or is religion to be employed as the means or the instrument of lust or revenge? The scene is laid in Italy; the contrivers and the perpetrators are Italians; and to give it more diabolical effect, a convent or a church is the stage, and clergymen of some description or other, are the actors of the tragedy.[10]

Too trivial and too numerous to be considered in any detail, a brief sketch of some of the more sensational examples of the genre will suffice to illustrate the accuracy of Eustace's sketch.

The Venetian setting of Edward Montague's *The Legends of A Nunnery* (1807) affords a convenient example of a typical lack in the author of familiarity with his material, for, although he does have boats on the canals, Montague has no sense of the incongruity – the impossibility – of having his characters occasionally chase each other through the streets of Venice in carriages. Montague's heroine

(Rosalia) scandalises her convent by being found to be pregnant. After being imprisoned by her father as a punishment, and escaping only to be captured by banditti, her cause is taken up by a benign agent of the inquisition, who vindicates her innocence, and at the same time avenges a past wrong done to his own family, by exposing the villainy of a monk from a neighbouring monastery who had access to Rosalia's convent and who had ravished her while she was under the influence of drugs. The monk's punishment in the dungeons of the inquisition is lifted almost verbatim from Mrs Radcliffe's *The Italian*, while Rosalia's 'long-suffering virtue' is suitably rewarded by a noble husband.

Less fortunate is another Rosalia, in Maturin's *Fatal Revenge; Or, The Family of Montorio* (1807), who stoically takes the veil despite being passionately in love, only to find eventually that she can no longer support the horrors and privations of the convent, which she flees in order to live pathetically disguised as a page in the house of the man she hopelessly adores; while less fortunate still is Helena, the heroine of Louisa Sidney Stanhope's *The Nun of Santa Maria di Tindaro* (1818), who flees the sinister Sicilian convent where her father wants her to devote her life to religion, in order to elope with a man who turns out to be the son of her own mother, who had been seduced away from her father while Helena was a child. The mother is punished for her infidelity, and the daughter for her disobedience, by a shattering series of torments, until, when everyone she holds dear is dead, Helena returns to the convent, where she herself dies in misery. The moral is carefully drawn for the reader's benefit: he (or, more likely, she) must beware the vile seducer, respect parental wisdom, and avoid the illusions of romance and the chimera of passion. 'To be good is to be happy', as the reader was told at the end of Mary Anne Radcliffe's *Manfrone; Or, The One-Handed Monk* (1809), whose heroine Rosaline happily survives the spine-chilling persecutions of the monk who glides – they always glide – furtively and ghost-like in and out of the narrative.

But the most whole-hearted indulgence in conventual horror comes in Anne Hatton's *Cesario Rosalba; Or, The Oath of Vengeance* (1819). Angelina is incarcerated in a convent on a cliff-top near Palermo in a vain attempt to stifle her love for the Count di Valvoni. The time she spends there is a constant succession of scenes of hypocrisy, flagellation, murder, and the burying alive of recalcitrant nuns, until she is rescued by the Count and lives with him as his mistress, bearing him a son, Cesario. When she is abandoned after the Count's marriage to another woman, she brings up her son to hate his father and everything to do with him, and on her death bed makes him swear the dreadful Oath of Vengeance, which he pursues throughout the rest of his life, in a relentless and incredibly unsuccessful series of attacks upon the Count and his legitimate offspring, until eventually he is arrested by the inquisition and poisons himself. Remote and unreal as the story may seem, its relevance is inexorably asserted in the penultimate paragraph of the novel:

> From the dreadful history of Cesario Rosalba and his erring mother, the young, the gay, and licentious, will be taught that seduction is a sin of the highest magnitude – they will shudder at indulging passions that lead to misery, to infamy, and death; but above all, they will be taught to suppress the first incitements to revenge, for they will see that Heaven, from whom no injuries are hid, will, in its own good time, avenge and redress.

The relevance of such novels to our recurrent theme of the inability of successive generations of writers fully to seize and assimilate the creative opportunities they detected in Italian material is evident: sensing the possibilities in an imaginary Italian environment of an escape into a more immediately exciting life than that of contemporary England, these novelists failed either to produce a credible realisation of the texture of such a life or to face the challenge of its moral implications. Equally evident is the relevance of these novels to Byron: his early narrative poems clearly grow out of the background of fictional sensationalism, but his work has the distinction, as we shall see, of following through the opportunities and implications of his material to achieve the fully developed poise of high Romanticism.

Apart from the overall relevance of this genre in providing part of the context of Byron's achievement, one novel in particular merits attention as probably standing in a specially significant relationship to the early Byronic hero. Matthew Gregory Lewis's short novel *The Bravo of Venice* (1805) is an adaptation of Heinrich Zschokke's *Aböllino Der Grosse Bandit* (1793), which had become an immediate success in the German theatre when dramatised by its author in 1795, and was subsequently translated into French, Spanish, Danish and Polish, as well as English. A version by the American playwright William Dunlap rapidly became popular in the United States and was first presented in England as *The Venetian Outlaw* in

1805. A dramatised abridgement of Lewis's novel, entitled *Rugantino*, 'thronged Covent Garden for many successive nights' in 1807[11], and the novel itself remained popular, especially as a schoolboy tale, throughout the nineteenth century. Despite this popularity, despite the fact that Lewis's hero seems far more Byronic than any other fictional hero of the period, and despite Byron's acquaintance with Lewis, whom he met in Switzerland in 1816 and who visited him in Venice the following year, the novel seems to have been rather neglected by enquirers into the genealogy of the Byronic hero.[12]

The Bravo of Venice is in no way great literature, but it is a very readable tale of adventure and love. It is the first literary use since Otway's *Venice Preserv'd* (1682) of the Venetian atmosphere of mystery and conspiracy, which a few years later fascinated Byron; and its hero, Rosalvo, has precisely those Byronic qualities which are lacking in Dr Moore's Zeluco or Mrs Radcliffe's Schedoni. He is self-consciously different from other mortals: 'To astonish is my destiny: Rosalvo can know no medium: Rosalvo can never act like common men.' He feels this distinction as a burden to be carried, and throughout the book he is surrounded by mystery. Since the story is nowadays forgotten, it can be summarised here.

Rosalvo arrives in Venice from Naples as a beggar. It is not until the end of the story that we learn that he has come to avenge himself upon an enemy who has cheated him of his princely inheritance. This enemy is coming to Venice to marry the Doge's beautiful niece, Rosabella. Under the assumed name of Abellino, Rosalvo joins a group of bravi in order to get money to live. Soon (his boundless ambition) he decides to use his position among the bravi to take over the government of Venice. He works with a group of conspirators against the state, and outrageously publicises his 'crimes': though, in fact, he kills none of his 'victims', but merely keeps them imprisoned in preparation for his *coup de grâce*. He does, however, kill his enemy in a duel and so regains his wealth. He then assumes a new disguise and appears as a handsome Florentine, promising to hand over the outlaw Abellino to the Doge at an appointed time, in return for the hand of Rosabella. When the time comes he reveals his triple identity, exposes the conspirators, and restores the men he is supposed to have murdered. He will now marry Rosabella, whom he has loved since he first set eyes on her when he was sent to kill her, and who has survived the test of pleading for mercy for him even when she believes him guilty of Abellino's crimes.

Though clearly superficial, the novel is significant for its confrontation of an exceptionally, almost superhumanly, active and competent hero with the sinister and violent environment of Venetian statecraft. It was largely from this sort of tension that Byron's treatment of Italy was to grow. But before coming to Byron we must look at the development of another facet of the literary background to his sojourn in Italy which, although mainly French in origin, was fundamentally important to English literary attitudes to Italy in the nineteenth century.

Throughout the nineteenth and early twentieth centuries the most obvious series of treatments of our theme of repeatedly frustrated attempts to re-invigorate Anglo-Saxon life by creating fruitful contact with the south was the succession of works treating the intimate relationships of representative figures of Britain (or America) and Italy. The subject, indeed, is the very embodiment of our theme, and we shall have frequently to return to it. Its first major treatment was by Madame de Staël.

Although all the novels we have yet mentioned have primarily concerned supposedly Italian characters, there had been occasional minor considerations in English fiction of the possibility of sex breaking down the cultural barriers between England and Italy. As early as 1754, the Italian sections of Richardson's *Sir Charles Grandison* had been concerned with the difficulties of love between the hero, a paragon of Protestantism, and an Italian girl who is equally a paragon of Catholicism, and who hopelessly adores the Englishmen. Grandison, 'the best of Men, of Friends, of Husbands,' marries an Englishwoman and does his rather feeble best to console the Italian. Unfortunately, the characters are far too flat and simple ever to come to life, and the 'Italian' setting is only the merest sketch. Similar problems render almost unreadable Charlotte Smith's *Montalbert* (1795) and Mary Young's *Right and Wrong; Or, The Kinsmen of Naples* (1803), both novels heavily indebted to Mrs Radcliffe, which deal with the problems afflicting Anglo-Italian marriages, ranging from earth-quakes to fabulously wicked mothers-in-law, after surviving which, in true Gothic novel fashion, the international married couple are left with the unconvincing prospect of living happily together ever after. None of these treatments bears comparison with Madame de Staël.

Her interest in an Italian subject was stimulated not only by visiting Italy but by Madame de Krüdener's *Valérie* (1803), the most successful French novel of its season, regarded as a master-piece by Sainte-Beuve, and now not unjustly forgotten. The story is very simple, and obviously derived from Goethe's *Werther*. Gustave, a young Swede, accompanies the Swedish ambassador to Venice. He falls madly in love with the ambassador's sixteen year old wife, Valérie, but hides his love because of his respect for the ambassador, who was the best friend of his late father. His anguish is expressed in a series of letters to a friend. Finally, the strain becomes too much, and he leaves Venice and languishes and dies in the mountains. The novel is insipid, and fails to exploit as much as it might the contrast between the apparent warmth and gaiety of Venice and Gustave's mental and emotional disturbance; but it does, at least, begin to explore this tension, and stimulates Madame de Staël to develop it more fully.

Her *Corinne* is one of the most important documents in the growth of the English Romantic image of Italy. The first English translation appeared in the same year as the first French edition (1807) and a French edition was printed in London in 1809. Commendatory references to *Corinne* were the first Romantic trait to appear in the English guide-books to Italy when the Continent was re-opened to tourists after the Napoleonic wars: the books which were issued then were still essentially eighteenth century in attitude (as opposed to those of only a few years later, which took account of the new kind of interest in Italy created largely by the work of Byron), yet the most popular of them recommends *Corinne* as the best available book on Italy[13], and it soon became 'a fashionable vade mecum for sentimental travellers in Italy'[14]; while as late as 1853 it could still be regarded as the best-known book on Italy[15], and it was one of the books which Mary Garland and Mrs Hudson read in preparation for Italy in James's *Roderick Hudson* (1875). Indeed, much of *Corinne* is unashamedly a guide to Italy, with long descriptions of the things to see in Rome, Naples, Florence and Venice. Against the background of these towns most of the rather thin story is set.

The male protagonist is a young Scottish lord whose life is diseased by a guilty fear that an affair he has had with a French girl in revolutionary France may have helped to hasten the death of his father. He is introduced as the very type of melancholy Romantic hero:

Il s' identifiait avec les idées qui avaient dû occuper son père dans les derniers temps de sa vie, et il portait l' ardeur de vingt-cinq ans dans les réflexions mélancoliques de la vieillesse.[16]

To try to escape his melancholy the young Lord Nelvil goes to Italy. There he meets and falls in love with the immensely popular *improvvisatrice*, Corinne, whom he first sees at her coronation with poetic laurels on the Capitol. Their love, potentially so satisfactory, is blighted by the scruples of Lord Nelvil, who cannot enter into a marriage which he fears may offend the ghost of his father. Corinne eventually reveals that she is, in fact, the daughter by a first marriage of his father's best friend, and that she had at one time been intended as Nelvil's bride, until his father decided that he should marry her younger half-sister instead. Nelvil returns to Scotland and discovers that his father's change of mind had come from a fear that Corinne was too vivacious, too Italian, to be happy in the narrower emotional climate of Britain, where he saw it as as his son's duty to live. Nelvil therefore marries the half-sister. Corinne, who has secretly followed him to Britain, is shattered by this betrayal, and returns to live out her days in Florence, where, years later, Nelvil and his wife find her, a physical and emotional wreck, and are present at her death. At the end of the novel the questions of whether Nelvil was really happy with the pleasures of his domestic British marriage, in comparison with what Corinne might have given him, and whether he was responsible for the misery of the last years of her life are ostensibly left open, but the implied answers are clear: he is unhappy and guilty.

Such, in outline, is the first novel to raise the important theme of the mutual destructiveness of northern ideals of duty and domesticity and spontaneous southern vivacity. In the course of introducing this scheme, Madame de Staël contributes greatly towards the establishment of a new, Romantic approach to Italy, which the novel did much to propagate, and whose timeliness clearly contributed to its immense success. Firstly, the novel calls into question the whole nature of travel. Hitherto, travel had been regarded as a self-justifying activity, in the spirit of the opening words of Bacon's essay; *Of Travel*:

> Travel, in the younger sort, is a part of education; in the elder, a part of experience.

In *Corinne* it becomes a different matter; travelling is 'un des plus tristes plaisirs de la vie . . . cette hâte pour arriver là où personne ne vous attend.'[17] Eighteenth century self-confidence is replaced by the world-weariness of Romantic melancholy; and not only in the story itself and in the general description of travel, but in the very texture of Madame de Staël's picture of Italy. The noble associations of Italy with classical literature are replaced by the recollection of the tragic and sombre events of more recent history. She was the first writer to stress consistently the aura of pathos lying over Italy, which we have already seen lightly sketched by the Della Cruscan poets; it was a stress which changed the habits of tourists and caused the guide-books to be re-written.

We have noted, for example, that Verona did not arouse memories of Romeo and Juliet in eighteenth century travellers. In the Romantic period, by contrast, such memories became so common-place that 'the source of an Englishman's feelings at Verona [was] that her tale of deep interest is immortalised in the language of his country.'[18] Ironically, it was the French novelist who first attracted widespread English notice to the association: 'C' est un sujet italien que Roméo et Juliette; la scène se passe à Vérone; on y montre encore le tombeau de ces deux amants.'[19] It is only a few years before one begins to find complaints about the dilapidation of the so-called tomb of Juliet caused by 'the zeal of the English for fragments.'[20] Byron himself was among the culprits.

The cell in the hospital of Saint Anne at Ferrara which was falsely claimed to have been that where Tasso languished in prison was another landmark which was put on the tourist map of Italy by *Corinne*. Goethe had been there and noted sceptically that 'instead of Tasso's prison we are shown a woodshed or coal cellar in which he was certainly not confined.'[21] But for Madame de Staël and the hordes of Romantic tourists who followed her to Ferrara the cell was accepted at its face value and the emotions that it inspired made the city 'une des villes d' Italie les plus tristes.'[22]

But most significant of all was Madame de Staël's treatment of Venice. It had traditionally been a city of little interest to the serious traveller. Its post-Roman origin deprived it of classical associations, and its canals struck the eighteenth century as rather disconcerting than enchanting; characteristically of his century, Dr Moore had commented that

there is no manner of doubt that a town, surrounded by water, is a very fine sight; but all the travellers that have existed since the days of Cain, will not convince me that a town, surrounded by land, is not a much finer.[23]

The fame, or notoriety, of Venice rested, indeed, less upon its intellectual and artistic attractions than on its reputation as the European capital of sexual licence. Roger Ascham, in the sixteenth century, had been horrified to find in nine days in Venice 'more libertie to sinne, than ever I heard tell of in our noble Citie of London in ix years',[24] and throughout the seventeenth and eighteenth centuries successive generations of Englishmen contributed their fair share to the perpetuation of so delightfully permissive on atmosphere.[25] But towards the end of the eighteenth century new attitudes towards Venice, the origin of the predominant modern feelings about the city, began to appear. Perhaps the very charming Spanish traveller Don Juan Andres, 'a pioneer in the discovery of the picturesqueness of Venice',[26] was the first to express the breath-taking architectural qualities of the city. '!Quan grande y estupenda no es aquella plaza!', he exclaimed of the Piazza San Marco,[27] whose gaiety and beauty were more fully evoked a few years later in an important passage of Mrs Piozzi, whom we have already met as one of the Della Cruscans:

> Whoever sees St Mark's place lighted up of an evening, adorned with every excellence of human art, and pregnant with pleasure, expressed by intelligent countenances sparkling with every grace of nature; the sea washing its walls, the moon-beams dancing on its subjugated waves, sport and laughter resounding from the coffee-houses, girls with guitars skipping about the square, masks and merry-makers singing as they pass you, unless a barge with a band of music is heard at some distance upon the water, and calls attention to sounds made sweeter by the element over which they are brought – whoever is led suddenly I say to this scene of seemingly perennial gaiety, will be apt to cry out of Venice, as Eve says to Adam in Milton,
> With thee conversing, I *forget all time,*
> All *seasons,* and their *change* – all please *alike.*[28]

Such novel enthusiasm for the gaiety of Venice was contagious, and the fashionable image of the city soon became one of a Piazza where elegant ladies strolled savouring the lights and sounds, casually surveyed by lounging Turks and Armenians quietly smoking cigars, as described by Madame de Krüdener in the twenty-first letter of *Valérie.*

This brilliant picture, however, soon darkened. Napoleon's

destruction of Venetian independence diminished the activity and gaiety of the city. Mrs Radcliffe adopted Mrs Piozzi's description, but made it part of a predominantly gloomy and threatening picture of Italy; Beckford had noted in his diary the Piranesian feel of the place, and Lewis exploited its cloak and dagger atmosphere. Madame de Staël achieves important developments in the creation of the sinister image of the city.

Firstly, she uses its exoticism, not as something exciting, but as a contribution to a feeling of boredom with the present state of civilisation. Looking from the campanile of San Marco towards Dalmatia, and talking of the savage ignorance of the Dalmatians, Corinne says,

> Je me plairais à voir tous les pays où il y a dans les moeurs, dans les costumes, dans le langage, quelque chose d' original. Le monde civilisé est bien monotone, et l' on en connaît tout en peu de temps; j' ai deja assez vécu pour cela.[29]

The association of Venice with gaiety is abandoned in favour of world-weariness; and with this feeling of ennui the novel combines a sustained symbolic exploitation of the threatening sadness of Venice, which set the pattern for the rest of the nineteenth century. It is the last city that Corinne and Nelvil go to together. It is there that he leaves her and returns to Scotland. The tragic memories of the city which Corinne will carry for the rest of her life are emphasised from the moment of their arrival in Venice, when they hear three cannon shots, announcing that in one of the convents a novice is in the process of renouncing the world and taking the veil. Everything in Venice becomes a symbol of sadness, of dissatisfaction with life; the lack of vegetation which other travellers had grumbled about as making them dis-oriented here becomes elegiac:

> Un sentiment de tristesse s' empare de l' imagination en entrant dans Venise. On prend congé de la végétation: on ne voit pas même une mouche en ce séjour; tous les animaux en sont bannis; et l' homme seul est là pour lutter contre la mer.[30]

The pathos of all Madame de Staël's Italian settings is at its strongest in Venice, and becomes a lasting part of the imaginative picture of the city. After *Corinne* only one element remained to be added to complete the full Romantic image of Venice – the awareness of the literary ghosts of the city. That was added by the next great literary visitor to Venice, who went there in 1816 after spending the summer in Switzerland in frequent contact with Madame de Staël, with whose novel he was familiar.[31] It is time to turn to Byron.

3 Byron

Wordsworth learnt Italian from the exile Isola at Cambridge and loved Italy all his life, but his 'Italian' poetry is for the most part disappointing. The elegiac sonnet *On The Extinction of the Venetian Republic* ('Once did She hold the gorgeous East in fee'), written in 1802, is the most memorable of his Italian writings, and doubtless contributed to the Romantic image of Venice as the city of recently departed grandeur; but otherwise one cannot but regret that Wordsworth did not visit Italy while at the height of his poetic powers. In his walking tour of 1790 he went only as far as Lake Como, whose beauty he recorded in *The Prelude* (Book 6, 660–726); in 1820 he went to Milan; but it was not until 1837, at the age of sixty-seven, that he made an extended tour of Italy with Crabb Robinson. But he was, for example, 'indifferent'[1] to Venice, and the poetry which resulted from these visits has very little interest; and even in the more spontaneous mode of letter writing he fails to display very much enthusiasm for what he is seeing.[2]

Coleridge, too, knew Italy and the Mediterranean, having lived from 1804 to 1806 in Malta, whither he had gone to escape from debts and from his unfortunate marriage, and for the sake of his health.[3] He travelled in Italy, and was one of the earliest admirers of the frescoes in the Campo Santo at Pisa, to which he frequently refers in his lectures. He was, moreover, devoted to the Italian epic poets, but, like Wordsworth, his feelings for Italy were only very peripheral to the main interests of his work. It was with the second generation of Romantic poets that Italy assumed a position of outstanding importance, and particularly with Byron.

Byron went to Italy in 1816 and left the country only to undertake his fatal expedition to Greece in 1823, and in the course of seven years' continuous residence came to know Italy and the Italians better than any previous English writer. The events of his life there are well known, and need only briefly be summarised here.

At first Byron settled in Venice, seeing few English, participating occasionally in the social life of the city, but mostly revelling in the

delights of a series of Venetian women, immortalised enthusiastically in his own letters and disgustedly in Shelley's. The kind of
pleasure and excitement he found in these women, and the general
quality of his life in Venice, may be suggested by his description to
Murray of his most tenacious Venetian mistress, La Fornarina, who
managed to continue to stimulate his passion and admiration
during two or three years when a constant stream of women was
flooding through his life:

> The reasons of this were firstly – her person – very dark – tall – the
> Venetian face – very fine black eyes – and certain other qualities
> which need not be mentioned. She was two & twenty years old –
> and never having had children – had not spoilt her figure – nor
> *anything else* – which is I assure you – a great consideration in a hot
> climate where they grow relaxed and doughy and *flumpity* in a
> short time after breeding. – – She was besides a thorough
> Venetian in her dialect – in her thoughts – in her countenance –
> in every thing – with all their naïveté and Pantaloon humour. –
> Besides she could neither read nor write – and could not plague
> me with letters – except twice that she paid sixpence to a public
> scribe under the piazza – to make a letter for her – upon some
> occasion when I was ill and could not see her. – – In other respects
> she was somewhat fierce and 'prepotente' – that is –
> overbearing – and used to walk in whenever it suited her – with
> no very great regard to time, place, nor persons – and if she found
> any women in her way, she knocked them down.[4]

Such was Byron's attachment to the attractions of this kind of life,
and of La Fornarina in particular, that even his visit to Rome, the
climax of his most extended piece of writing about Italy, in the
fourth Canto of *Childe Harold's Pilgrimage*, was cut short by his desire
to return to Venice, where his palazzo was pointed out to English
visitors[5] and his daily rides on the Lido became famous:

> There are only eight horses in Venice; four are of brass, over the
> gate of the cathedral; and the other four are alive in Lord Byron's
> stable.[6]

Byron put an end to this dissipated way of life in 1819, when he
became devoted to Teresa Guiccioli, a far more cultivated and
respectable woman than his previous Italian mistresses, whom he

followed to Ravenna, a town quite off the tourist routes of the day, where he spent two years in a completely Italian environment, adoring la Guiccioli and getting involved in the activities of the revolutionary Carbonarist movement.[7] Under constant surveillance by the Austrian secret police, he was elected a leader of the local cell, contributing funds to the cause and storing insurrectionary arms in his apartment. When her family was banished from the Romagna for their revolutionary sympathies, Byron accepted Shelley's suggestion and went with Teresa and her brother to live near the Shelleys at Pisa. There they stayed until after Shelley's death, removing then to Genoa, whence Byron sailed to Greece in 1823. His seven years in Italy had been not only adventurous, but extremely productive.

Poetically, the essential thing about Italy, to Byron, was that there his whole environment seemed to be a stimulating embodiment of the anguished tension which he felt within himself. Italy was the country upon which Nature had lavished her blessings, which was full of the delights of wine, women and sun, where men had attained some of the peaks of civilisation, but whose achievements, stranded in political degradation and economic backwardness, were now almost a mockery of the magnificent confidence which had created them. Similarly, man himself, the finest of Nature's creations, gifted with astonishing mental and emotional faculties, with an imaginatively felt potential for immense activity and experience, is hopelessly doomed to realise only a pitiful fraction of his aspirations, by the sheer limitations of his physical capabilities. Childe Harold goes to Italy 'to meditate amongst decay, and stand/ A ruin amidst ruins.' (IV.25) The notion of ruin is at the centre of Byron's work, and his attitude to the ruins of Italy is utterly different from that of the classical Grand Tourists. For man himself, to Byron, is a ruin.[8] The crumbling palaces of Venice, the monuments of ancient Rome, are sad fragments of what was once so great and vital but now is inevitably and irretrievably lost. The sight of the ruin or dilapidation of man's greatest achievements stresses the feeling of debility in the individual soul facing the discrepancy between its boundless desires and its pathetic limitations. No longer are the ruins and decayed buildings emblems of past glory to be contemplated and emulated in the modern context. They have become metaphors of the human condition, helping to define the anguish which follows the Romantic realisation which comes to Childe Harold that

. . life's enchanted cup but sparkles near the brim.
His had been quaff'd too quickly, and he found
The dregs were wormwood. (III.8–9)

Such feelings make the Romantic a solitary figure, a stranger to other men going about their daily business. In some ways Byron's life in Italy was the very type of this Romantic situation: scandalous to his own countrymen, from whom he had exiled himself, mysterious to those he had chosen to live amongst, suspicious to the State, misunderstood by all; and the work he produced in this situation did more than any other writer's to define the Romantic dilemma and create the Romantic credo.

Shelley wrote to Byron in 1816 that the French Revolution 'may be called the master theme of the epoch in which we live.'[9] It was, indeed, the focal point of the Romantic crisis. In a period when all kinds of established order – philosophical, theological, socio-political – were being radically questioned and torn apart, the Revolution, the most violent and tangible attack on the old order, was a crucial growth-point of thought, at the centre of the process of emergence of the problematic modern world from the confident world-picture of the Enlightment. The Romantic period replaces the ordered world of secure systems based on absolute and agreed values by a world of relative values and existential attitudes. The demand made on the literature of the time was to analyse the crisis and try to find a valid way forward out of the trauma of un-certainty.

Wordsworth offered the solace of the bliss of solitude. When all intellectual systems are called into doubt, when the problems of living seem too over-bearing, there is always, he proclaimed, something deep within oneself which can give a reassuring sense of sanity and rightness in the universe. Solitary communion with Nature will fill the soul with the 'sense sublime of something far more deeply interfused.' Byron, too, is aware of the deep sense of calm which comes from wandering in the pathless woods and along the lonely shore,

To mingle with the Universe, and feel
What I can ne'er express, yet cannot all conceal.
(C.H.IV. 178)

But Byron goes more deeply into the problem. Wordsworth's 'self-sufficing power of solitude'[10] is a very selective kind of solitude, that of the man – indeed, perhaps, of the Englishman – voluntarily alone with Nature. He does not concern himself with the other kind of solitude, the involuntary feeling of loneliness of one man in the midst of others, which was to be so important a feature of the growth of urban society. Byron, however, does know the feeling when solitude is not a blessing but an affliction, when he is alone

> . . midst the crowd, the hum, the shock of men,
> To hear, to see, to feel, and to possess,
> And roam along, the world's tired denizen,
> With none to bless us, none whom we can bless;
> Minions of splendour shrinking from distress!
>
> (C.H.II.26)

Byron approaches closer to the problems of modern living, problems we have largely inherited from the Romantic period, than Wordsworth can. Far more in the mainstream of European Romanticism than Wordsworth, it has been observed of Byron that 'he, among the great English poets, was the first of our true contemporaries.'[11] His modernity is in his stress on the need, in an era when there are no absolutes left to put faith in, for the individual constantly to create and re-create his own values. The only way, says Byron, to deal with the tensions and frustrations which such an era forces upon us is to try to fuse them into some sort of creative activity, on whatever level it might be.

Politically, for example, one can give sense to one's life by joining in the struggle for liberty. By Byron's time the ruins of Greece and Rome were no longer stirring reminders of past glory, but galling reminders of the present slavery of Greeks and Italians. After the French Revolution there was no longer any question of using the ruins to preach self-satisfied allegories of liberty; rather, it was a matter of concerning oneself with the political struggle to throw off foreign oppression. This Byron did with admirable enthusiasm, going far beyond the earlier poetical protests of the Della Cruscans. From the *Ode on Venice* (1818) onwards, he frequently laments the political desolation of Italy and urges the Italians to do something about it; in *The Prophecy of Dante*, (1819) for example, he uses the persona of the Italian poet to exhort Italy to rise unitedly against oppression:

Oh! my own beauteous land! so long laid low,
So long the grave of thy own children's hopes,
When there is but required a single blow
To break the chain, yet – yet the Avenger stops,
And Doubt and Discord step 'twixt thine and thee,
And join their strength to that which with thee copes;
What is there wanting then to set thee free,
And show thy beauty in its fullest light?
To make the Alps impassible; and we,
Her sons, may do this with *one* deed – Unite.

(Canto 2, 136–45)

Passages like this are not the vain liberal crying in a void that the political poems of *The Florence Miscellany* had been, but attempts to make a constructive contribution to a potentially revolutionary situation. In 1821 Byron sent, though it never arrived, an exhortatory address and an offer of money to the revolutionaries in Naples. In Ravenna he was actively involved with the local Carbonari, and whatever the mixture of sincere commitment and dare-devil exuberance in his revolutionary zeal, it was a zeal serious to the point of dying in Greece, a death which became an inspiration to revolutionary movements throughout the nineteenth century, not least to the Italian Risorgimento: Mazzini declared that it was the finest symbol of the destiny of Art in modern times.[12]

On the imaginative plane, Byron proposes artistic creation as a means of fulfilling desires which the physical conditions of life otherwise frustrate:

'Tis to create, and in creating live
A being more intense, that we endow
With form our fancy, gaining as we give
The life we image, even as I do now.
What am I? Nothing: but not so art thou,
Soul of my thought! with whom I traverse earth,
Invisible but gazing, as I glow
Mix'd with thy spirit, blended with thy birth,
And feeling still with thee in my crush'd feelings dearth.

(C. H. III. 6)

In Italy he found a rich and colourful environment which provided a constant succession of stimuli to such creative activity, and which became absorbed into the texture of the work he produced there. Not least was he aware of the emotional strata built into the Italian landscape by previous writers who had found inspiration there, and, indeed, one of his major contributions to the English apprehension of Italy was to develop Madame de Staël's work, making his readers aware of the thick literary atmosphere of Italy, the association of almost every town with some great author or some fictional character: an atmosphere which Byron's own life and work themselves appreciably enriched. One of his earliest responses to Italy, a letter from Verona to Tom Moore, is typical:

> I have been over Verona. The amphitheatre is wonderful – beats even Greece. Of the truth of Juliet's story, they seem tenacious to a degree, insisting on the fact – giving a date (1303), and showing a tomb. It is a plain, open, and partly destroyed sarcophagus, with withered leaves in it, in a wild and desolate conventual garden, once a cemetery, now ruined to the very graves. The situation struck me as very appropriate to the legend, being blighted as their love. I have brought away a few pieces of the granite, to give to my daughter and my nieces. Of the other marvels of this city, paintings, antiquities, etc., excepting the tombs of the Scaliger Princes, I have no pretensions to judge. The gothic monuments of the Scaligers pleased me, but 'a poor virtuoso am I' and ever yours . . .[13]

No eighteenth century traveller would have treated the amphitheatre so cavalierly, dismissed the art treasures so nonchalantly, or, above all, dwelt so much on the blight and decay which accompany the recollection of the Shakespearean immortality of the city's star-crossed lovers. The contrast between the shabbiness and melancholy of the site of the tomb and the emotional power of its associations, an image of the contrast between man's physical frailty and imaginative sublimity, is the kind of tension which spurs Byron to his own creative achievement.

Similarly in Venice. Byron had loved Venice since boyhood, as the scene of vivid, dramatic action. It was 'the greenest island of my imagination'; 'a poetical place; and classical, to us, from Shakespeare and Otway'; 'Otway, Radcliffe, Schiller, Shakespeare's art/Had stamp'd her image in me'.[14] Byron had chosen to settle in Venice largely because of the vivid presence of its literary ghosts; and partly because so few English went there at that time, a fact which the popularity of his work was to change radically. His two Venetian tragedies, *Marino Faliero* (1821) and *The Two Foscari* (1821) combine all the elements of previous literary images of Venice to re-create the unique atmosphere of the city beneath whose alluring beauty and gaiety festered the diseases of political corruption and sordid, violent intrigue. While

> The high moon sails upon her beauteous way,
> Serenely smoothing o'er the lofty walls
> Of those tall piles and sea-girt palaces,
> Whose porphyry pillars, and whose costly fronts,
> Fraught with the orient spoil of many marbles,
> Like altars ranged along the broad canal,
> Seem each a trophy of some mighty deed
> Rear'd up from out the waters,

conspirators gather to rise against 'this monster of a state' where 'private wrongs have sprung from public vices,' since

> . . . fatal poison to the springs of life,
> To human ties, and all that's good and dear,
> Lurks in the present institutes of Venice.[15]

What in Lewis's *Bravo of Venice* had been the background to an adventure story here becomes the very substance of the drama. It is not simply the exciting stories of Faliero or the Foscari, but the tension of the contrast between forces of life and death, light and dark, purity and corruption, which creates the vitality and the significance of the dramas, for in Italy 'decay/Is still impregnate with divinity.'[16] Not only at Venice and Verona, but at Arquà, where Petarch declined and died, at Ravenna, where Dante died, and at Ferrara, where, as we have seen, Tasso lived and suffered; wherever Byron goes in Italy there is this constant tension, particularly apparent in the Florence section of the fourth Canto of *Childe Harold's Pilgrimage*, between decay and death, the sad mortality of genius on the one hand, and vitality, beauty and the immortality of art on the other. Nowhere more than in Italy could the Romantic traveller feel himself a ruin amid ruins; and in Italy nowhere more than at Rome. In the famous opening stanza of the Roman section of *Childe Harold* Byron ostensibly preaches the old Renaissance doctrine of subduing individual sorrow by contemplat-

ing the great movements of history; but the effect of the poetry is
quite the opposite. Its tone is so mournful that individual anguish
is intensified by having added to it the sadness of the passing of
nations:

> Oh Rome! my country! city of the soul!
> The orphans of the heart must turn to thee,
> Lone mother of dead empires! and control
> In their shut breasts their petty misery.
> What are our woes and sufferance? Come and see
> The cypress, hear the owl, and plod your way
> O'er steps of broken thrones and temples, Ye!
> Whose agonies are evils of a day –
> A world is at our feet as fragile as our clay.
>
> (C. H. IV. 78)

This stanza creates the complete Romantic image of Rome. The
advice to sublimate one's sorrow is an effective control against
sentimentality; while the real movement of the verse is towards
internalising the sorrow of dead empires. The orphan of the heart –
the Romantic, finding himself alone in a world where there are no
values left to rely on – will feel at home in a city where he has
constant reminders of such sadness. Byron has here created the most
powerful modern literary image of Rome, more immediately
accessible and strikingly vivid than that of Gibbon, from which it
partly derives, and completely different from that of the Grand
Tour.

Before going to Italy, Byron had already worked out the
character of the suffering Romantic hero, in the magnificently
narrated early tales, with very Faustian overtones in *Manfred*, and in
the earlier Cantos of *Childe Harold*. The fourth Canto is a hymn to
Italy as the country which can offer the greatest stimulus to the
melancholy imagination for those vivid flights of feeling which seem
to give it a reason for continuing to live. When Harold dies at Rome,
he sets the pattern for a succession of nineteenth century heroes to
find Italy to be the country which offers so much satisfaction with
one hand while it destroys with the other the life that might have
enjoyed it.

But there were other sides to Italy than this. It was also the
country of warmth and relaxation, a country of sensual delight,
enthusiastically contrasted with England in stanzas 41–9 of *Beppo*:

With all its sinful doings, I must say,
That Italy's a pleasant place to me.

In Italy sunshine is strong and guaranteed, the country is beautiful
and luxuriant, the language is 'soft bastard Latin,/Which melts like
kisses from a female mouth,' and the women themselves,

> From the rich peasant cheek of ruddy bronze,
> And large black eyes that flash on you a volley
> Of rays that say a thousand things at once,
> To the high dama's brow, more melancholy,
> But clear, and with a wild and liquid glance,
> Heart on her lips, and soul within her eyes,
> Soft as her clime, and sunny as her skies,

are a more inviting prospect than the 'chilly women' of expensive,
over-taxed, damp England. Despite all the gloomy and violent
literary associations, Italy is still the nearest thing we have to
Paradise:

> Thou art the garden of the world, the home
> Of all Art yields, and Nature can decree;
> Even in thy desert, what is like to thee?
> Thy very weeds are beautiful, thy waste
> More rich than other climes' fertility;
> Thy wreck a glory, and thy ruin graced
> With an immaculate charm which cannot be defaced.
>
> (C. H. IV. 26)

It is part of the fullness of Byron's writing that it gives strong
expression to both sides of this apparent paradox: to the ruins of
Rome and the women of Venice. The different aspects of Italy are
placed, in Byron's poetry, in fruitful relationship. It is not just that
in Italy the women are more attractive, the sun more pleasant, and
the ruins more impressive than in England. More than that, sensual
satisfaction is more acute in an environment which constantly
recalls its own transitoriness; pleasures do not become domesticated
and taken for granted, but are enhanced by a sense of being victories
over Time, whose destructive power is seen in the ruins and the
crumbling palaces. And this decay itself is felt the more vividly for
one's being the more aware of the life-values which are being

destroyed. Each feeling deepens the other, and in Italy Byron finds the most stimulating co-existence of both. The richness and variety of stimuli are suggested by the ease with which he moves from devastation to delight in describing why he likes Venice despite its evident decay:

> I have been familiar with ruins too long to dislike desolation. Besides, I have fallen in love . . .[17]

This kind of felt tension gives Byron the basic structural principle of *Don Juan*. The splendid hero, young, handsome, passionate, noble, courageous, is contrasted with the older, worldly, rather weary (but never wearisome) narrator. The narrator creates his ideal hero the more lovingly because through Don Juan he is living imaginatively those delights of whose fragility and brevity he is so aware, and that awareness is made the more poignant precisely by the vitality of his creation. *Don Juan* is full of the flow of diverse feelings which constitutes the experience of living, and its basis is in this contrast, of the sort which Byron constantly felt around him in his life in Italy. For Italy, like *Don Juan*, was a matter of colourful life going on in the context of the decay of previous generations, a decay which is a constant reminder of the inevitable fate of all feeling, and thus a symbol of Romantic anguish.

Moreover, Italy also offered Byron the model of the literary technique which enabled him to incorporate a wide variety of stimuli within his poetic achievement. The versatility of Italian epic poetry had attracted him since the beginning of his poetic career; as early as 1811 he had written of *Childe Harold* as being 'intended to be a poem on *Ariosto's plan*, that *is* to *say*, on *no plan* at all.'[18] But it was not until he was in Italy that he fully discovered the magnificent resourcefulness of the ottava rima. Byron was not the first English Romantic to use the form, and his interest in it was partly aroused by an English model, J. H. Frere's *The Monks and The Giants* (1817–8), but he exploited more creatively than any other English poet the lessons to be learnt from his study of Pulci (from whose *Morgante Maggiore* he translated an extract), Berni and Casti. From them he learnt the value of the fluidity of the burlesque method, of the juxtaposition of terse narrative and loose digression, lofty and colloquial language, the sincere and the ludicrous, the ribald and the tearful; and from them he learnt the use of self-assertive narrators and of run-on lines and stanzas, and outrageous rhymes.[19] The

Italian epic writers gave Byron a technique which would adapt to
any material, and whose life was precisely in the variety of material
it embraced. In *Beppo* (1818), his first significant attempt at using
the burlesque mode, the bulk of the poem, and almost all its vitality,
is in the digressions woven around the slight fabric of the narrative
structure. In a casual, conversational manner, witty comments and
striking vignettes succeed each other as the observations prompted
in his mind by the events of his simple story flow off Byron's pen.
Despite the apparent flippancy and facility of the verse, the poem's
achievement is fundamentally serious. The vivacity of its style is an
implicit criticism of any attitude to life that is less all-embracing and
vigorously joyful. ('One hates an author that's *all author*': *Beppo*,
LXXV.) The contagion of Byron's vitality is a stimulus to a similar
responsiveness to the pulse of life in his reader, and, particularly, the
constant target of his satire is a narrow-mindedness and lack of
spontaneity which he found in English life, from which the example
of the poems aims at helping his English readers to liberate
themselves. Throughout *Beppo*, England is contrasted with Italy,
and specifically with Venice. We have already noticed something of
the attraction to Byron of the beauty of Venetian women and the
freedom of the social mores which encouraged the development of
their winning personalities. By contrast, he evokes the behaviour
and educational background of an English girl emerging into
society:

> 'Tis true, your budding Miss is very charming,
>   But shy and awkward at first coming out,
> So much alarm'd, that she is quite alarming,
>   All Giggle, Blush; half Pertness, and half Pout;
> And glancing at *Mamma*, for fear there's harm in
>   What you, she, it, or they may be about,
> The nursery still lisps out in all they utter –
> Besides, they always smell of bread and butter.
>
> (*Beppo*, XXXIX)

Italy cultivates the enjoyment of life, while Puritanical England
attempts to repress the instinct to enjoyment. Byron, of course, had
never been a Puritan, but it was largely his experience of the
richness of life in Italy which gave him the vigorous impulse of his
maturest criticism of English life, as well as the example of Italian
poetry which gave him the ideal technique for the embodiment of

his constant plea for a more vibrant openness to living.

Thus, although his greatest work, *Don Juan*, has little ostensibly to do with Italy, the possibility of its achievement grows directly out of Byron's experience of the country in which it was written. The tension which is consistently at the basis of his work is the apprehension of the discrepancy between the immensity of man's imaginative power and the pathetic limitations of his physical capabilities. Stated on another level, the contrast is between the crippling hypocrisy and cant Byron found in cloudy England and the pleasures of life under an Italian sun. While the former contrast is absolute, part of the condition of life, the second is susceptible of remedy: it is possible to escape into a fuller life, represented by that of Italy. But within Italy itself there is a further contrast. Fittingly, the country which seems to offer the greatest possibilities of fulfilment also offers the most constant reminders of devastation and decay. Italy is the country where the conflict of forces of life and death is most constantly and vividly felt in the fabric of everyday existence, where the individual who goes there, like Childe Harold, disconcerted by the problems of living is most likely to come to an awareness of the nature of his own existence as a brief and fragile synthesis of the two, and of the need to risk himself upon the flood of life and to seek his values from the experience of living rather than by reliance on supposed absolutes whose claims to authority are mocked both by the vigour of life with which they are inadequate to deal and by the atmosphere of ruin which recalls the relativity of all things.

Hence the immense significance of Italy to Byron. Of all the English poets since Shakespeare, Byron is the most fully responsive to the whole range of the experience of living, to its self-evident delights and its anguished complexities, its deepest and most universal feelings and its ephemeral chatter; and Italy was to Byron the country where all the ingredients of existence were most suggestively mixed together. No other English writer threw himself so completely into the physical and imaginative enjoyment of Italy, and in comparison with Byron all those who followed him there in the nineteenth century seem to be fragmentary in their attitudes both to Italy and to life. With any of these writers their response to Italy is an index of their response to life; despite having the vivid example of Byron's work before them, none could accept that fullness of joyous acceptance of the South, which is an acceptance of the conditions of life itself, which characterises Byron's work and is the index of his health and sanity. Byron himself summed up the diseased mentality of his compatriots which had perennially prevented them from floating on the tide of sensuous Mediterranean philosophy:

> The Italians do not understand the English; indeed, how can they? for they (the Italians) are frank, simple, and open in their natures, following the bent of their inclinations, which they do not believe to be wicked; while the English, to conceal the indulgence of theirs, daily practise hypocrisy, falsehood, and uncharitableness; so that to *one* error is added many crimes.[20]

A century later, D. H. Lawrence was to proclaim much the same thing, with the air of discovering something new; but Lawrence was trying painfully to re-create that pagan sanity which to Byron had come so naturally, and at just that moment of the breaking up of the old order when the time might have been ripe for it. Lawrence was crippled by the fact that he had to will it: and to will the exaltation of the flesh above the will is clearly a tragically vicious circle. He had to struggle against the history of a century of inability to follow the Byronic example and embrace the entirety of life.

4 Shelley; and the Minor Romantics

It is a remarkable testimony to the importance of Italy to the second generation of English Romantics that in the years 1821 and 1822 the most significant centre of English literary activity was not in England but in the sleepy town of Pisa. When Byron arrived there at the beginning of November, 1821, Shelley was finishing the manuscript of *Hellas*. A few months earlier he had written *Adonais* in Pisa in memory of Keats who, almost symbolically for our subject, had died in Rome on his way to meet Shelley there, having seen scarcely anything of the beauty of Italy for which he had longed so much. Walter Savage Landor had left Pisa for Florence a few months before Byron's arrival. In Pisa, Byron worked on *Don Juan*, while Mary Shelley was writing her novel *Valperga*. Samuel Rogers, with whom Byron had made part of the journey from Ravenna, stopped in Pisa on his way home from Rome, and Leigh Hunt came down from England in the spring of 1822 to try to found a new liberal journal with the help of Byron and Shelley. Then Shelley drowned off Livorno, everyone went away, and Pisa's brief literary eminence was over.

Shelley spent the last four years of his life in Italy, a country which he, like Byron, regarded as the 'Paradise of exiles'.[1] In general, however, their reactions to the country were as different as their poetry. Shelley, for example, thought Italian women

> perhaps the most contemptible of all who exist under the moon; the most ignorant, the most disgusting, the most bigotted, the most filthy. Countesses smell so of garlic that an ordinary Englishman cannot approach them.[2]

Even when Shelley approaches closest to the Byronic atmosphere, in *The Cenci* (1819), the play is still distinctly different from Byron's Italian dramas. It has a deeper and more subtle psychological

44

interest than any of Byron's plays, and a different kind of interest in the Italian material. The play is pervaded, for example, by a study of the nature of Italian Catholicism, which in the *Preface* Shelley explicitly contrasts with English Protestantism:

> Religion in Italy is not, as in Protestant countries, a cloak to be worn on particular days; or a passport which those who do not wish to be railed at carry with them to exhibit; or a gloomy passion for penetrating the impenetrable mysteries of our being, which terrifies its possessor at the darkness of the abyss to the brink of which it has conducted him. Religion coexists, as it were, in the mind of an Italian Catholic, with a faith in that of which all men have the most certain knowledge. It is inter-woven with the whole fabric of life. It is adoration, faith, submission, penitence, blind admiration; not a rule for moral conduct. It has no necessary connexion with any one virtue. The most atrocious villain may be rigidly devout, and without any shock to the established faith, confess himself to be so. Religion pervades intently the whole frame of society, and is, according to the temper of the mind which it inhabits, a passion, a persuasion, an excuse, a refuge; never a check.

The analysis is presented with a clarity, precision, and lack of prejudice quite beyond the ability of the majority of writers who tried to describe Italian religion to an English audience, and quite different from Byron's more exuberant approach to Italy.

Essentially, *The Cenci* comes from the tradition of the Gothic novel. In his youth Shelley had composed two nugatory Gothic romances, *Zastrozzi* (1810), which took the cloak and dagger image of Venice from Charlotte Dacre's *Zofloya, or The Moor* (1806), and *St Irvyne* (1811). In *The Cenci* he combines the trappings of the Gothic novel, particularly in the evocation of the Castle of Petrella, with his observation of Italian life and his deep psychological insight, to produce a more exciting Italian atmosphere than any of the novelists had managed to achieve in prose. The mood established in the opening lines –

> That matter of the murder is hushed up
> If you consent to yield his Holiness
> Your fief that lies beyond the Pincian gate, –

is sustained throughout the play, through the description of

> That savage rock, the Castle of Petrella:
> 'Tis safely walled, and moated round about:
> Its dungeons underground, and its thick towers,
> Never told tales; though they have heard and seen
> What might make dumb things speak, (II. i. 168–72)

to the murder of the Count –

> –They are about it now.
>   –Nay, it is done.
> –I have not heard him groan.
>   –He will not groan.
>
>   (IV. ii. 1–2) –

and Beatrice being led off to execution. The oppressive, violent image of Italy, derived from Shakespeare and developed by the novelists, is here united to a dramatic style which is itself indebted to the Shakespearean model. The two lines of development fittingly re-unite in this, the last major work of Gothic Romanticism.

The Cenci, however, is rather outside the main stream of Italian influence on Shelley. Though in this play he showed himself capable of exploiting the violent episodes in the country's history, he was much more deeply interested in the beauty of Italy. Far from being horrific as in *The Cenci*, the atmosphere of Italy was extremely congenial to him, to the extent of his feeling more at home there than in England: 'Our roots were never struck so deeply as at Pisa,' he wrote to Mary in 1821.[3] Based in Pisa, Shelley travelled quite widely in Italy, and everywhere found imaginative stimulus of the most pleasant kind. Often – it is in the nature of his abstract, intellectual poetry – there is nothing in the verse itself to suggest this: but it is constantly evident from Mary's notes to the poems, his own prefaces, and the enthusiasm of the magnificent series of letters to Peacock. Rome, for example, was to Shelley the 'capital of the vanished world,' 'moral degradation contrasted with the glory of nature and the arts,' 'a great city, where the imagination is kept for ever active and awake.[4] In the Preface to his master-piece, *Prometheus Unbound* (written 1818–9; published 1820), he is vividly explicit:

This Poem was chiefly written upon the mountainous ruins of the Baths of Caracalla, among the flowery glades, and thickets of odoriferous blossoming trees, which are extended in ever winding labyrinths upon its immense platforms and dizzy arches suspended in the air. The bright blue sky of Rome, and the effect of the vigorous awakening spring in that divinest climate, and the new life with which it drenches the spirits even to intoxication, were the inspirations of this drama.

The Piranesian reference in the dizzy arches is evident; but Shelley's response to the ruins is quite different from those of other English admirers of Piranesi. Far from being terrific, the arches are seen in a context which is eminently attractive; the inspirational qualities of the site lie not in its physical reminder of decay, but in its beauty. The ruins, the sun and the flowers provide an idyllically conducive ambiance for Shelley's poetical work, although the poetry which grows out of this stimulus has nothing specifically Italian about it. Similarly, the *Ode To The West Wind* 'was conceived and chiefly written in a wood that skirts the Arno, near Florence,'[5] and the famous skylark was heard one evening in the lanes near Livorno, but although meteorologists may detect in *The West Wind* descriptions of cloud formations peculiarly characteristic of the region[6] there is nothing self-evidently Italian in the poetry.

Sometimes, however, Shelley does describe directly in verse his feelings about Italy: about Venice, for example. Despite the haunting figure of the lunatic in *Julian and Maddalo*, a poem which is to some extent a record of his stay there with Byron, Shelley's Venice – 'sweet Venice . . . bright Venice' – is quite a different place from Byron's. Shelley is not interested in the literary ghosts of the city, nor in the oppressive presence of the prisons and the shades of the Consiglio dei Dieci, nor the gaiety of Carnival. He is a little troubled by the threat of the ultimate destruction of Venice by the sea, but, above all, he is enthralled by the magic of the city. His Venice is not a city of gloom or death, nor of sensual pleasure; it is a city stupendously responsive to the lighting effects of the sun on water and marble. What is memorably Venetian in *Julian and Maddalo* is not the lunatic languishing in the mad-house but the beauty of the sunset over Venice as the protagonists watch it from the Lido:

> As those who pause on some delightful way,
> Though bent on pleasant pilgrimage, we stood,

Looking upon the evening and the flood,
Which lay between the city and the shore,
Paved with the image of the sky; the hoar
And aery Alps, towards the north, appeared,
Through mist, an heaven-sustaining bulwark, reared
Between the east and west; and half the sky
Was roofed with clouds of rich emblazonry,
Dark purple at the zenith, which still grew
Down the steep west into a wondrous hue
Brighter than burning gold, even to the rent
Where the swift sun yet paused in his descent
Among the many folded hills – they were
Those famous Euganean hills – which bear,
As seen from Lido, through the harbour piles,
The likeness of a clump of peaked isles –
And then, as if the earth and sea had been
Dissolved into one lake of fire, were seen
Those mountains towering, as from waves of flame,
Around the vaporous sun, from which there came
The inmost purple spirit of light, and made
Their very peaks transparent. (63–85)

In a poem of the previous year the view had been reversed, when
Shelley had looked down from the Euganean hills at dawn across
the 'sun-girt city':

Lo! the sun upsprings behind,
Broad, red, radiant, half reclined
On the level quivering line
Of the waters crystalline;
And before that chasm of light,
As within a furnace bright,
Column, tower, and dome, and spire,
Shine like obelisks of fire,
Pointing with inconstant motion
From the altar of dark ocean
To the sapphire-tinted skies;
As the flames of sacrifice
From the marble shrines did rise,
As to pierce the dome of gold
Where Apollo spoke of old.[7]

The stress on the shimmering quality of light marks a notable stage in the growth of the literary apprehension of Italy. We have seen how, in the previous century, the change from viewing ruins as emblems of former greatness to seeing them as reminders of human transience had been reflected in a growing tendency to describe them in the setting sun or the pale light of the moon, but no-one before Shelley had dwelt so lovingly on the sheer miracle of the effects of light. With descriptions such as these we are clearly much closer to Turner's Venice than to Canaletto's.

It is moments like this, or like the days spent writing *Prometheus Unbound* in the Baths of Caracalla, that delighted and inspired Shelley in Italy, rather than any qualities of Italian life, with which his contact was slight, and quite unlike Lord Byron's. One interest in contemporary Italy, they did, however, share: its revolutionary politics. The *Lines Written Among The Euganean Hills* in 1818 had warned the Venetians and Paduans against the dangers of falling into irrecoverable decline unless they soon threw off the Austrian yoke, and when in 1820 and 1821 insurrection did break out in Italy and Spain, Shelley 'looked upon the struggle . . . as decisive of the destinies of the world, probably for centuries to come.'[8] Shelley greeted the short-lived Naples revolt of 1820 with an *Ode To Naples* exhorting the revolutionaries to set an example which would arouse all Italy against her tyrants. For Shelley liberty and beauty went hand in hand; his poem ends with an appeal to the Spirit of Love and Beauty:

> Great Spirit, deepest Love!
> Which rulest and dost move
> All things which live and are, within the Italian shore;
> Who spreadest heaven around it,
> Whose woods, rocks, waves, surround it;
> Who sittest in thy star, o'er Ocean's western floor,
> Spirit of Beauty! at whose soft command
> The sunbeams and the showers distil its foison
> From the Earth's bosom chill;
> O bid those beams be each a blinding brand
> Of lightning! bid those showers be dews of poison!
> Bid the Earth's plenty kill!
> Bid thy bright Heaven above,
> Whilst light and darkness bound it,
> Be their tomb who planned

To make it ours and thine!
Or, with thine harminizing ardours fill
And raise thy sons, as o'er the prone horizon
Thy lamp feeds every twilight wave with fire
By man's high hope and unextinct desire,
The instrument to work thy will divine!
Then clouds from sunbeams, antelopes from leopards,
    And frowns and fears from Thee,
    Would not more swiftly flee
Than Celtic wolves from the Ausonian shepherds.
    Whatever, Sprit, from thy starry shrine
    Thou yieldest or witholdest, Oh let be
    This city of thy worship ever free!

The contrast with Byron is clear. Both respond enthusiastically to the same political events, but their responses are quite different. Byron attempts to involve himself in events, because commitment to the struggle of a people he admires to attain an end he feels to be desirable is a self-justifying activity. Shelley's approach is more purely intellectual: his concern is much less for the people involved, or the day to day realities of the situation, than for the beauty of the abstract principle of freedom. Byron could not have written a stanza like this of Shelley's without immediately writing another to undercut it and bring it down to earth – a potential criticism of which Shelley was aware: 'You talk Utopia', says Maddalo to Julian. Byron's view of life is broader and tougher than Shelley's vision, which is more intense. But, though Shelley distilled into his verse much of the essence of the beauty of Italy in a way quite beyond the range of Byron's art, one cannot help feeling that, for all its exquisite value, this response to Italy – to life – is fragmentary and partial in a way that Byron's is not.

Samuel Rogers travelled in Italy in 1814–5 and 1821–2 and published his poem *Italy* in 1822. At first a commercial failure, the book achieved popularity in the lavishly produced edition of 1830; but it was a success which came less from the poetry than from the illustrations which Rogers had commissioned from Turner. It is these vignettes which have made the volume famous, not only as a stage in the development of Turner's career but, especially, for the impression they made on the young Ruskin. To these subjects we shall return later, but for the moment we must consider the poem itself which, long neglected, has of recent years begun again to find admirers.[9]

The first observation to be made is that, although it lacks the stature of the work of Byron or Shelley, the poetry is attractive and readable, by comparison with other poets of the period who wrote on Italy. Rogers can still be read and enjoyed, while works like John Chaloner's *Rome* (1821) or William Sotheby's *Italy* (1828) have become mere documents of literary history. Rogers' distinctive quality is that he was a connoisseur of Italian art, who was also a moderately gifted poet. Of his connoisseurship there is no doubt: a rich banker, his private collection was one of the artistic attractions of London, and from it he left a Giorgione, a Titian and a Guido Reni to the National Gallery. In his notes on Florence he rather charmingly observes that a Cimabue in Santa Croce was just like his own,[10] and the soundness of his taste is evidenced by his starting the Florentine section of his poem by praising the Masaccio frescoes in the Carmine, paintings which hold a crucial place in the history of art, but which were almost totally ignored by travellers of the time. The attractiveness of the poem is that it conveys vividly and gracefully the gentle affection and deep admiration of such a man for Italy. Rogers has often been reproached for being old-fashioned in his attitudes to Italy; but though he was born in 1763 and thus in his fifties when he first went to Italy, the reproach is more justly applicable to some younger poets than to Rogers. On the contrary, his *Italy* is a significant growth-point of feeling, since it applies the viewpoint of the wealthy, cultivated Grand Tourist not to Classical but to Renaissance Italy. The eighteenth century had found inspiration for its self-confidence in the grandeur of ancient Rome; the nineteenth would seek refuge from the ugliness of the new industrial society in the beauty of Italian culture. Rogers' *Italy* is the pleasant link between two quite different attitudes: a more interesting link between two ages than the better-known one that in his youth he almost met Dr Johnson and in old age he blessed the infant Swinburne.

Italy, to Rogers, was the country where 'the memory sees more than the eye,'[11] and he evokes the mysterious process by which places absorb the feel of the events that have taken place in them, in his *St Mark's Place* in the *Italy* sequence:

> Over how many tracts, vast, measureless,
> Ages on ages roll, and none appear
> Save the wild hunter ranging for his prey;
> While on this spot of earth, the work of man,
> How much has been transacted! Emperors, Popes,

> Warriors, from far and wide, laden with spoil,
> Landing, have here performed their several parts,
> Then left the stage to others. Not a stone
> In the broad pavement, but to him who has
> An eye, an ear for the Inanimate World,
> Tells of past ages.

This is the note which dominates the poems; everywhere, Italy is redolent of the past, whether it is at Venice, among the ruins of Rome, or, above all, at Florence:

> Of all the fairest Cities of the Earth
> None is so fair as FLORENCE. 'Tis a gem
> Of purest ray; and what a light broke forth,
> When it emerged from darkness! Search within,
> Without; all is enchantment! 'Tis the Past
> Contending with the Present; and in turn
> Each has the mastery.

Clearly, this is not great poetry; but it is fluent and attractive, the first English poetic celebration of those qualities of Italy which would increasingly become a solace to sensitive Englishmen as the century progressed. Rogers' affection for Italy, and his need of its spiritual resources, are movingly suggested by the opening lines of his *Farewell*:

> And now farewell to Italy – perhaps
> For ever! Yet, methinks, I could not go,
> I could not leave it, were it mine to say,
> 'Farewell for ever!'

But as well as these eloquent meditations on the history and beauty of Italy, Rogers' *Italy* also contains a number of short narrative poems on Italian subjects, all but one in a vein of pathos which is the principal characteristic of 'Italian' poetry in the years after Waterloo. One's impression is that the remarkable growth of interest in the pathetic in the poetry of the time is a development of an aspect of the Gothic novel, which had, of course, stressed at considerable length the sufferings of its heroes and especially its heroines. Like the Gothic novelists, the poets of this genre sought a great deal of their material in Italian subjects, and characteristically claimed an excessively simple and self-satisfied moral purpose behind their apparently morbid interest in suffering: Laetitia Landon, in her *The Venetian Bracelet* (1829), summed up their moral claims in asserting that

> The heart of vanity, the head of pride,
> Touch'd by such sorrow, are half purified;
> And we rise up less selfish, having known
> Part in deep grief, yet that grief not our own.

Though these works are too trivial to detain us long, some suggestion of their quantity will indicate the astonishing amount of attention devoted to this extremely narrow aspect of Italy. We have already noted William Parson's translation of Dante's Francesca da Rimini episode; Byron himself re-translated the passage, and in 1816 Leigh Hunt expanded the story to 1,700 lines in his *Story of Rimini*, entirely losing the poignancy of Dante in a mass of pathetic detail. The story of Dante's Pia dei Tolomei was retold by Mrs Hemans as *The Maremma* in *Tales, & Historic Scenes, In Verse* (1819), and again by William Herbert in *Pia della Pietra* (1820), while the Ugolino episode was treated by Edward Wilmot in *Ugolino; or, The Tower of Famine* (1828). The pathetic tales of Boccaccio similarly attracted attention, two versions of the Pot of Basil story appearing in 1820, Barry Cornwall's *Sicilian Story* and Keats' *Isabella*, the undoubted master-piece of the genre, followed by versions of two other tales, *The Garden Of Florence* and *The Ladye of Provence*, by Keats' friend and collaborator John Hamilton Reynolds in 1821. Also in 1821, John Chaloner's *Rome: A Poem* contains a translation of Verri's *Story of A Vestal Virgin* who dies after receiving her lover in the temple; while Barry Cornwall's *The Letter of Boccaccio* (in *The Flood of Thessaly & Other Poems*, 1823) is supposedly a letter from the poet to a girl he hopelessly adores, and Cornwall's *Marcian Colonna* (1820) and Laetitia Landon's *The Improvisatrice* and *Rosalie* (both 1824) are all tales of thwarted Italian love.

Nor was the craving for pathos, and its association with Italy, confined to poetry. The ceremony of a novice taking the veil became for a while one of the principal tourist attractions of the country, and no traveller's diary was complete without a detailed, poignant account of the ceremony.[12] Rogers got up early one morning to see the ceremony in Rome,[13] and recorded his impressions in *The Nun*, addressing the novice in terms of sombre compassion:

In thy gentle bosom sleep
Feelings, affections, destined now to die,
To wither like the blossom in the bud,
Those of a wife, a mother; leaving there
A cheerless void, a chill as of the grave,
A langour and a lethargy of soul,
Death-like, and gathering more and more, till Death
Comes to release thee.

Although this is one of the best of such poems, the limitation of its attitude, its failure to make even a gesture towards imaginative understanding of the Roman Catholic point of view, is shocking; the whole genre, indeed, is depressing in its unremitting stress on the negation of the positive values of life. There could scarcely be a greater contrast with the treatments of Italy by Byron and Shelley, within whose shadow these poets fall.

We have already twice mentioned Leigh Hunt in passing, and must now consider for a moment his slight place in our story. As well as *The Story of Rimini*, Hunt produced throughout his career a series of translations and adaptations from the Italian poets, of a quality which was at best mediocre and could fall to levels of bathos suggested by his calling *The Divine Comedy* 'the Italian *Pilgrim's Progress*.'[14] There was, however, a healthy streak of vitality in his work, which was not entirely devoted to the cultivation of pathos; as, for example, in his translation of Redi's *Bacchus in Tuscany* (1825), with its energetic celebration of Tuscan food and wine, or his adaptation of the song *Se monaca ti fai* as *The Nun* (1821), beginning

If you become a nun, dear,
    A friar I will be;
In any cell you run, dear,
    Pray look behind for me.

Doggerel, indeed, but a change from the usual mournful image of conventual life.[15]

Hunt spent the years 1822–5 in Italy, at first at Monte Nero and Pisa with Byron and Shelley, then at Genoa with Byron, and finally with Landor and Charles Armitage Brown at Florence, where he thought of founding an English newspaper, but abandoned the idea as soon as he had enough money to allow him to return to England. A much lesser poet and much less attracted to Italy than Byron and

Shelley, no valuable poetry resulted from his living there. Indeed, his motive for going there in the first place had been practical rather than poetical. With Byron and Shelley's help, he had hoped to found a new radical magazine, *The Liberal*, which could appear with more impunity in Pisa than had been the case with his brother's *Examiner* in London. But the plan was disrupted by the death of Shelley and departure of Byron, and only four numbers of the magazine appeared. The most distinguished contribution was Byron's *Vision of Judgment*, but much of the material related to Italy: for example, a translation of Ariosto, an article on Casti, stories of medieval Italy, and Hunt's *Letters From Abroad*, the first of which is perhaps the most eloquent and enthusiastic account of the beauties of Pisa to have appeared in English, though unfortunately much too long to be quoted effectively here.[16] Had the Pisan circle continued to flourish, and *The Liberal* got properly off the ground, the subsequent story of this study might have been very different; as it is, Hunt and *The Liberal* are merely transient phenomena in the history of Italy in English literature.

5 Italy in English Fiction, 1820–37

The pathos which characterised English poetic treatments of Italy in the 1820s was also a feature of the 'Italian' novel in the same period. Though they had the example of Byron before them, the tendency of the novelists' exploration of Italy in these years was towards a feeling that any such creative relationship with Italy as Byron had achieved was purely exceptional, and that the more general truth lay rather in the direction of Madame de Staël's finding, that the life-values represented by Italy were tragically unattainable to the northern spirit, however great its yearning for them.

Lord Normanby was the first English writer to take up seriously the *Corinne* theme, particularly in his very popular collection of stories, *The English in Italy* (1825). Normanby spent two years in Italy as a young man, when his liberal political views had made him embarrassing to his family, and in these stories he cleverly and attractively exploited the English enthusiasm for Italy at a time when 'Jenkinsons and Tomkinsons tumble down the Alps in living avalanches.' (Vol. 2, p. 221) The best of the stories is the first, *L' Amoroso*. Though rather contrived, melodramatic and moralising, the lightness and economy of its style make a delightful contrast with most English fiction of the time. The heroine, Matilda Euston, full of Romantic notions, persuades her parents to make the tour of Europe, and becomes infatuated with Italy and contemptuous of her own country. The description of her initial response to Italy is both a good specimen of Normanby's ironic style and a partial portrait of the first of a long line of post-Romantic Anglo–Saxon heroines which includes James's Daisy Miller, Forster's Lilia Herriton and Lawrence's Alvina Houghton:

Foreign address, foreign adulation, foreign enthusiasm capti-vated her. Italy too was the land of the arts, and Italians alone understood the finer feelings inspired by those intellectual sisters. The verses of Tasso had ever been familiar to Matilda; she knew of no English poetry that touched the heart, without a smack of foreign in it. Byron was a self-adopted Italian – the muse of Moore revelled either in oriental or occidental fancy, and the northern scenes of Scott, so flexible was her geography, she placed in the same poetic latitude, at least with those of Ariosto. Of Italian music, too, Miss Euston had become an admirer: her mother had of course a box at St Carlos, over-flowing each evening with crowds of critical amateurs, and the comparative merits of Davide and Nozzari, of Cimarosa and Paësiello often disturbed her rest. She made the most vigorous efforts at comprehending the occult merits and excellencies of the art of painting; but this lay all together too deep for her, and on this point, at least, Matilda was doomed to reluctant ignorance. (Vol. 1, pp. 36–7)

In Naples, Matilda forgets the lover she has left in England and falls in love with the Count Avellino. The English lover turns up rather dramatically, but though he wounds the Count in a duel he fails to destroy Matilda's plans to marry and drops dead of a broken heart on seeing her wedding procession. The marriage is a disaster: the illusions of courtship had not anticipated the hopeless confrontation between the English ideal of domestic comfort in marriage and the Italian notion of great social freedom for each partner, based on the tradition of the cavalier servente. It is not long before Matilda finds the strain intolerable and runs away to seek refuge aboard a British warship, from which she sees taking place on shore a duel in which her husband is killed by an English friend of whom he had become groundlessly jealous. As the novel ends, Matilda is living in chronic melancholy in London,

> her fate a striking, and, it is to be hoped, not a useless example to the British fair, who learn, in their enthusiasm for foreign climes and habits, to contemn the domestic virtues of their country, – who mistake the mere charms of novelty for sources of lasting happiness, and who blush not to forfeit the name of English women, in yielding up their hearts and hands to the fickle keeping of a stranger. (Vol. 1, p. 220)

Clearly, the explicit moral is disappointingly trite, and the action melodramatic, but the story has a certain charm: it is still readable in a way that most of the sensational novels referred to earlier are not; and it is interestingly representative of the growing stress on Italy as a land of blight. To the Gothic novelists Italy had been a country of danger and sensation, but with a self-contained society which did not include English people, who could therefore enjoy the thrills and suspense without feeling fundamentally threatened. But now, following the example of *Corinne*, Italy becomes a country apparently offering the English beauty and happiness, but actually giving only disappointment or even death. In *Change of Air*, another of the *English in Italy* stories, a young Oxford graduate goes to Italy in search of a healthy, convalescent climate which he finds, too late, to be malignant: his death there is not only a reflection of an all too common phenomenon of the time (as one sees, for example, in the appalling number of graves of young Englishmen of the period in the Protestant cemetery at Livorno[1]), but also an image of the way in which Italy is used to focus the Romantic anguish by appearing to offer access to a more totally fulfilled life while in fact only dealing death.

Similarly, in Normanby's novel *Matilda. A Tale of The Day* (1825) Italy appears to give the heroine the opportunity of escaping from a frustrating marriage and eloping with the man she had always loved. But her happiness is short-lived. She becomes pregnant and, thinking she sees her lover drown in the Mediterranean, gives birth prematurely. Both mother and child die, and the distraught lover goes off to fight in Greece. This last detail clearly recalls the life of Byron, and, indeed, Byron pervades Normanby's fiction: but, significantly, the fiction describes not the fulness of Byron's response to Italy but the frustration of people who cannot attain it. In doing so, it helps set the literary pattern for at least the next hundred years.

Similar *Corinne*-based patterns occur in Mary Shelley's work. Her novel *Valperga* (1823) traces in a medieval setting the *Corinne* theme of two lives being blighted by the man's rejection of the possibilities of love. Euthanasia and Castruccio (suggestive names), friends since childhood, would make an ideal Lord and Lady of the happy estates of Valperga, in Tuscany, but Castruccio rejects marriage and domestic happiness in favour of politics and power. From a handsome, noble youth he declines into a cruel, vicious tyrant, obliged constantly to defend himself against external attack and internal revolt. Euthanasia is forced eventually to renounce her hopes for him and becomes involved in a conspiracy against his outrageous behaviour. He penetrates the plot and sends the woman who could have made his ideal wife into exile. As she begins her journey she is drowned off the coast of Tuscany. The story is typical of the genre: its pathetic ending is quite different from the happy ending with which Mrs Radcliffe had always managed to stave off the realities of her material.

In a more contemporary context, the sub-plot of *Lodore* (1835) provides an interesting variation on Madame de Staël's story. Disappointed in his love for Lady Lodore, Horatio Saville goes to Italy, where he meets the lovely and passionate Clorinda, who

> was shut up in a convent through the heatless vanity of her mother, who dreaded her as a rival, to wait there till her parents should find some suitable match, which she must instantly accept, or be doomed to seclusion for ever. (Vol. 2, p. 174)

The Neapolitan girl (whose fictional plight recalls that in real life of Emilia Viviani, who had inspired Shelley's poem, *Epipsychidion*) falls in love with the Englishman, who agrees to marry her on the remarkable understanding that his real love is for the unattainable Lady Lodore. The thought of her rival drives Clorinda to furious fits of jealousy, including an attempt to stab her husband reminiscent of an event in Byron's life in Venice. Horatio eventually obeys the call of his family to return to his duties as an Englishman, and their journey has scarcely begun when Clorinda kills herself in despair. But, unlike the *Corinne* pattern, the Englishman whose lack of passion has killed her is not in turn destroyed by it. On the contrary, Mary Shelley tacitly approves his father's condemnation of his stay in Italy

> until the very flower of his youth seemed to be wasted in aimless rambles, and an intercourse with foreigners, that must tend to unnationalize him, and to render him unfit for a career in his own country (Vol. 1, p. 85)

and she eventually rewards his return to England with the hand of Lady Lodore. Such a complacent and bourgeois attitude (to be found in a different form in her travel books about Italy) is somehow sadly disappointing from the woman who had written *Frankenstein* and gone to Italy with Shelley: though perhaps understandable when one recalls the tragic pattern of their own life there.

The events of that shared life reappear in one of the novels of

Disraeli, a central figure in the post-Romantic apprehension of Italy. When Disraeli went to Italy in 1826, after the failure of *Vivian Grey*, it was to the Italy of Byron and Mrs Radcliffe. The Italian mountains were 'the Apennines of Mrs Ratcliffe (sic)',[2] while Byron, whom he idolised, and whose boatman he sought out on Lake Geneva,[3] had early filled him with an enthusiasm for Venice which emerges fascinatingly in *Contarini Fleming* (1832). The Scandinavian hero of the novel, which proclaims itself as the autobiography of a genius, longs from childhood to go to Venice, a city he associates with his illustrious ancestors, the Contarini, and with the excitement of artistic creation. In a way which would have been inconceivable before Byron had put Venice vividly before the English literary imagination, Fleming's feelings for the city dominate the first part of the novel. He runs away from school to try to get there and when, as a young man, he does go to Italy his feelings of enchantment are sustained in crescendo until they reach a climax in his response to Venice. When he has spent some time there he reflects on the unique fascination of the place in a passage which embodies the essence of post-Byronic Venice:

> If I were to assign the particular quality which conduces to that dreamy, and voluptuous existence, which men of high imagination experience in Venice, I should describe it as the feeling of Abstraction which is remarkable in that city, and peculiar to it. Venice is the only city which can yield the magical delights of Solitude. All is still and silent. No rude sound disturbs your reveries; Fancy, therefore, is not put to flight. No rude sound distracts your self-consciousness. This renders existence intense. We feel everything. And we feel thus keenly in a city not only eminently beautiful, not only abounding in wonderful creations of Art, but each step of which is hallowed ground, quick with associations, that, in their more various nature, their nearer relation to ourselves, and perhaps their more picturesque character, exercise a greater influence over the imagination, than the more antique story of Greece and Rome. We feel all this in a city too, which, although her lustre be indeed dimmed, can still count among her daughters, maidens fairer than the orient pearls with which her warriors once loved to deck them. Poetry, Tradition, and Love, these are the Graces which have invested with an ever-charming cestus this Aphrodite of cities. (Vol. 3, pp. 5–6)

Venice 'renders existence intense' and it is Byron who has shown how. The contrast with pre-Byronic Italy is evident. Venice has become more stimulating than Rome as the character of the sensitive observer has changed. The classical tourist of the eighteenth century had felt himself distinguished from other men by the achievements of the civilisation he represented and whose ancient models he was interested in viewing. The Romantic traveller, however, is a solitary, not a social, creature, set apart from others by the individual quality of 'high imagination' and seeking the stimulus of vivid experience. Contarini Fleming is the most eloquently self-conscious of the followers of Childe Harold; and, like the Byronic hero, he learns from Italy that the more intensely one lives the more intensely he suffers. Enamoured of a beautiful Venetian cousin, he seizes her from her vows to take the veil, marries her, and flees with her to Candia (Crete); but after only a short period of idyllic existence she dies in still-born childbirth. Since the days of Othello, the Venetian bride has brought her husband sorrow.

The rest of the novel is rather disappointing. Fleming returns to Italy, where he again finds the beauty of the country seducing him into suffering – the constant reminders in Florence of the great achievements of the Renaissance, and the 'elegant melancholy' of Pisa, stimulate him to write, but the creative exertion soon exhausts him and leads to a nervous breakdown. When he comes back to Italy again at the end of the novel, after a desultory tour of the middle East, intending to create near Naples a modern Villa Adriana, a centre of all the intellectual pleasures, where he will seize every opportunity of serving his fellow men, it is impossible, as Leslie Stephen observed,[4] to lend to his project the enthusiasm and credence which Disraeli seems to invite. He seems temporarily to have forgotten the consistent tendency of Italy to stimulate her admirers to activity which will lead them only to disaster.

Five years later, however, Disraeli returned to this theme in his two novels of 1837. In *Henrietta Temple* the heroine falls in love in Italy with a man whom she abandons on her return to England, but more interestingly *Venetia* is partly set in Italy, and, indeed, the heroine's name is derived from a vague ancestral connection with the city of 'graceful towers/Loved by the bard and honoured by the sage.' (Ed. 1853, p. 98) Rather tenuously, Disraeli had by this time elaborated a theory that he himself had Venetian ancestors. The descriptions of Venice in the novel are virtually identical to the impressions of Contarini Fleming, but the interest of *Venetia* lies in the two characters Cadurcis and Marmion Herbert, who are freely but distinctly based on Byron and Shelley. The Shelleyan figure, Herbert, speaks of the Mediterranean in a passage which is comparable, in its relation to the attitudes of the previous century, with Fleming's description of Venice:

> There is a spell in the shores of the Mediterranean Sea which no others can rival. Never was such a union of natural loveliness and magical associations! On these shores have risen all that interests us in the past: – Egypt and Palestine, Greece, Rome, Carthage, Moorish Spain and feodal Italy. These shores have yielded us our religion, our arts, our literature, and our laws. If all that we have gained from the shores of the Mediterranean was erased from the memory of man, we should be savages. (Ed. 1853, p. 302)

But the reward that Herbert receives for such adoration of the life-giving sea is death by drowning: in a fictional exaggeration of the actual death of Shelley, both Herbert and Cadurcis are drowned in the Gulf of Spezia. The drowning of Cadurcis has a symbolic value which resounds beyond the confines of the internal structure of the novel: to have the character who represents the man who had got more than anyone out of Italy drowned in the Italian sea might be seen as the dream-fulfilment of an envy towards Byron for having attained a fulness of living which his followers could not find it in themselves to achieve. But whatever depth of symbolical significance one may want to read into the ending of *Venetia*, one thing is certain: namely, that it fittingly closes a generation of English literary response to Italy, a generation characterised by a rather negative stress on the associations of Italy with death and despair. The strength of these associations was to trouble literary explorers of Italy throughout the rest of our period, but later generations of writers would try more constructively to locate and relate to the life-giving sources of Italy than had been the case with these writers, who were doubtless over-awed by the example of Byron. The process, indeed, had already begun. But before we go on to consider it we must notice one other work which also, in its way, marks the end of Romantic Italy.

This was Bulwer Lytton's *The Last Days of Pompeii* (1834). In 1833 Lytton began, in Rome, a novel on *Rienzi, The Last of The Tribunes*, an historical figure who, he felt, had been consistently under-rated. (The novel, however, published in 1835, was no more than a mediocre historical romance, chiefly notable for having suggested to Wagner the subject for his opera.) But in Naples in the spring of 1834, he put aside the medieval novel in favour of the more compelling subject of the destruction of Pompeii, a subject which gave him an opportunity to attempt an equivalent in fiction of the vast apocalyptic paintings of John Martin, the artist whom he considered 'the greatest, the most lofty, the most permanent, the most original genius of his age.'[6] Indeed, Lytton must have had in mind when choosing this subject Martin's *Destruction of Pompeii*, painted in 1822. The painting represents another link between English literature and Piranesi, whose influence on the architectural imagination of Martin was fundamental.

We may note in passing that Martin's painting was a manifestation of the widespread interest in Pompeii caused by the publication of Sir William Gell's *Pompeiiana* (1817–9), another result of which was that the subject of the destruction of Pompeii was set for the Cambridge prize poem of 1819. The prize was won by Macaulay, though with a poem much less impressive than the *Lays of Ancient Rome* which later (1842) became an obvious companion piece to Lytton's novel.

The Last Days of Pompeii has of course no claim to be considered as a great novel. Immensely popular in its own day, it still makes an exciting schoolboys' tale; but it exists purely on the level of the sensational, and, indeed, its success on that level was symptomatic. For the novel completed the process by which the traveller was provided with local associations, in whatever part of Italy he was likely to visit, with either the authors or the characters of modern (i.e. post-classical) literature. Lytton told his readers that in Pompeii 'still, after the lapse of ages, the traveller may survey that airy hall, within whose cunning galleries and elaborate chambers once thought, reasoned, dreamed, and sinned – the soul of Arbaces the Egyptian!' (Ed. 1834, Vol. 3, p. 312) After 1834, the Arbaces the tourist conjured up among the excavations of Pompeii was not the historical but the fictional character. The classical Grand Tourists had been replaced, even on a classical site, by the Romantic tourists with their Byron and their novels. When Mary Shelley, returning to Pompeii in 1843, found that the place impressed her more vividly than it had done in 1820, it was not that the excavations were more extensive, but that the 'City of the Dead'[7] had been re-peopled by

Lytton's novel. By re-creating the last days of Pompeii in terms of the Romantic imagination, Lytton put a last touch to the thick new layer of literary associations which, in less than half a century, the English writers had spread over all the tourist sites in Italy.[8]

6 Developments in the 1830s

In half a century, then, and particularly in the twenty years since the opening of the Continent after Waterloo, the range of response to Italy in English literature had been considerably extended, and the dominant image of Italy in contemporary writing radically changed. The next major revaluation of Italy by English writers came around the mid-century, notably in the works of Ruskin and the Brownings, rejecting Romantic sensationalism, and seeking new modes of experiencing Italy, more relevant to the needs of a rapidly changing society. The available picture of Italy, however, by no means remained static between Lytton's *Pompeii* and Ruskin's *Modern Painters*, and before going on to consider Ruskin's importance to our subject we must consider three very different contributions to the developing apprehension of the South: those of Landor, Turner and George Sand.

WALTER SAVAGE LANDOR (1775–1864)

Landor's involvement with Italy extended over a longer period than that of any other writer who comes within our scope. Twentysix of his eightynine years were spent in Italy, mostly at or near Florence: from 1815 to 1835, and again from 1858 until his death. As a young man he had known Bertie Greatheed of the *Florence Miscellany* group[1]; his early years in Italy were the years when Byron and Shelley were celebrating the country; and for the last few years of his life his best friend was Robert Browning. With Byron and Shelley he had hoped for great things from the Naples insurrection of 1821, which he hoped to encourage with a rather disorganised pamphlet written in Italian (*Poche Osservazioni*, 1821), while towards the end of his life he enthusiastically followed the progress of the Risorgimento, writing poems on Garibaldi and letters to *The Times*. Landor loved the beauty of Italy, though he detested its Church; he read widely in Italian literature and history, and regarded himself as a connoisseur of Italian painting. Roughly a quarter of his voluminous work is in some way concerned with Italy.

This work has called forth judgments as various as Eliot's claim that Landor is a grossly under-rated master of the English language and Leavis's belief that his enduring repuration is pernicious 'in a world where there is more literature worth attention than anyone can hope to find time for.'[2] A less extreme view suggested by a reading of the Italian material would accord with that of Leslie Stephen, that, although passages of magnificent prose are occasionally to be found, they are surrounded by a formidable waste of pettiness and tedium. To the latter category we may immediately dismiss the seven plays and dramatic fragments on Italian subjects, listed in the bibliography, on which Landor worked over a period of twenty years. Devoid of any impressive poetic, psychological or dramatic quality, they turgidly attempt to exploit the violence-incest-murder-prison paradigm of Gothic Italy, a kind of material with which the musing, classically-minded Landor was singularly not at home.

Nor, in another sense, did Landor really feel at home in contemporary Tuscany. His distaste for the majority of English society in Florence and his constant petty quarrels with the Tuscan authorities are all too evident in his epistolary novelette, *High and Low Life in Italy*, written in 1831. Despite the title, the work has little, and nothing original, to say about Italian life, but consists of a series of outbursts resulting from Landor's cantankerous inability to get on with other people; it never comes to life as fiction, and is memorable only for the exclamation of one of the characters: 'A man to leave Italy and not to write a book about it! Was ever such a thing heard of?'[3]

Landor did, however, contribute something of value to the fashion of writing about Italy. Not, indeed, the *Imaginary Conversations*, whose fault is that they are imaginary without being really imaginative: they lack the verve of creative imagination. Their form presents Landor with a minimum of artistic difficulties, and they are deprived of the intensity which can result from a writer successfully grappling with the problems of his material. The speakers in the dialogues are used merely to expound Landor's own feelings and ideas, few of which are sufficiently profound or original to justify the demands made on the reader's time. But where Landor does sometimes succeed in genuinely creative use of language is in the atmosphere he builds up around the dialogue itself. This is particularly the case in *The Pentameron* (1837), a five day dialogue between Petrarch and Boccaccio, the apotheosis, and the most charming, of the *Conversations*. The principal subject of their talks is their own writing and that of their predecessors – topics on which their own real opinions would clearly command interest, while Landor's are much less engrossing. The merit of the piece, however, is in its evocation of Renaissance Tuscany – the quiet happiness of Boccaccio's estate, where Petrarch is visiting him, the freshness and beauty of the country, or Petrarch's reception when he goes to the village church on Sunday morning:

As they approached the walls of the town the whole country was pervaded by a stirring and diversified air of gladness. Laughter and songs and flutes and viols, inviting voices and complying responses, mingled with merry bells and with processional hymns, along the woodland paths and along the yellow meadows. It was really the *Lord's Day*, for he made his creatures happy in it, and their hearts were thankful. Even the cruel had ceased from cruelty; and the rich man alone exacted from the animal his daily labour. Ser Francesco made this remark, and told his youthful guide that he had never been before where he could not walk to church on a Sunday; and that nothing should persuade him to urge the speed of his beast, on the seventh day, beyond his natural and willing foot's-pace. He reached the gates of Certaldo more than half an hour before the time of service, and he found laurels suspended over them, and being suspended; and many pleasant and beautiful faces were protruded between the ranks of gentry and clergy who awaited him. Little did he expect such an attendance; but Fra Biagio of San Vivaldo, who himself had offered no obsequiousness of respect, had scattered the secret of his visit throughout the whole country. A young poet, the most celebrated in the town, approached the canonico with a long scroll of verses, which fell below the knee, beginning,
How shall we welcome our illustrious guest?
To which Ser Francesco immediately replied, 'Take your favourite maiden, lead the dance with her, and bid all your friends follow; you have a good half-hour for it.[4]

There is a pleasant feeling in *The Pentameron* of two great and sympathetic intellects enjoying each other's company amidst these pastoral surroundings and domestic bliss – an idealised happiness quite the opposite of Landor's own disastrous marriage. It is an attractive, and rather noble, beginning to a body of work that was to grow up in the nineteenth century, devoted to inviting its readers to enter imaginatively into the life of a period so different from their own, a time when rural beauty was unthreatened by the blight of industrialisation, when intellectual discovery supposedly filled the air, and individual excellence was valued and encouraged. One can only regret that Landor did not spend more of his energies in this fruitful direction, though he did indeed follow up *The Pentameron* with an interesting biographical and critical sketch of *Francesco Petrarca* in the *Foreign Quarterly Review* in 1843. But he does at least have the distinction of having provided a valuable starting point from which Browning could develop one of the most important aspects of the later nineteenth century literary attitude to Italy.

JOSEPH M. W. TURNER (1775–1851)

The most importantly new and lastingly impressive English response to Italy in the 1830s came not from literature but from Turner, whose paintings of Venice occupy so important a position between Byron and Ruskin that no study of literary attitudes to Italy can afford to ignore them. Ruskin remarked in *Praeterita* that 'my Venice, like Turner's, had been chiefly created for us by Byron'[5] and what concerns us here is to look into the relationship between the Venetian work of Byron and of Turner.

Turner first visited Italy, including Venice, in 1819, a visit of immense significance to his artistic development – indeed, 'the most significant turning point in his art'[6] – since his discovery of the qualities of Italian light led him to concentrate increasingly on the exploration of light in his painting. In Venice he made a large number of sketches in his note-books, and four water colours, but as yet no oil paintings. In Venice the light was at its most magical, filtering through the Adriatic mist or glimmering on the water, lighting the exotic architecture and the profusion of boats. It was the period of Byron's residence in Venice, and the fourth Canto of *Childe Harold* had appeared the year before, but there is nothing of Byron's Venice in Turner's drawings. For Turner there is nothing sinister, tragically ruinous or violently Shakespearean about the city; it is a city of magic and beauty, the city of light par excellence. It is much more Shelley's Venice than Byron's. From his sketches it is obviously a city he loves.

Yet for thirteen years Turner made no major use of the notes he had sketched in Venice. It is impossible to be sure why he did not exploit this material sooner. Perhaps he felt that his artistic technique had not yet developed to the point where he could do justice to the magical subject; certainly, when he did come to paint Venice in oils in 1832, he became obsessed by the city and found it was the ideal subject into which to put 'his full perception of atmosphere and light.'[7] His creative interest in the city seems eventually to have been aroused by a variety of stimuli. Work on the vignettes for the 1830 edition of Rogers' *Italy* was one, for the illustrations to the volume included the Rialto and the Ducal Palace. Reynolds suggests[8] that the main incentive to take up the Venetian subject came from Bonington's paintings of Venice, exhibited at the Royal Academy in 1828. These paintings, which had previously been exhibited in Paris and, with Constable's works, were to have a deep influence on the development of French landscape painting, are brightly coloured works celebrating the beauty and exoticism of Venice. In the two versions of *The Doge's Palace*, for example, interest is divided between the architecture of the palace, luminous even under the cloudy sky which persisted during all of Bonington's stay in the city, and foreground groups of colourfully dressed Turks. The scene is viewed from a point very near the Bridge of Sighs where Childe Harold stands at the beginning of the fourth Canto, but the bridge itself is not included, and by contrast with Byron's poem only the brilliance òf the city is recorded. The poem, however, must have influenced Bonington's desire to travel to Venice. When he went to Italy in 1826 it was not, as most previous painters had gone there, to study the works of the great masters and absorb Italian light and landscape. Despite the academic attractions of Florence and Rome, Bonington's single-minded purpose was to make straight for Venice and stay there as long as possible.[9] So strong a desire to visit the city which had traditionally been regarded as of at best only secondary artistic interest could only have been a response to Byron's enthusiasm for Venice.

But Byron also had a more direct influence on Turner's decision to paint Venice, for in 1830 the artist worked on a series of illustrations to Byron's poems, and his familiarity with the fourth Canto is shown by his 1832 painting of *Childe Harold's Pilgrimage – Italy*. Working on illustrations to Rogers and Byron must have prompted Turner to revisit Venice in 1832, when he fell again under its spell and realised that, at the point which his art had reached, Venice was his ideal subject. The constant painting of Venetian scenes which began that year was a direct response to the qualities of the city, not indebted in essence to anyone else's view of it. His biographer, Finberg, was unaware that Turner revisited Venice in 1832 and overstresses the debt to Byron, commenting, for example, on the subject of the painting *The Bridge of Sighs*, shown at the Royal Academy in 1833: 'It is not likely that the Bridge of Sighs would have taken precedence of the Ducal Palace and the Dogana but for the opening lines of the 4th canto and the first of the *Historical Notes* with which the poem was "elucidated".'[10] This may be true; but it is also true that the picture is a view of the whole water-front of that part of Venice, that its joyous light suggests nothing of the gloomy story of the bridge, and that the figure of Canaletto painting in the bottom left-hand corner is a strong reminder of more purely pictorial influences than Byron's. He was doubtless largely responsible for Turner's initially taking up the subject; but the treatment of it is entirely Turner's own.

Turner revisited Venice in 1835 and 1840. Between 1832 and 1846 he painted Venetian scenes with a frequency which amounted to obsession. These paintings sometimes reflected his current interests; in the mid-thirties, for instance, when he was for a time interested in painting night scenes, he produced a painting of *Juliet and Her Nurse*, in which they are set against a background of the Piazza San Marco by night. (His only other 'Shakespearean' painting of Venice was the encounter between Shylock and Antonio in *Scene – A Street in Venice*, a painting so poor that even Ruskin did not like it.) But for the most part the paintings form the well-known series of studies of light and water, of graceful architecture and captivating boats, a world half fairyland and half reality, the most delightful of all visions of Venice. Turner's finest art was devoted to the ephemerally beautiful, the perfect moment of a fiery sunset, or the second when a ship putting to sea stands in its most poignant relation to the shore it is leaving behind. In contrast with the classical artists before him, Turner does not seek the immutable beau idéal, but gives permanent form to the ideality of passing perception. Like Byron, he refuses to rely on illusory absolutes; but whereas Byron holds in tension the exhilaration of creation and the inevitability of decay and death, Turner seizes the moment when the beautiful has reached its fullest expression and is on the point of waning, and records it as a fine example of the fragile but magnificent potentiality of beauty. Fundamentally, both men are pursuing the same task: the assertion of a deeply serious role for art in a world becoming increasingly conscious of its own relativity; and thus each is a figure of crucial artistic importance, although Turner's centrality to the development of painting is perhaps more readily apparent than Byron's comparable position in literature because his example was more vigorously taken up by a series of followers. The nature of their work, however, differed widely, as a result both of their different personalities and of the nature of their media.

Both men found in Venice a wealth of material for their differing artistic needs. Byron's celebration of the city had been largely responsible for Turner's initial interest in Venice; he in turn created one of the most powerful English visions of the city, led Ruskin to become enamoured of it, and, by the nature of his stress on the potential beauty of the passing moment, deeply influenced the pattern of subsequent English interest in Italy and the growth of aestheticism. But before following this up in Ruskin, we must look at one other, less well-known but very important, growth-point of attitudes.

GEORGE SAND (1804–76)

In literature, the closest parallel to the change of attitudes to Italy, and particularly to Venice, represented by Turner's paintings, is to be found in the work of George Sand. Though little read in England now, she was probably the best-known French novelist in the last century. Introduced to the English audience by her friend Mazzini, the enthusiasm with which her work was received was so great that almost all the subsequent English writers we shall consider expressed admiration of, and often indebtedness to, her novels. The new picture whch many of these gave of Italy made, therefore, an important contribution to the growth of the English consciousness of Italy.

A character in one of her later novels sums up the change of attitudes towards Italy which had taken place, in France as well as in England, during the first half of the nineteenth century – largely as a result of George Sand's work. He contrasts his own response to the Campo Santo at Pisa with the response of the Romantic writers to the phenomenon of ruin in Italy:

> J'avoue que je suis très-las des réflexions imprimées, sur les destins de l' homme et la chute des empires. Ce fut la grande mode, il y a quelque quarante ans, sous notre empire à nous, de *pleurer* les vicissitudes des grandes époques et des grandes sociétés. Pourtant, nous étions, nous-mêmes, grande société et grande époque, et nous touchions aussi à des désastres, à des transformations, à des renouvellements. Il me semble que regretter ce qui n' est plus, quand on devrait sentir vivement que l' on doit être quelque chose, est une flânerie poétique assez creuse. Le passé qui, en bien comme en mal, a eu sa raison d' être, ne nous a pas laissé ces témoignages, ces débris de sa vie, pour nous décourager de la nôtre. Il devrait, en nous parlant par ses ruines, nous crier: *agis et recommence*, au lieu de cet éternel: *contemple et frémis*, que la mode littéraire avait si longtemps imposé au voyageur romantique des premiers jours du siècle.
> L' illustre Chateaubriand fut un des plus puissants inventeurs de cette mode. C' est qu' il était une ruine lui-même.[11]

In English literature the comparison is obviously with the kind of sentimental pathos we have considered earlier. Byron, of course, had transcended the limitations of this attitude, and set precisely the example for which this passage pleads, but although George Sand and her lover, the poet Alfred de Musset, were aware of the Byronic associations of Venice when they went there in 1834, she seems not entirely to have realised this. Certainly, the image of Venice she created in her own work was very different from Byron's. She did not feel that the aspect of decay and the recollections of a history rendered claustrophobic by its constant sordid intrigue and brutal oppression were significant elements in the experience of Venice: on the contrary,

> J' aimai cette ville pour elle-même, et c' est la seule au monde que je puisse aimer ainsi, car une ville m' a toujours fait l' effet d' une prison que je supporte à cause de mes compagnons de captivité. A Venise on vivrait longtemps seul, et l' on comprend qu' au temps de sa splendeur et de sa liberté, ses enfants l' aient presque

personnifiée dans leur amour et l' aient chérie non pas comme une chose, mais comme un être.[12]

Nor, despite her notorious love affair with the Venetian doctor, Pagello, did she emphasise, like Byron, the sensual attractions of the city. What was important to her about Venice was a beauty, and gaiety, which inspired creative activity – an inspiration less vigorous than that we have seen in Byron, but which valuably permeates much of her finest work. Her initial reaction to Venice gave her the image of the city which remained with her throughout her life:

Je n' ai pas été charmée de la Toscane, mais Venise est la plus belle chose qu' il y ait au monde. Toute cette architecture mauresque en marbre blanc au milieu de l'eau limpide et sous un ciel magnifique, ce peuple si gai, si insouciant, si chantant, si spirituel, ces gondoles, ces églises, ces galeries de tableaux, toutes les femmes jolies ou élégantes, la mer qui se brise à vos oreilles, des clairs de lune comme il n' y en a nulle part; des sérénades sous toutes les fenêtres, des cafés pleins de Turcs et d' Arméniens, de beaux et vastes théâtres, où chantent Mme Pasta et Donzelli; des palais magnifiques; . . . des huîtres délicieuses, qu' on pêche sur les marches de toutes les maisons; du vin de Chypre à vingt-cinq sous la bouteille; des poulets excellents à dix sous; des fleurs en plein hiver, et, au mois de février, la chaleur de notre mois de mai.[13]

The experience of Italy was the greatest imaginative stimulus of George Sand's life,[14] providing material and inspiration for over twenty novels. Some of these were simply vivid tales of passion and adventure, such as *L' Uscoque* (1837), a story of seventeenth century Venetian brigands based on Byron's early tales of *Lara* and *The Corsair*. But the more substantial achievements were not only inspired by Italy but took as their central theme the exhilaration of creative artistic life which seemed in Italy to have sprung spontaneously from an enchanted environment. *Les Maîtres Mosaïstes* (1837), for example, concerns the relations of rival groups of mosaic artists employed on the decoration of the interior of St Mark's in 1570. Titian and Tintoretto appear among the characters; where Byron and his contemporaries had chosen to represent in their work the sufferings of past artists (notably Tasso[15]) George Sand presents her readers with figures associated more entirely with fruitful creation. Attention is moved away from Tasso's cell to the artist's studio and the mosaicist's atelier. At one point in the novel the brothers who are its heroes suffer unjust imprisonment in the infamous Venetian prison; but, unlike the Romantic writers, the prison is not a dominant image in the novel, but rather emphasises by contrast the prevailing colour, creativity and good humour of the life of the majority of Venetian artists and artisans.

It is characteristics like this – quite different from any that English writers had been used to attribute to Italians – that typify George Sand's principal Italian figures. Italian artistic life is repeatedly presented in her novels, especially in *Les Maîtres Mosaïstes*, *La Dernière Aldini*, *Lucrezia Floriani*, *Le Piccinino* and *Consuelo*. The last, and best-known, of these may be taken as representative, though, in fact, the heroine is not Italian, but of Spanish gipsy origin, and only the first twenty-one chapters are set in Italy. These opening chapters create a scintillating portrait of the musical life of eighteenth century Venice. The city where earlier travellers had grumbled of a disturbing silence becomes in this novel indelibly the city of delicious, pervasive music – music which ranges from the constant lapping of the wavelets in the canals, through the spontaneous if atonal singing of the people as they come and go about their business in the side-streets and the campi, to the most gorgeous of Venetian operas. The whole atmosphere is music: we hear singing from the gondoliers; from the poor workmen of the Corti Minelli, a populous quarter of the city where George Sand herself lived for a time; at the lavish first nights of the Opera; and from the school of the maestro Porpora, one of the many historical characters who appear in the novel. (Others include Frederic II of Prussia, Maria-Theresa, Voltaire and Haydn.) Everything is art and vitality, the people rather than the ghosts of the city become important, in this exciting new picture of Venice.

George Sand several times satirises the English in Italy for their boorishness, their false feeling of superiority to the Italians, and their general lack of sensitivity to the creative stimulus of Italy. The majority of tourists in Italy have, of course, continued to qualify for, and have frequently received, such satirical condemnation. But for those who sought seriously to discover and explore the life-values of Italy, George Sand's work had shown the way forward by releasing Italian material from the over-worked and uncreative obsession with melancholy and frustration, and revealing some of the possibilities of learning to improve the quality of one's own life through sympathetic contact with the contemporary life of Italy, and with the great art-works of her past.

MRS JAMESON (1794–1860)

It was a major change in attitudes, and its effect is nowhere seen more graphically than in the work of George Sand's early English admirer, Elizabeth Browning's close friend, Anna Jameson. In the twenties Mrs Jameson's best-selling *Diary of An Ennuyée* (1826), which is largely set in Italy, had been part of the vogue for portraying the sufferings of a broken heart against a guide-book background, in the manner of *Corinne* and *Childe Harold*; the Venetian scenes in the *Diary* are full of langour and decay. Revisiting Venice twenty years later, however, having read Sand's 'beautiful tale' of *Les Maîtres Mosaïstes*, she displays a totally different attitude towards the city in her eloquent essay on *The House of Titian*.[16] The essay is flooded with the colour and translucence of Venice, by which she is entranced. Titian is her hero because of the correspondence she feels between the colours of his paintings and the colours of the city; though he rarely depicted the city itself, he is the only artist whose work conveys a true feeling of the place. 'Canaletti gives us the forms without the colour or light. Turner, the colour and light without the forms.' Everyone, says Mrs Jameson, should penetrate the back canals of Venice on a pilgrimage to Titian's house.[17] Twenty years earlier she had meditated conventionally in Tasso's cell at Ferrara; now she attempts to establish a new shrine on the tourist map of Italy, but one conducive to joyous reflection on creativity rather than to morbid dwelling on artistic suffering. *The House of Titian* explicitly rejects her own earlier attitude, the attitude of people who gaze on 'the falling or fallen palaces of Venice, and moralise on the transitoriness of all human things,' and recommends rather that they should make the most of what survives, seizing every opportunity to respond to the enduring vitality of works of genius. She abandons the Romantic and helps introduce the mid-Victorian feeling towards Italy.

Mrs Jameson herself, however, was not equipped to develop the new feeling very much further. She did produce, between 1848 and 1860, a series of iconographical works whose summaries of the treatments of the Christian legends in art are still fascinating and useful, but she was terribly limited, as Ruskin, who knew her in

Venice, delightfully remarked, by her 'pleasant disposition to make the best of all she saw, and to say, compliantly, that a picture was good, if anybody had ever said so before.'[18] Nor did George Sand consider at all deeply the possible means of relating the experience of past art to the problems of the present day; she is content merely to convey the colour and exhilaration of her material, without exploring its implications. Such exploration was to be the preoccupation of a succession of English writers; firstly, and notably, of Ruskin.

7 Ruskin

Since first the dominion of man was asserted over the ocean, three thrones, of mark beyond all others, have been set upon its sands: the thrones of Tyre, Venice, and England. Of the First of these great powers only the memory remains; of the Second, the ruin; the Third, which inherits their greatness, if it forget their example, may may be led through prouder eminence to less pitied destruction.

These first sentences of *The Stones of Venice* (1851–2) read almost like a challenge thrown out by Ruskin to Gibbon. Ruskin was always contemptuous of the earlier writer, whose style he described to Carlyle as being 'like the most tasteless water-gruel, with a handful of Epsom salts strewed in for flowers, and served with the airs of being turtle,'[1] and their tastes and interests were completely opposite. Gibbon's beloved classical Rome was to Ruskin a heap of rubbish:

The Capitol is a melancholy rubbishy square of average Palladian – modern; the Forum, a good group of smashed columns, just what, if it were got up, as it might easily be, at Virginia Water, we should call a piece of humbug – the kind of thing that one is sick to death of in 'compositions'; the Coliseum I have always considered a public nuisance, like Jim Crow [a popular negro song]; and the rest of the ruins are mere mountains of shattered, shapeless bricks, covering miles of ground with a Babylon-like weight of red tiles.[2]

Venice, on the other hand, which Gibbon had found the least attractive city in Italy, was to Ruskin 'the Paradise of cities.'[3] Between the two men lay the treatments of Italy we have been considering, with which Ruskin was intimately acquainted.

Ruskin's interest in both Italy and Turner was aroused by the vignettes in the 1830 edition of Rogers' *Italy*, which he received for his thirteenth birthday; when he was first taken to Italy in 1835, at the age of sixteen, his preparation for what he found there had been

Turner, Shakespeare and Byron.[4] The precocious youth considered that Bulwer's *Pompeii* gave its readers 'a clearer idea of the manners prevailing at that period than they ever obtained from their classical studies',[5] saw Italy in true Romantic fashion as 'a land of tombs [where] the air is full of death',[6] wrote a short story, *Leoni. A Legend of Italy*, in the conventional pattern of fatal love and sensational banditti, and began a drama of Venetian conspiracy on the model of Byron, whose title, *Marcolini*, was taken from Rogers. On his first visit to Pisa in 1840 he was much less interested in the Duomo and the Campo Santo than in the association of the city with the lives of Byron and Shelley.[7]

As he became better acquainted with Italy, however, and particularly with Venice, Ruskin began to attack the hold on the literary imagination of this fallaciously sensational Romantic picture which had so vividly impressed him as a youth.

> The Venice of modern fiction and drama is a thing of yesterday, a mere efflorescence of decay, a stage dream which the first ray of daylight must dissipate into dust.[8]

Venice was a sinister oligarchy only for a short period of her history, and that in her decline; the physical appearance of the city has changed out of recognition since its days of greatness; no nobly poignant prisoner or stupendous villain ever crossed the Bridge of Sighs, which was not built until the end of the sixteenth century: such were the disillusioning truths which Ruskin told his readers, while one of his letters to his father destroys one's delight in one of the most powerful scenes of Cooper's *The Bravo*, which we shall come to later, by protesting that the lagoons are too shallow for anyone to be wilfully drowned there without having his head held under water. 'It is marvellous how ridiculous the common novel-sentiment about Venice appears to anyone who really knows anything about it', he commented.[9]

Yet, despite his attacks on these illusions which owed their popularity very largely to the work of Byron, Ruskin always insisted on his admiration of and debt to the poet. 'My Venice, like Turner's, had been chiefly created for us by Byron,' he wrote in *Praeterita*,[10] and though there he is talking less about any substantial specific influence than about the fact that Byron was the first modern writer to make great imaginative capital out of the city and to make his readers vividly aware of its magnificence, in a late

Epilogue (1881) to *The Stones of Venice* Ruskin claims that although he deprecated Byron's ignorance about Venice he nevertheless owed a great deal to his poems and 'still felt exactly as Byron did, in every particular.'[11] The claim may seem rather startling. Certainly, the lines quoted at the head of this chapter are a paraphrase of Byron's

> In her youth she was all glory, – a new Tyre;
> . . . [addressing Albion] in the fall
> Of Venice think of thine, despite thy watery wall.[12]

But one can scarcely exaggerate the contrast between the lives led in Venice by these two men of utterly different temperament. To the city where Byron had revelled in the delights of women picked up for him by his gondoliers, Ruskin went with a wife whose charm and beauty made her an outstanding social success but with whom he never consummated his marriage. The mornings which Byron had spent sleeping off the excesses of the previous night were spent by Ruskin in detailed study of the paintings and architecture, with prayers prompt at ten. Byron relaxed by riding on the Lido, while Ruskin had never been allowed on a horse in case he should fall and hurt himself; and Byron certainly never wrote home to explain what arrangements he had made for the religious welfare of his household in the absence of an English church in Venice.

Yet beneath these differences, and much deeper than their shared enthusiasm for the beauty of Venice, their excitement at the grandeur of her history, and their concern for the sadness of her decay, lay a fundamental similarity between the two men. Ruskin was one of the rare Victorians who appreciated Byron's poetry. In an early essay he asserted that,

> with the sole exception of Shakespeare, Byron was the greatest poet that ever lived, because he was perhaps the most miserable man. His mind was from its very mightiness capable of experiencing greater agony than lower intellects, and his poetry was wrung out of his spirit by that agony. We have said that he was the greatest poet that ever lived, because his talent was the most universal. Excelled by Milton and Homer only in the vastness of their epic imaginations, he was excelled in nothing else by any man. He was overwhelming in his satire, irresistible in the brilliancy of the coruscations of his wit, unequalled in depth of pathos, or in the melancholy of moralising contemplation. We

may challenge every satirist and every comic poet that ever lived
to produce specimens of wit or of comic power at all equal to some
that might be selected from *Don Juan*.[13]

As his own work developed Ruskin himself came strikingly close
in many ways to fitting a description of this kind. As a descriptive
prose writer he is unequalled in English, his unerring eye for the
significant detail and the precise epithet, and his power of ordering
them in long rhythmic phrases which give each its appropriate stress
make glowing master-pieces of passages like the description of
Alpine life and landscape in *The Mountain Gloom*, the comparison of
the approach to an English cathedral and the approach to St Mark's
in *The Stones of Venice*, or the wonderful evocations of the sea,
especially of the sea exhausted after days of ceaseless storm in *Of
Water As Painted By Turner*. The vividness of such passages makes
them feel closer to painting than to other prose: they are, as it were,
painting with the controlled extension in time which the painter is
denied and which gives the writer a stricter control of the attention
of his reader.

Ruskin, like Byron, lived in a state of scornful opposition, to his
age. Both attacked insensitivity, vulgarity, and the industrial and
commercial degradation of humanity. Their interests and many of
their beliefs are different, but they are at one in openly identifying
and fearlessly attacking their enemies in the name of humanity; and
they are most alike in the comprehensiveness of their weapons and
methods of attack – in their ability to bring a wide range of material
under the unifying command of a central creative urge.

The central unifying theme of Ruskin's work is a concern with the
nature and problems of the intellectual life. Though he still seems to
be widely regarded as an interesting if erratic art critic who
wandered into political economy before degenerating into lunacy,
the fact is rather that his initial outrage at an imbecile journalistic
notice of Turner led him into a long process of thought, study and
writing, to produce what is still in many ways the most stimulating
analysis we have of the privileges and responsibilities of the sensitive
intellectual, with regard to art, morality and society.

His championship of Turner in *Modern Painters* causes Ruskin first
to explore both the minutiae of the technical details of landscape
painting and the overall nature of man's delight in beauty and the
arts. The precision and clarity of his analysis of the forms of leaves
and clouds, mountains and waves, must surely shock most readers

into a realisation of the insensitivity of their own normal perception as objects whirl past them on the tide of life. Stressing one's duty to see things as fully and clearly as possible, and demonstrating the reward for fulfilling this duty, in the form of enhanced appreciation of beauty, Ruskin goes on to consider the philosophical context of such activity. Though few modern readers would share Ruskin's evangelical beliefs of the 1840s and 50s, and therefore could not follow him in maintaining that landscape painting should help one to admire the beauty of God's creation, and thus of God himself, nevertheless precisely this necessary disagreement provides a powerful stimulus to justify one's own view of art. Though much of value can be written about art without raising any fundamental questions, any significant attempt at serious thought on the subject must relate its propositions about art to propositions about life: one's sense of significance in art cannot ultimately be dissociated from one's feeling for values in living. Most of the time, of course, it is easier and convenient to work within a framework of vague assumptions that 'culture' is good and therefore worth writing about; and, indeed, it would be intolerable if everyone who set out to write on the arts should feel obliged – or licensed – to pour out his inmost thoughts on the nature of existence. But this presents a danger: the risk that in writing about art only within the tacit conventions which support the vast 'culture' industry whose interest is rather in flattering its consumer into a belief that he knows something about art than in provoking him to confront the mediocrity and insensitivity of his own life with the shattering forces of great art, criticism may lapse into just that state of damaging irrelevance which prompted Ruskin to his defence of Turner. Ruskin, by constantly stressing the basis of significance in art in the nature of beliefs about morality and metaphysics, forces his reader to examine and try to define his own position, to refuse merely to take works of art as tokens in a cultural game, and to look at them critically and keep them in a dynamic relationship with his own widest and deepest beliefs.

Having forced his reader to treat art as something of the highest importance and to think about it in the most serious way as a central phenomenon to which all the problems of living can and should be related, Ruskin goes on in the works of his middle period to explore the necessarily consequent question of the relation of the man who has followed through such a process of thought to life in a society motivated principally by interests which are increasingly divergent from and destructive of the beliefs in the nature of the good life to which this study is likely to have led him. The transition is natural and smooth from Ruskin's insistence on the relationship between the quality of life in a society and the quality of its art to a concern with the problems of Victorian society, where craftsmanship was being replaced by machine production, and whose architecture was mostly so wretched. His concern that a man should be happy in his work, expressed in *The Seven Lamps of Architecture* and in the *Nature of Gothic* chapter of *The Stones of Venice*, led to his frontal attack on an economic order based on capitalist profit motives in *Unto This Last* and his various lectures of the period. Again, though the modern reader is likely to be uneasy with the paternalistic tone of *Unto This Last* and of the *Fors Clavigera* series of letters to 'The workmen and labourers of Great Britain', and dubious of Ruskin's readiness to reduce every problem to the simplest terms, overlooking the scale of complication given to them by their magnitude in reality, the provocation to disagree is a more valuable stimulus to thought than is provided by more circumspect and less outspoken authors.

Ruskin's experience of Italy was fundamental to the development of this work, and the work itself changed the direction of English interest in Italy almost as radically as Byron had done a generation earlier. We have seen that in his first visits to Italy in 1835 and 1840 Ruskin was chiefly interested by the country's associations with the work of Byron and Turner, and that he was relatively uninterested in the art and architecture of the early Renaissance; yet by the early fifties he had become absorbed in the latter, was eagerly exposing the inaccuracies of the Romantic image of Italy, and had set out to direct attention away from the sensational, and from the classicism of Gibbon, to what he thought the enduring ideals of early Christian art. The turning point was his visit of 1845.

In preparation for this visit Ruskin read Rio's *De la poésie chrétienne* (1836), the first book on Italian art to refer fluently and familiarly to most of the works and places one expects to find in such a book – the Campo Santo at Pisa, the Arena Chapel at Padua, the Brancacci Chapel at Florence, the Mantegna triptych in San Zeno at Verona, and so on. Ruskin's enthusiasm for the book, which he often mentions in his own work and which was translated into English in 1854 as a result of his references to it, doubtless stems from Rio's association of great art with the spirit of Christianity (though for Rio this meant Roman Catholicism, not Ruskin's Protestantism), his praise of Venice which 'malgré tout ce qu' on a pu dire de ses

tribunaux secrets, de ses courtisanes célèbres, et de son machiavél-
isme commercial, a été la plus chrétienne des républiques,' (p. 528)
and his horror at the paganism of the Renaissance which sets in with
the late works of Raphael.

His interest aroused by Rio, one of the crucial moments in
Ruskin's career came when he studied the tomb of Ilaria di Caretto
at Lucca in 1845. There, he wrote almost thirty years later,[14] he
really began his study of art. Going down to Pisa he discovered in
the Campo Santo 'the entire doctrine of Christianity, painted so
that a child could understand it. And what a child cannot
understand of Christianity, no one need try to.'[15] Then at Venice in
September he was overwhelmed by the genius of Tintoretto. This
revelation of the power of Italian art made the second volume of
Modern Painters (1846) quite different from the first (1843). There he
had championed Turner against the lifeless conventions of the
classical tradition; now he develops the attack on classicism in a
different way by arguing, on the evidence of the work that had so
impressed him in Italy, that the greatest art can only be derived
from the Christian moral view of God. By this realisation Ruskin
was led into a massive ten years' digression away from the subject of
Modern Painters, a digression, however, which was to prove to be in
the main line of development of his thought.

Cultivating his interest in Gothic architecture produced first the
laying down of principles in *The Seven lamps of Architecture* (1849) and
then the great *Stones of Venice* (1851–3). In order to demonstrate in
practice the operation of the principles enunciated in *The Seven
Lamps*, Ruskin takes the example of Venice not because its Gothic is
the most beautiful – the styles of Verona and of Florence he
considered far superior – but because the Ducal Palace, containing
equal elements of Roman, Lombard and Arab architecture is 'the
central building of the world.'[16] The first volume, in preparation for
the exploration of the city's architecture, is mostly taken up with a
treatise on the elements of the subject, until in the final section, *The
Vestibule*, Ruskin describes in magnificent prose the approach from
Mestre by gondola across the lagoon towards Venice. This dream-
like journey, however, has already become a thing of the past: the
railway had reached Venice in 1845, a fact which Ruskin deplores
as he concludes his description with the arrival in Venice at the
beginning of volume two. A large part of Ruskin's self-appointed
task in *The Stones of Venice* is simply to record as much as possible of
the beauty of Venice before it is too late and it is all destroyed – a

catastrophe which he felt to be very near at hand: 'I don't think the Ducal palace will stand 5 years more – its capitals are so rent and worn,' he wrote to his father in 1852.[17] Ruskin records Venice in his drawings and water colours, in his precise descriptions of the most minute and obscure details, and in splendid passages of prose, particularly, perhaps, the magnificent contrast of the approach to an English cathedral (Salisbury) with the approach to St Mark's, a passage full of the shimmering beauty of Venetian architecture, and of the crowded, noisy life of her alley ways and of the Piazza. Unfortunately, its length forbids its quotation in full, but its central moments, as the writer emerges from the narrow Venetian alleys into the miracle of the Piazza, may stand as representing something of the quality of Ruskinian Venice:

> A yard or two further, we pass the hostelry of the Black Eagle, and, glancing as we pass through the square door of marble, deeply moulded, in the outer wall, we see the shadows of its pergolas of vines resting on an ancient well, with a pointed shield carved on its side; and so presently emerge on the bridge and Campo San Moisè, whence to the entrance into St. Mark's Place, called the Bocca di Piazza (mouth of the square), the Venetian character is nearly destroyed, first by the frightful façade of San Moisè, which we will pause at another time to examine, and then by the modernising of the shops as they near the piazza, and the mingling with the lower Venetian populace of lounging groups of English and Austrians. We will push fast through them into the shadow of the pillars at the end of the 'Bocca di Piazza', and then we forget them all; for between those pillars there opens a great light, and, in the midst of it, as we advance slowly, the vast tower of St. Mark seems to lift itself visibly forth from the level field of chequered stones; and, on each side, the countless arches prolong themselves into ranged symmetry, as if the rugged and irregular houses that pressed together above us in the dark alley had been struck back into sudden obedience and lovely order, and all their rude casements and broken walls had been transformed into arches charged with goodly sculpture, and fluted shafts of delicate stone.
>
> And well may they fall back, for beyond those troops of ordered arches there rises a vision out of the earth, and all the great square seems to have opened from it in a kind of awe, that we may see it far away; – a multitude of pillars and white domes, clustered into

a long low pyramid of coloured light; a treasure-heap, it seems, partly of gold, and partly of opal and mother-of-pearl, hollowed beneath into five great vaulted porches, ceiled with fair mosaic, and beset with sculpture of alabaster, clear as amber and delicate as ivory, – sculpture fantastic and involved, of palm leaves and lilies, and grapes and pomegranates, and birds clinging and fluttering among the branches, all twined together into an endless network of buds and plumes; and, in the midst of it, the solemn forms of angels, sceptred, and robed to the feet, and leaning to each other across the gates, their figures indistinct among the gleaming of the golden ground through the leaves beside them, interrupted and dim, like the morning light as it faded back among the branches of Eden, when first its gates were angel-guarded long ago. And round the walls of the porches there are set pillars of variegated stones, jasper and porphyry, and deep-green serpentine spotted with flakes of snow, and marbles, that half refuse and half yield to the sunshine, Cleopatra-like, 'their bluest veins to kiss'. . .[18]

The Shakespearean reference is fittingly different from those which earlier writers had associated with Venice. Where the Romantics had found a city, indeed beautiful, but predominantly mysterious and melancholy, a city that for Byron had been a metaphor of his own feeling of vitality inseparable from decay, Ruskin finds a city which is very much Turner's in its unique beauty, and whose beauty is to be an inspiration, a re-awakening, in an age which is becoming increasingly inured to ugliness. Venice is, indeed, in an appaling state of neglect, decay and destructive 'restoration': from the moment his interest in Italy was aroused, Ruskin never ceased to protest against these evils, whether in print, in lectures, or by directly berating the people he felt were responsible for them – in 1872 he was restrained from friends from attacking astonished workmen 'restoring' the church of La Spina at Pisa, only to return to his hotel and lecture the landlord on his wickedness in allowing such things to go on in his town.[19] But his reaction to such phenomena is always one of wrathful indignation, never the morbid absorption in decay which had characterised some of the writers considered earlier. For Ruskin was intent upon salvaging from what he regarded as the ruin of Venice whatever was left of beauty which could recall his own age from its squalor to a realisation of the true dignity and magnificence of life.

Thus it was that the exotic beauty of Venice became related to the life of the factory floor in Victorian England. Meditation on the contrast between the spirit which created Venice and that which was afoot in industrial England brought to a head Ruskin's thoughts on the evil in the latter of 'the degradation of the operative into a machine', and produced the great creative protest of the *Nature of Gothic* chapter of the second volume of *The Stones of Venice*. The gradual changes in the English image of Italy we have been considering have brought us from the eighteenth century use of the grandeur of ancient Rome as an exhortation to England to attain a comparable degree of magnificence to Ruskin a century later, contemptuous of the irrelevance of the Roman remains, urging the example of the beauty of early Italian art as a possible means of recalling contemporary England from its accelerating decline into degradation and ugliness.

As we have seen, Ruskin opened *The Stones of Venice* with a warning that if this light were not followed destruction would follow. The third volume (1853) closes on a note of qualified optimism. In its last chapter Ruskin sees the so far miserable developments of the nineteenth century as merely the first stages of an ultimately admirable progress which could be helped on its way by the careful introduction of a new national school of architecture drawing its strength from the example of the vitality of the great Gothic buildings of the middle ages. Unfortunately, he was to be disappointed, for the influence of the book was not what he had hoped. Twenty years later he almost regretted having written the book, which, in the *Preface* to the 1874 edition, he regarded as responsible for the proliferation of wretched Venetian Gothic public houses and red and black striped chimneys: a curious variation on the common pattern of devotion to the beauty of Italy producing results disastrously different from those that had been hoped for. But although the book perversely had the effect of encouraging the spread of ugliness, and though his notes for the 1847 edition of Murray's *Handbook For Travellers in Northern Italy* doubtless helped encourage the propensity for 'doing' art galleries of those people whom he castigated in his 1858 *Cambridge Inaugural Address*[20] for never spending more than three-quarters of a minute before even the greatest master-piece, nevertheless Ruskin had provided in his Italian writing invaluable material for the serious traveller and had effected that change of emphasis from Romantic sensationalism to a more constructive interest in art which stimulated so much important work on Italian cultural history, which we shall consider later.

Though he continued to visit and write about Italy until his final mental breakdown, and although it was at Turin that his famous 'unconversion' took place in 1858, Ruskin's later Italian writing, while often locally admirable, consists simply of repetitions or minor developments of the positions outlined above. In the *A Joy For Ever* lectures (1857), for example, he attacks his Manchester audience for their lack of interest in the beautiful and recommends the study of Italy as the source of all the beauties of post-classical art, and especially of Verona as the city which contains 'at this moment the most singular concentration of art-teaching and art-treasure.'[21] In the third volume of *Modern Painters* (1856) he draws attention to Dante in the tour de force in which he compares the treatment of Nature in Homer, Dante and Milton, and in the fifth volume (1860) he has his famous comparison of the childhoods of Turner and Giorgione, and re-appraises Titian, having become more sympathetic to sixteenth century art after the abandonment of his evangelicalism. His *Giotto and His Works at Padua* (1854) put the Arena Chapel frescoes firmly on the tourist map of Italy, but had nothing new or important to say about them. (They were already well-known to serious students from books such as Maria Callcott's *Description of The Chapel of The Annunciata dell' Arena*, 1835). Apart from an infatuation with Carpaccio which resulted largely from his associating the painter's St Ursula with his beloved Rose La Touche, nothing new is to be found in the subsequent work – the Oxford lectures, the *Fors Clavigera* letters, and the popularising *Mornings in Florence* (1875–7) and *St Mark's Rest* (1877–84), and guide to the Venetian Academy (1877).

During the 'eighties Ruskin was disproportionately impressed by the sketches and writing of a young American artist Francesca Alexander, whose *Story of Ida* (1883), *Roadside Songs of Tuscany* (1884–5) and *Christ's Folk in The Apennines* (1887–9) are aetherealised, patronising idealisations of Tuscan peasants, such as could only be admired by someone quite out of touch with the realities of their harsh life. Ruskin, in fact, never had any real contact with Italian life, didn't speak Italian, and in so far as he had ever thought about the Italians of his own day tended to be contemptuous of their insensitivity to the monuments among which they lived, and of their laziness; in an appendix to *The Stones of Venice* on *Austrian Government in Italy* he observed that

The misery of the Italians consists in having three festa days a week, and doing in their days of exertion about one-fourth as much as an English labourer,[22]

and his 1859 letters on *The Italian Question* were quite unoptimistic about the prospects of the Risorgimento. His range of response to Italy was distinctly limited; but contemporary readers were not restricted to his intense but narrow view of Italy, for Browning's work effectively acted as its complement.

8 Browning

> I know no other piece of modern English, prose or poetry, in which there is so much told, as in these lines [*The Bishop Orders His Tomb*], of the Renaissance spirit – its worldliness, inconsistency, love of art, of luxury, and of good Latin. It is nearly all that I said of the central Renaissance in thirty pages of the *Stones of Venice*, Browning's being also the antecedent work.[1]

Such was Ruskin's opinion, reciprocated by Browning's admiration of *Modern Painters*[2] and by their subsequent friendship in London, of the poet who has often been regarded as speaking for himself in the lines he gave to the persona of *De Gustibus*:

> Open my heart and you will see
> Graved inside of it, 'Italy'.

The lines appear on the tablet erected to his memory on the Palazzo Rezzonico in Venice where Browning died in 1889, more than half a century after he had been moved and fascinated by his first visit to that city in 1838. Much of that half-century Browning had spent in Italy where, of course, he is particularly associated with Florence, his and Elizabeth's home for fourteen years – almost the whole – of their married life. He was well acquainted with Italy from the Bay of Naples northwards, and absorbed by Italian history; and devoted much of his literary effort to Italian subjects, drawing from an Italian critic the opinion that

> Roberto Browning è certamente il più italiano dei poeti inglesi, quando per *italiano* voglia intendersi sentimento non nazionalità. Nessun scrittore straniero ha amato l' Italia con l' intensità di passione che rivive nell' opera d' arte di Roberto Browning.[3]

and from a British scholar the observation that

> Italy provided Browning in his prime with what he needed as a poet, a refuge from the distracting pressures of Victorian England

from which Tennyson was fated never to escape. Italy saved Browning from becoming just another Eminent Victorian.[4]

Browning first came to know Italy at much the same time as Ruskin, and in some ways their literary preparation for the country was similar. Byron and Shelley were the dominant figures: when he went with Elizabeth to live in Pisa in 1847, it was to a city full of the memory of the two poets; and a week before sailing for Italy in 1838 Browning had seen *The Two Foscari* at Covent Garden. Landor too was important in his approach to Italy. Browning, who became Landor's closest friend during his final months of senility in Tuscany, always admired the older writer: 'I know no finer reading than Landor' was a typical comment, and Elizabeth noted that 'Robert always said that he owed more as a writer to Landor than to any contemporary.'[5] Landor's frequent use of Italian personae must have encouraged Browning's interest in Italy, and particularly in the Renaissance, while the form of the *Imaginary Conversations* may have led him to consider the possibilities of the dramatic monologue.

Browning's first visit to Italy, in 1838, was ostensibly to gather material for *Sordello*. That his first creative interest in Italy should have been aroused by Sordello, the poet who greets Virgil as a fellow Mantuan in Dante's *Purgatorio*, – an interest in the medieval, not the classical, poet – is characteristic of the early Victorian period, a product of the Romantic revolution in feeling that we have considered above. It parallels Ruskin's rejection of the achievements of classical Rome in favour of those of medieval Italy.

The composition of *Sordello* occupied Browning over many years, years which saw, symptomatically of the period's interest in Italy, the publication of another poem of the same name by one Mrs Busk in 1837. Hers is a straightforward, undistinguished narrative of the course, ultimately successful, of Sordello's love for Princess Cuniza, a narrative whose events are carefully adjusted to fit the moral proprieties of nineteenth century England. Though nugatory, it at least has the advantage over Browning's poem of being comprehensible. For the notorious difficulties of Browning's *Sordello* – Mrs Carlyle is supposed to have read it without being able to make out whether Sordello was a man, a city or a book – are such that it has no effect on contemporary attitudes to Italy, and little to offer the modern reader. The significance of the 1838 visit is not in terms of its effect on *Sordello* – mainly, the introduction of the episodes connected with Ferrara, which Browning did not visit – but rather as an introduction to the country which was to be so important to Browning, and especially for the radical change of outlook which resulted from his experience of Venice. His biographers observe that

> Venice, though unconnected with the subject of his poem except for a few and quite unimportant details, laid such a spell upon Browning that the fortnight he spent there was destined to lead to a revolution in his work.[6]

The experience is described in Book 3 of *Sordello*: sitting on the steps of a decaying Venetian palace, Browning was overwhelmed by a sense of the vitality of the working people around him. The realisation of the thickness and vigour of life won him away from the lofty speculation and romance of his early work to a concern, which marks his major poetry, with the subtle feel of life. He began to change – *Pippa Passes* (1841), that curious picture of life in his favourite town, Asolo, is a transitional work – from formal drama towards the dramatic monologue, though still continuing to write conventional dramas, two of them, *Luria* and *A Soul's Tragedy* (1846), Landor-like dramatisations of Italian history. Luria himself is the Moorish commander of the Florentine army, a confessedly Othello figure, and both plays exploit unashamedly the old 'Machiavellian' picture of Italian political treachery.

The poems, however, create a more vivid and compelling picture of the Italian past, quite deserving Ruskin's praise. Nothing presents representative figures of the Italian Renaissance so strikingly as *My Last Duchess* and *The Bishop Orders His Tomb at St Praxed's Church*.[7] The speaker in *My Last Duchess* has been convincingly identified[8] as Duke Alfonso II of Ferrara, and the Duchess as his second wife, Lucrezia dei Medici. The poem is a master-piece of economy in which each detail can be accounted for (the reference to the sculptor Claus of Innsbruck in the last line, for example, fits perfectly, since Alfonso's third wife was Austrian and in the poem he is speaking to the emissary who has been sent from Innsbruck to arrange the marriage), but whose ease and assurance appear quite unlaboured and need no elucidation from the authentic documents whose essence they distil. The portrait of the Duke, lover of pleasure and, in an egoistic way, of art, civilised, charming, yet jealous and sinisterly powerful ('I gave commands;/Then all smiles stopped together.'), is technically brilliant, psychologically stimulating, and historically, as a Renaissance type, convincing. Similarly, *The Bishop Orders His Tomb* presents the worldliness of the Renaissance Church, critically yet sympathetically, in a way that it would be fruitless and presumptuous to try to describe more precisely than Ruskin has done. It needs to be pointed out, however, that Browning's picture is not precisely the same as Ruskin's in *The Stones of Venice*. Ruskin castigated the high Renaissance as a period when pride, pleasure and paganism had replaced in art and life a Christian morality and the worship of God through the appreciation of the beauty of Nature. Browning, however, has an imaginative sympathy which allows him to adopt the voice of the Bishop or Duke and give his reader the illusion of seeing the experience of living through the eyes of a Renaissance man.

At times, indeed, Browning goes quite against Ruskin. The speaker in his *Pictor Ignotus*, condemned to painting

> These endless cloisters and eternal aisles
> With the same series, Virgin, Babe, and Saint, (59–60)

and envious of the fame and financial success of worldlier artists, is quite other than Ruskin would have one believe the religious painters to have been; and in his monologue *Fra Lippo Lippi* he makes the artist protest with splendid humour and vigour against the artificiality and stifled emotions of religious painting. The priests condemn Lippi's work for being too realistic and insufficiently spiritual:

> Your business is not to catch men with show,
> With homage to the perishable clay,
> But lift them over it, ignore it all,
> Make them forget there's such a thing as flesh.
> Your business is to paint the souls of men. (179–83)

Lippi, though, believes that the way to worship God is to celebrate the life he has created,

> The beauty and the wonder and the power,
> The shapes of things, their colours, lights and shades,
> Changes, surprises, (283–5)

for, in a painting,

> If you get simple beauty and nought else,
> You get about the best thing God invents, –
> That's somewhat. And you'll find the soul you have missed,
> Within yourself when you return Him thanks!
>
> (217–20)

Ruskin, too, believed that God was to be praised through the study of his creation, but he approached that study with an earnestness and awe far removed from the spontaneous joyfulness of Browning's hero. Browning's sympathies are quite different from Ruskin's and so, of course, is the nature of his work. Not concerned with expounding wide and fundamental ideas, Browning uses his command of the verse monologue to create an imaginative insight into human psychology at representative points. Those of his portraits with Italian subjects have doubtless contributed more to the English image of Italy than all of Ruskin's work – result partly of their convenient, accessible brevity, but also of their consummate art and sensitivity. Such, indeed, is their insight and authenticity that authorities of our own day have recommended *Andrea del Sarto*, the pathetically moving speech of the artist to his wife, as 'probably the best explanation of [Andrea's] failure to live up to his great promise.'[9] Taken together, Browning's Renaissance personae give the English reader his most vivid imaginative entry into the appreciation of the period, giving a human thickness to its atmosphere which helps to prevent its artistic remains from becoming mere museum pieces.

Nor is it only the Renaissance that Browning makes vivid in this manner. *A Toccata of Galuppi's* is a poem whose charm and sadness parallel the gaiety and lack of spiritual resource of the eighteenth century Venice it describes:

> As for Venice and its people, merely born to bloom and drop,
> Here on earth they bore their fruitage, mirth and folly were the
> crop,
> What of soul was left, I wonder, when the kissing had to stop?

The Italian in England, the monologue of an Italian exile, gives a human reality to the events of the Risorgimento: idealistic dedication, betrayal, the nervous life of the hunted man, the touching

devotion of the peasant girl who risks her life to help him, and the
bitter realisation of the pliancy with which his former comrades
bend under the yoke of Austrian tyranny:

> If I resolved to seek at length
> My father's house again, how scared
> They all would look, and unprepared!
> My brothers live in Austria's pay
> – Disowned me long ago, men say;
> And all my early mates who used
> To praise me so – perhaps induced
> More than one early step of mine –
> Are turning wise; while some opine
> 'Freedom grows licence,' some suspect
> 'Haste breeds delay,' and recollect
> They always said, such premature
> Beginnings never could endure!
> So, with a sullen 'All's for best,'
> The land seems settling to its rest. ·

Though consistently sympathetic to the Italian cause, Browning
wrote little about it; but his power to convey poetically the feelings
of its heroes was such that Mazzini translated this poem for his
followers to show them how deeply a foreigner could understand
their struggle.

On the brighter side, *The Englishman in Italy* is a luscious
evocation of life in the country near Sorrento, a hymn to the
sensuous delights of the sunny and fertile south. The poem marks a
crucial stage in the development of English attitudes to Italy. Two
things particularly are likely to strike one in comparing the
attractions of Italy to the modern English tourist and those things
which attracted his eighteenth century predecessor. The first is the
shift of taste, which we have followed, from the classical to the
medieval and Renaissance; and, secondly, the modern traveller is
likely to enthuse over the sun, the sea, the mountains, and the food
and wine of Italy, all of which to the eighteenth century were not
merely uninteresting, but positive disincentives to going to Italy; the
mountains and sea being obstacles to travel, the sun oppressive, and
the fare indigestible, in their view. The modern who admires the
eloquent stoicism of the Italian peasant would have found no
sympathisers among the Grand Tourists with their blanket con-

tempt of living Italians. His feelings are the fruit of a tradition which reaches its climax, as we shall see, with D. H. Lawrence, and which effectively starts as late as Browning.

Byron, of course, had celebrated the Italian sun and the joys of the south, but his case was rather different. The countrymen he admired were the fierce clansmen of Albania, and the women the ubiquitous dark-eyed peasant girl, suggestive of violent passion. Temperamentally, he was not the man to relax appreciatively among the peasants of the plain of Sorrento whose life forms the texture of *The Englishman in Italy*. It is since Browning's day that much of the attraction of Italy has been seen to lie in the kind of meal he mouth-wateringly describes:

> With lasagne so tempting to swallow
>   In slippery ropes,
> And gourds fried in great purple slices,
>   That colour of popes.
> Meantime, see the grape-bunch they've brought you, –
>   The rain-water slips
> O'er the heavy blue bloom on each globe
>   Which the wasp to your lips
> Still follows with fretful persistence.

It is the season when the Sirocco blows over the south, but its oppressiveness is not resented, since it is a part of the natural pattern, a pattern which is translucently clear in a country of sunny mountains where

> No rampart excludes
> Your eye from the life to be lived
>   In the blue solitudes!

and on whose sea-shore, past which Ulysses once sailed on his Odyssey, there is still to be heard

> The birds' quiet singing, that tells us
>   What life is, so clear!
> The secret they sang to Ulysses,
>   When, ages ago,
> He heard and he knew this life's secret,
>   I hear and I know!

Browning has re-connected his age with the classics, not through the study of the ruins of Italy, but through his delight in those sensuous, pagan qualities which had remained scarcely changed since the days when they had inspired the classical poets themselves. It is this kind of delight in living which gives Browning his sympathy with the Renaissance, makes him so different, and shapes a new type of interest in Italy, which we shall consider later, which derives much of its critical view of Italian art from Ruskin, but combines it with a sensuous appreciation of Italy which follows the model set by Browning's shorter poems.

Indeed, not only do these poems place these kinds of material vividly before the English literary imagination; they also provide the touchstones against which to judge later treatments of Italy. The Renaissance portraits we have already mentioned; *Up At A Villa – Down In The City* provides a model with which to compare later accounts of contemporary Italian life, whether they are perceptive, sentimental, patronising, or rather silly, as Lawrence (normally one of the acutest observers of Italy) becomes when, noticing the narrowness and darkness of Italian village streets, he theorises about the inner darkness of the Italian soul, apparently not realising that the important thing about these streets is that their darkness makes them cool.[10] In Browning's poem the speaker is 'An Italian Person of Quality', quite unenamoured of life in the country, where he spends his time dreaming of the city where, if only he could afford it, he would love to live:

> Ere you open your eyes in the city, the blessed church-bells begin:
> No sooner the bells leave off, than the diligence rattles in:
> You get the pick of the news, and it costs you never a pin.
> By and by there's the travelling doctor gives pills, lets blood, draws teeth;
> Or the Pulcinello-trumpet breaks up the market beneath.
> At the post-office such a scene-picture – the new play, piping hot!
> And a notice how, only this morning, three liberal thieves were shot.
> Above it, behold the archbishop's most fatherly of rebukes,
> And beneath, with his crown and his lion, some little new law of the Duke's!

It is the first sympathetic evocation in English of the compulsive Piazza life of the Italian, that delight in communal lounging, at which Dr Moore had hinted, so alien to the Englishman whose home is his castle, but without a feeling for which one cannot begin to appreciate Italian life. Browning led the way, and his account remains one of the most vivid and perceptive.

Browning's stimulating revaluation of Italy was the work of the eighteen-forties and early 'fifties. (*Dramatic Lyrics*, 1842; *Dramatic Romances & Lyrics*, 1845; *Men & Women*, 1855.) It was consolidated in the 'sixties by *The Ring and The Book* (1868–9). The poem is based upon a manuscript account of a Roman murder trial of 1698, which Browning had picked up in the market in Florence in 1860. In some ways, the story of the fatal marriage of Count Guido Franceschini and Pompilia, which ends in his murdering her, is a typical subject of Italian romance, which would have appealed to the sensational Romantic novelists. Browning, however, treats his material with greater skill and sophistication than any of those had possessed. He creates a series of personae – protagonists in the events of the story, lawyers, the Pope who must judge the case, and the Piazza loungers of Rome who discuss it – each presenting or considering the story from his own point of view. There is a certain gracefulness about the work. There is none of the suspense one usually expects from a murder story: on the contrary, Browning is explicit about the Count's guilt from the beginning, where he outlines in advance the plan of the whole work. Thenceforth the poem proceeds like a geometrical demonstration. Every speaker, each a fully rounded character, appears in his appointed place, and following the poem from one to the next, the reader is led through a demonstration of the elusiveness of truth and the ease with which, whether wilfully or innocently, it can be obscured by the individual viewpoint. But though the poem is attractive and fascinating, though any poem which sustains interest through twenty thousand lines is worthy of admiration, it lacks the force and feeling of significance of some of the earlier, shorter poems. Though it is an important document in the history of English literary use of Italy, it is on those shorter works, rather than on *The Ring and The Book*, that Browning's importance to our subject, as well as his claim to high poetic rank, must rest.[11]

9 The other Victorian Poets

Not all Victorian poets, of course, were so profoundly influenced by Italy as Browning. Tennyson is the obvious contrast. His friend Hallam, commemorated in *In Memoriam*, had been an early visitor to the graves of Keats and Shelley in 1827–8 and a pioneering admirer of the early Italian painters, whom he praised in his *Oration* at Trinity College, Cambridge in December, 1831, a stimulating survey of the influence of Italian models on English literature, which argues the value of comparative literary studies, and is full of admiration for Dante. Despite sharing this enthusiasm for Dante, claiming Garibaldi as a friend, and having an elder brother, Frederick, who married an Italian and lived for twenty years in Florence, where he knew the Brownings and occasionally produced mediocre verses on Italian subjects, Tennyson's visit to Italy in 1851 produced a solitary poem on that very English flower, *The Daisy*, while, according to Browning,

> after he got to Florence, on his way to Rome, he was so disquieted because he could not find a particular tobacco he liked that he turned back to England and never went to Rome.[1]

Matthew Arnold knew Italy rather better, travelling there several times, notably on business in 1865 and on holiday in 1873. His admiration for Italy is clear from the letters of these periods, which declare, for example, that

> Here in Italy one feels that all time spent out of Italy by tourists in France, Germany, Switzerland, etc., etc., is – human life being so short – time misspent.[2]

From 1869 to 1871 Prince Thomas of Savoy, the young Duke of Genoa, stayed in Arnold's home, while attending school at Harrow, hospitality rewarded by King Victor Emmanuel with the Order of Commander of The Crown of Italy. But his experience of Italy is quite incidental to Arnold's work. It has no appreciable effect on his poetry; there is, of course, nothing Sicilian about *Empedocles on Etna* (1852), though it is interesting that he should have taken a nominally Italian setting for his exploration of the difficulties of coming to terms with life at the same time that his friend Clough was working on *Dipsychus*, with its Venetian setting. Arnold's pamphlet, *England and The Italian Question* (1859), though sympathetic to the Italians, reflects the tendencies of his mind in being less about Italy than about France, and, anyway, essentially about England. The Italian section of *Schools and Universities on The Continent* (1868), the report of his journey of 1865, is an interesting, but purely professional, account of the growth and state of Italian education.

Four poets, however did respond significantly to Italy: Elizabeth Browning, Clough, Rossetti and Swinburne.

ELIZABETH BARRETT BROWNING (1806–61)

Elizabeth Barrett Browning is no longer regarded, as she was by many of her contemporaries,[3] as a greater poet than her husband. Her poems lack the mastery of self-effacing art which distinguishes Robert's best work; one has almost always the feeling that the genuine interest of her ideas and feelings is blunted by her inability fully to fuse them into compelling poetic form. Yet she is a significant poet; and particularly for our subject, since so large a proportion of her work concerns Italian material, and that in an interesting way.

Some of her incidental references to Italy provide a convenient index of the changes of attitude to Italy that we have considered. Some lines of her youthful poem *An Essay on Mind* (1826) unwittingly stress the change in feeling towards the Roman ruins which had been effected by the Romantic poets; she bids her reader think of Rome and

> See the crushed column and the ruined dome –
> 'Tis all Eternity has left of Rome!
> While travelled crowds, with curious gaze, repair
> To read the littleness of greatness there!
>
> Alas! alas! so Albion shall decay,
> And all my country's glory pass away!

So shall she perish, as the mighty must,
And be Italia's rival – in the dust. (Bk. 1, 233–40)

The eighteenth century verse form is curiously employed to express a thoroughly Romantic sentiment; a quarter of a century later, a letter from Venice in 1851 marks the development from this melancholy Romantic response to decay to the post-Turner delight in the magical beauty of the city:

> Venice is quite exquisite; it wrapt me round with a spell at first sight, and I longed to live and die there – never to go away. The gondolas, and the glory they swim through, and the silence of the population, drifted over one's head across the bridges, and the fantastic architecture and the coffee-drinking and music in the Piazza San Marco, everything fitted into my lazy, idle nature and weakness of body, as if I had been born to the manner of it and to no other. Do you know I expected in Venice a dreary sort of desolation? Whereas there was nothing melancholy at all, only a soothing, lulling, rocking atmosphere which if Armida had lived in a city rather than in a garden would have suited her purpose. [4]

Elizabeth would have liked to live in Venice, but the humidity was bad for Robert's health and they settled at Florence, where her sympathy with the Italian people and support for their political cause were so deeply appreciated that her death in 1861 was regarded as a national loss, lamented by the Florentine newspapers. 'L' Italia perdeva una delle più fervide, più calde, più costanti sostenitrici della sua causa,' said *La Gazzetta del Popolo*. [5] The tribute was won by her pre-occupation with the ambitions and fortunes of Italian nationalism. *Casa Guidi Windows* (1851), *Poems Before Congress* (1860) and the posthumous *Last Poems* (1862) are dominated by the subject. The poems chart the course of the hopes and deceptions of the Italian movement – the enthusiasm of 1848 in the first part of *Casa Guidi Windows*, and the sense of inadequacy in the second part, written in 1851 when hopes in the revolutionary zeal of the Italian people, in foreign support, and in liberal policies from the new Pope Pius the Ninth had all proved unfounded; and again, in the later poems, the hopes for the war of 1859 and the disillusion with the Treaty of Villafranca and loss of faith in Napoleon the Third. The interest of the poems is unfortunately more as documents than for any intrinsic merit. Though poetically ephemeral, none of them having the lasting vividness of Robert's

The Italian In England, the prominence of Italian affairs in her later work shows a major redirection of her poetic energies brought about by contact with Italy, and presented the English reader with a sustained plea for sympathy with the Italian cause: her verse, according to Tommaso Tommasei's inscription on the Casa Guidi, became 'a golden ring linking Italy and England.' The poems are one of the principal literary manifestations of the enormous English interest in Italian politics in mid-century, testified to in other ways by the activities of the exile Antonio Panizzi, by Gladstone's *Two Letters To The Earl of Aberdeen on The State Prosecutions of The Neapolitan Government* (1851), and by the phenomenal welcome given to Garibaldi on his visit to England in 1864.[6] In total contrast with the tendency of eighteenth century contemplation of Italy to feed a self-satisfied English sense of superiority to the rest of the world, and in defiance of the mercantilist doctrine of splendid isolation, Italy had become one of the focal points of the growing feeling of mutual dependence and responsibility, the recognition that no man or country can be truly free while another is in chains. The increasing acceptance of such truths and principles which Byron had seen and fought for is one of the great movements of the nineteenth century, and its importance is nowhere more nobly asserted than in Elizabeth Browning's refusal to support inward-looking policies of non-intervention which implicitly condone the oppression and inhumanity practised by other states:

> I love no peace which is not fellowship,
> And which includes not mercy. I would have
> Rather, the raking of the guns across
> The world, and shrieks against Heaven's architrave;
> Rather, the struggle in the slippery fosse
> Of dying men and horses, and the wave
> Blood-bubbling . . . Enough said! – by Christ's own cross,
> And by this faint heart of my woman-hood,
> Such things are better than a Peace that sits
> Beside a hearth in self-commended mood,
> And takes no thought how wind and rain by fits
> Are howling out of doors against the good
> Of the poor wanderer. What! your peace admits
> Of outside anguish while it keeps at home?
> I loathe to take its name upon my tongue.
> 'Tis nowise peace. 'Tis treason, stiff with doom.[7]

In passages of this sort, concern with the political state of Italy plays an important part in the education of those feelings of equality and communal moral responsibility, whose emergence in the forms of communism, socialism and liberal idealism marks one of the greatest differences between the beginning and the end of the nineteenth century.

Italy also contributed substantially to Elizabeth Browning's longest poem, *Aurora Leigh* (1856). The heroine is the daughter of a Florentine beauty and an Englishman who had gone to Florence for a month and fallen in love with the country and with the woman whom he stayed to marry. Aurora is brought up in Italy until she is orphaned at the age of thirteen, and she returns to Italy towards the end of the poem; in the central part, set in England, Italy stands always as the land of beauty, of poetry, and of the full life, in damning contrast to the opposite qualities to be found in England. From the first, the loss of the vigorous, sunny life the girl had led in the Tuscan mountains is registered implicitly in the description of the aunt by whom she is to be looked after in England:

> She had lived, we'll say,
> A harmless life, she called a virtuous life,
> A quiet life, which was not life at all
> (But that, she had not lived enough to know),
> Between the vicar and the country squires,
> The lord-lieutenant looking down sometimes
> From the empyrean to assure their souls
> Against chance-vulgarisms, and, in the abyss
> The apothecary, looked on once a year
> To prove their soundness of humility.
> The poor-club exercised her Christian gifts
> Of knitting stockings, stitching petticoats,
> Because we are of one flesh after all
> And need one flannel (with a proper sense
> Of difference in the quality) . . .[8]

The child soon discovers that 'Italy/Is one thing, England one', that in England all the fields are gardens, nature is 'Tamed/And grown domestic like a barn-door fowl', 'And if you seek for any wilderness/You find, at best, a Park'. The child's familiarity with the more expansive and less domesticated life of Italy allows her to feel that crippling constriction of English life which, as she grows into a woman, becomes the principal concern of the poem. She feels, and in the course of time fulfils, aspirations to become a poet, and in pursuit of her vocation rejects the conventionally handsome prospect of marriage with her cousin Romney Leigh, preferring the imponderable risks of attempting to create an independent life of her own to the mundane security of becoming a wifely chattel. She disagrees with Romney about the effect of his magnanimous philanthropy, arguing that the appeal to men's minds through art has far greater reforming power than do the practical measures of poor relief.

After many difficulties and complications the poem vindicates her beliefs and, symbolically, she returns to live again in Italy, where Romney, his charitable projects in pathetic ruins, comes to confess that she was right, and to marry her on her own terms. The ending of the poem is unsatisfactory; it is lamely conventional in a poem whose whole strength is in its analysis of the difficulties of refusing to be stifled by convention, and the symbolical blinding of Romney is a lamentably crude piece of work. This and other criticisms of the poem – on the grounds of the banality of much of the verse, the frequent feebleness of characterisation, inconsistency, invraisemblance, and confusion – have adequately been made in Gardner B. Taplin's *Life of E. B. Browning*. It remains true, nevertheless, that some of the verse is quite distinguished – the passage quoted above, for example, or the visit to St Giles in Book 3, which Virginia Woolf thought the best passage in the poem,[9] or the 'wedding' scene in Book 4 – while the presentation of the problems facing a woman with a vocation is not only historically fascinating but still directly stimulating and relevant. If one observes that the poem leaves one with a more vivid realisation of those problems than do the modern advocates of Women's Lib, it is only to support Aurora Leigh's point that art is more powerful than propaganda.

In this poem as in the political poems, Elizabeth Browning is writing from a position quite the opposite of the English attitude to Italy in the previous century. No longer is Italy the poor down-trodden country whose glory has passed to England; it is a country whose beauty, openness to life, and struggle for national liberty can be used to criticise the stiff conventionality, laissez-faire indifference, and industrial squalor of the country which had used to feel so superior. The Italy of the middle ages with Ruskin, of the Renaissance with Robert Browning, and modern Italy with Browning and his wife had become in the 1850s the image of that

Eden of which the Industrial Revolution had been the forbidden tree.

ARTHUR HUGH CLOUGH (1819–61)

The Protestant cemetery at Florence received in 1861 not only the body of Elizabeth Browning but also that of Arthur Hugh Clough, who, like the hero of some nineteenth century novel, had gone to Italy at the age of forty-two in search of health, only to find there his death. His last, short visit to Italy produced no poetical work of any note, but two of his earlier visits, to Rome in 1849 and to Venice in 1850, had provided material and settings for his two major poems, *Amours de Voyage* and *Dipsychus*. Both of these poems were first drafted in Italy, then extensively re-worked in manuscript, and not published until appreciably later, *Amours de Voyage* partially in 1858 and fully in 1862, and *Dipsychus* in expurgated form in 1865 and not in full until 1951. They had, therefore, little or no immediate effect on the development of literary attitudes to Italy; but to put them in the context of this development may provide a new perspective for looking at the poems.

Clough was in Rome between April and July, 1849, having gone there, furnished with an introduction and a cigar case from Carlyle to Mazzini, to observe the progress of Mazzini's Roman Republic. It was a visit which, together with his visit to revolutionary Paris the previous year, rather dented Clough's earlier radicalism and republicanism.[10] He was shocked, for example, at the indifference of the majority of Romans to the fate of their – to Clough, 'our' – Republic, and particularly at the fact that it was the French, who a year before had been fighting for liberty, who were now restoring the Pope to Rome. His letters of the period vividly describe the siege and occupation of the city, and the experience of these events provides a major theme of *Amours de Voyage*.

The excitement of a city under attack gives rise to passages like the following description by the poem's hero, Claude (who, though he shares some traits of his creator, is not to be confused with Clough, who places him with careful touches of irony like that in the second half of the third line):

> Twelve o' clock, on the Pincian Hill, with lots of English,
> Germans, Americans, French, – the Frenchmen, too, are
> protected,
> So we stand in the sun, but afraid of a probable shower;

So we stand and stare, and see, to the left of St Peter's,
Smoke, from the cannon, white, – but that is at intervals
only, –
Black, from a burning house, we suppose, by the Caval-
leggieri;
And we believe we discern some lines of men descending
Down through the vineyard-slopes, and catch a bayonet
gleaming.
(Canto, 2, 115–22)

It is a picture of Rome strikingly different from any of those we
have hitherto met, a picture used not only to create a vivid piece of
reporting but to undercut both the character of the speaker (Claude
is writing to his friend Eustace) and the reader's assenting interest in
the description. For there is something repellent in the utterly
touristic manner in which Claude treats matters of life and death.
Ironically, the battle is watched from the Pincian, the most touristic
viewpoint in Rome; the tourists watch the smoke of the cannon
and of burning houses – and are afraid of a shower; Clough
echoes Milton's 'They also serve who only stand and wait', but these
people only stand and stare. The contrast is with Byron. Claude
hates Childe Harold (Canto 1, 209); by contrast with the significance which Byron had found in the Roman ruins, Claude wanders
through Rome, *Murray* in hand, and finds the city 'rubbishy'.
(Clough himself called Rome 'a rubbishy place' in a letter to his
mother.)[11] Like the political and military action of which he is a
mere spectator, the city offers him little that he can really relate to
his own life, for he is fundamentally incapable of involvement with
anything outside himself.

This is a dominant aspect of the relationship, or non-relationship,
between Claude and the flirtacious Mary Trevellyn, around which
the poem is built. The long process of his coming to a decision that
he does love her and then, when it is too late, chasing madly round
north Italy trying to find out where she has gone, draws out the
pathos of the hero who is unable to take the risk of floating on the
tide of life. Claude himself uses the Shakespearean image in one of
his letters to Eustace:

There is a tide, at least, in the *love* affairs of mortals,
Which, when taken at flood, leads on to the happiest fortune, –
Leads to the marriage-morn and the orange-flowers and the
altar,

And the long lawful line of crowned joys to crowned joys
succeeding, –
Ah, it has ebbed with me! Ye gods, and when it was
flowing,
Pitful fool that I was, to stand fiddle-faddling in that way!
(Canto 4, 33–8)

But this is only one level of the pathos; deeper is the fact that this self-pity is mis-guided, for had he committed himself to the tide, Claude would surely have found not married bliss but that the light-headed Mary, as the reader knows from the evidence of her letters, was hopelessly unsuited to him. He might at best have gained some useful experience of life which would have spared him from writing such nonsense as

Ah! she was worthy, Eustace, – and that, indeed, is my comfort, –
Worthy a nobler heart than a fool such as I could have given,
(Canto 5, 68–9)

when he decides to give up the search for Mary and to devote himself rather to a search for knowledge. Clough has taken the novelistic convention of Italy as a country which is prone to break people's hearts by leading them into ill-considered love affairs to a level of sophistication much higher than the novel had yet attained.

A Byronic hero in Claude's situation would doubtless have become Garibaldi's right-hand man in the defence of Rome and made love to Mary, and probably both her sisters, too. He would, at least, have acted, and have based his moral beliefs on the experience he had gained. The Victorian Claude, however, lost in a world without moral landmarks, wants to establish his beliefs before committing himself to action; he is worried by the Byronic example: '*ACTION will furnish belief*, – but will that belief be the true one?', he asks. (Canto 5, 20). The result, of course, is that his actions are irrelevant and fruitless, and what beliefs he has are invalidatingly untried by experience.

John Goode has suggested[12] that Clough intends the reader of *Amours de Voyage* to contrast the poem with Goethe's *Römische Elegien*. Though there seems to be nothing in the poem to support this, the comparison is useful. Goethe's Roman poems celebrate the whore whom he had taken as a mistress and whose body provides him with a stimulating contrast to the study of antiquities. The persona of the *Elegien* was able easily and delightedly to integrate dead stones and living flesh into a healthful total experience. It is precisely this kind of thing that Clough's heroes need urgently to do, but are quite unable to do; and Dipsychus even more so than Claude.

No letters appear to have survived from the period of Clough's visit to Venice in 1850, and nothing is known of the details of his stay there. But whatever his personal feelings about the city may have been, Clough's literary response to Venice is interesting. *Dipsychus* presents the struggle of its hero to come to terms with life without being corrupted by life, and for this struggle Venice provides an ideal setting. But it is necessarily a very different Venice from that which Byron had made the scene of so open an acceptance of the fulness of life. Dipsychus, indeed, shares the post-Byronic apprehension of the beauty of Venice:

> O beautiful, beneath the magic moon,
> To walk the watery way of palaces!
> O beautiful, o'ervaulted with gemmed blue,
> This spacious court; with colour and with gold,
> With cupolas, and pinnacles, and points,
> And crosses multiplex, and tips and balls
> (Wherewith the bright stars unreproving mix,
> Nor scorn by hasty eyes to be confused);
> Fantastically perfect this low pile
> Of oriental glory; these long ranges
> Of classic chiselling, this gay flickering crowd,
> And the calm Campanile. Beautiful!
>
> (Scene 10, 12–23)

But he is tormented by the sense of the ephemeral nature of such beauty, that all of life cannot be spent in delighted contemplation. He struggles to accept, without becoming demoralised, that much of life is wretched or repulsive; and the much harder truth that much that he knows he ought to be repelled by is in fact irresistibly attractive.

This leads Clough to lay considerable stress on the pre-Byronic attitude to Venice as the city of tempting sin, the European capital of licentiousness. The tormenting spirit who undercuts all of Dipsychus's attempts to work out a consistent and self-respecting view of life, by ironically demolishing all his rationalisations and exposing his self-righteousness, tempts him with the attractions of the Venetian whores, 'if 'twere only just to see/The room of an Italian fille.' (Scene 2a, 103–4). The heavily sexual atmosphere is strongly evoked, and recalls much more the old protests against the wickedness of Venice than Byron's exuberant reports from what was essentially the same ambiance. We observed earlier that much of the history of nineteenth century English attitudes to Italy was to be measured in terms of varying kinds of fragmentation of Byron's comprehensive response, and *Dipsychus* is very much a case in point. For the misery of Dipsychus is precisely that he is obsessed by his inability to embrace life in the way that Byron had done. Byron, we have suggested, had known how to exploit the problems posed by the breaking up of ordered systems of thought by harnessing the exhilaration of a constant dynamic process of making and remaking of personal values as the pulse of experience dictated. Dipsychus is a figure, at once very Victorian in the nature of the particular issues which trouble him and representatively post-Romantic – that is, modern – in a way which makes him enduringly relevant, whose anguish is a result of an attempt to salvage something of the old order of values in a world in which they are increasingly disintegrating, and which itself is becoming increasingly confusing through having lost their guide-lines.

Byron's acceptance of life had been so full as to lead him to protest against the condition of life itself, the discrepancy between desire and responsibility. Goethe's Faust characterises Romanticism when he cries, 'Zwei seelen wohnen, ach! in meiner brust!', feeling the imprisonment of his imagination within the feeble physical limitations of a human body. But Clough's Dipsychus and Mephistopheles have quite different problems from those of Goethe's drama. Dipsychus's anguish comes not from a sense of the impossibility of taking up more than a minuscule fraction of the potential experiences of life, but, quite the opposite, from a wish completely to reject vast numbers of those potentialities because they impinge too pressingly upon the narrow range he has elected to try to follow. His pre-occupation with not becoming corrupted by life is symptomatic: Byron could not consider life as corrupting, but Dipsychus is 'the over-tender conscience [which] will, of course, exaggerate the wickedness of the world.'[13] The city which in Byron is an image of the magnificent broad fecundity of life in *Dipsychus* splits into opposite poles of attraction, the aethereal qualities of its beauty, and the dark, fleshy qualities of its sensuality. The poem characterises vividly the type of the Victorian dilemma, a tension, not like that of the Romantics, between the potential and the limitations of life, but between 'higher' and 'lower' selves, each afraid of the other, and unable to merge into a healthful, total individuality. If Italy was in some sense a paradise, it was one which might be agonisingly unattainable.

DANTE GABRIEL ROSSETTI (1828–82)

The work of Dante Rossetti and Swinburne represents the last serious engagement of Victorian poetry with the stimulus of Italy. Verse continued to be written, of course, on Italian subjects. There were even attempts at producing epic poems on the events of the Risorgimento, like Mary Braddon's *Garibaldi* (1861), Harriet King's *Aspromonte* (1869) and *The Disciples* (1872) and Alfred Austin's *Rome or Death!* (1873). But nothing of value was produced, and essentially the terrain lay fallow until it was richly cropped in the present century by Ezra Pound's *Cantos*.

Dante Gabriel Rossetti's creative relationship with Italy is quite unlike that of any other writer who falls within our scope. Born in London in 1828, he never visited Italy, although in temperament and appearance he was often regarded by his contemporaries as typically Italian. He spoke Italian from childhood; his father was an Italian patriotic poet in exile from the Kingdom of Naples, who lived in London teaching Italian and elaborating an increasingly involved and extravagant theory that all Renaissance literature was the coded propaganda of a vast secret Carbonarist society with Dante at its centre. About the age of seventeen, Dante Gabriel began to penetrate beyond the obscurities of his father's theories, to reach an immediate contact with the vitality of Dante's work, and from that time on the spirit of Dante's adoration of Beatrice permeated his whole emotional life and artistic activity. In the poetry we may note the two major aspects of this phenomenon.

Firstly, throughout his early manhood Rossetti devoted a considerable amount of effort to the study and translation of Dante and the other early Italian poets. Published in 1861 as *The Early Italian Poets* and revised in 1874 as *Dante and His Circle*, the translations offer a sensitive and useful introduction to the Italian poetry of the period. The volume made an important contribution to the growing interest in Italian Renaissance culture, whose further developments we shall consider presently; and to the present day the energy and immediacy of the translations are an irresistible invitation to read further into the work of the original poets. Rossetti's version of one of the sonnets of Cecco Angiolieri, for example, must surely make the reader who does not already know him curious to know more of the work of the tempestuous Sienese poet:

> If I were fire, I'd burn the world away;
> If I were wind, I'd turn my storms thereon;
> If I were water, I'd soon let it drown;
> If I were God, I'd sink it from the day;
> If I were Pope, I'd never feel quite gay
> Until there was no peace beneath the sun;
> If I were Emperor, what would I have done? –
> I'd lop men's heads all round in my own way.
> If I were death, I'd lock my father up;
> If I were life, I'd run away from him;
> And treat my mother to like calls and runs.
> If I were Cecco (and that's all my hope,)
> I'd pick the nicest girls to suit my whim,
> And other folk should get the ugly ones.

Secondly, as well as offering the English reader a valuable means of access to the Italian poets, Rossetti's translations also had a fundamental influence on the development of his own poetic personality. On a stylistic level the debt to Dante is self-evident in such characteristically Rossetti lines as

> the spirits of mine eyes
> Before thy face, their altar, solemnize
> The worship of that Love through thee made known,

recalling, for example, Dante's

> Degli occhi suoi, come ch' ella gli muova,
> Escono spirti d' amore infiammati.[14]

More generally, the whole of Rossetti's poetic work (as well as his painting) centres around the concept of the fascinating woman, unattainable yet obsessive, which clearly relates to Dante's adoration of Beatrice. But there is a crucial difference in the relationships of the two poets to their heroines. Beatrice represents an ideal of womanhood in a clearly structured universe where such ideals can be accepted and adored because they reflect the basic fecundating ideal of the Divinity. But Rossetti's magnificent women are ideal lovers in a more purely physical world where ideals only frustrate because they are denied an existence in reality: the poignant absence is ironically emphasised by the recurrent reference to the Dantesque model. Like Byron relating his own anguish to the destruction of Roman grandeur, or like Ruskin deploring the contrast between English industrialism and Italian Gothic, but in his uniquely personal way, Rossetti, especially in *The House of Life*, succeeds in evoking the greatness of Italian achievement in the past in order imaginatively to express his sense of the plight of the contemporary situation. We have already used images of Eden to help suggest the relation to Italy of Clough and Elizabeth Browning; the tragic realisation which Rossetti's poetry enacts is that no Beatrice can exist within the corrupted conditions of earthly experience.

ALGERNON CHARLES SWINBURNE (1837–1909)

Swinburne's work took up in a stimulating manner both Elizabeth Browning's concern for liberty and Rossetti's fascination with women.

> Liberty
> Is no mere flower that feeds on light and air
> And sweetens life and soothes it, but herself
> Air, light, and life, which being withdrawn or quenched
> Or choked with rank infection till it rot
> Gives only place to death and darkness,

proclaims the hero in Act 5, Scene 2 of his *Marino Faliero* and, on one level, the mass of Swinburne's work is concerned to establish contact with this source of light and life, which he sees as emanating particularly from Italy, and outstandingly from the person of Mazzini. To Swinburne, Mazzini was much more than the hero widely acclaimed by Victorian Englishmen; he was

The ideal of selfless heroism – of infinite pity, helpfulness, love, zeal, and ardour as divine in the heat of wrath as in the glow of

charity – set before us in the life and character of Jesus . . .
[showing] . . . how divine a thing human nature may be when
absolutely and finally divorced from all thought or sense of self:
made perfect in heroism and devotion, even to the point, not
merely unattainable but unimaginable for most men, of dis-
regarding even the imputation of selfishness and cowardice;
'gentle, and just, and dreadless' as Shelley's ideal demigod, with
the single-hearted tenderness and lovingkindness of a little
child.[15]

This astonishing adulation of Mazzini appears to have its origins in
Oxford, in Swinburne's conversations with his fellow under-
graduates, and through his contact with Aurelio Saffi, Mazzini's
trusted friend, who was lecturing there. Though he did not meet
Mazzini himself until 1867, Swinburne's growing enthusiasm for all
things Italian – he wrote later that 'I have always loved Italy above
every other land'[16] – was consolidated by two short visits, his only
visits, to northern Italy from Genoa to Venice in 1861, and to
Tuscany in 1864, journeys which left an enduring impression of the
beauty of Italian art, landscape, and women.

Georges Lafourcade has described how, after the scandal caused
by the publication of *Poems and Ballads* in 1866, Swinburne so
entirely devoted his attention to Italian affairs that

the great fact which from 1866 to 1871 gives unity to the life of
Swinburne lies in his relations with Mazzini, and consequent
composition of more or less 'political' poems, which were later to
form a whole and become *Songs Before Sunrise*.[17]

Collected in 1871, the majority of these poems celebrate the heroes
and events of the Risorgimento, and look forward hopefully to the
establishment of a Mazzinian republic in Italy. On this local level
the volume is unimpressive. The rhythms of the verse are frequently
distressingly banal, and Swinburne tends to offer slogans rather
than insight. But as the subject opens out the poetry becomes more
significant. Around the Italian republican movement crystallise all
the larger issues of man's enduring struggle for liberty. Events in
Italy provide an uncommonly valuable focal point, not only
because of their contemporary immediacy, but because they are, in
the 1860s, a concrete political manifestation of the underlying
intellectual problem of the day – the need to revolt constructively

against the oppressive, reactionary weight of established power and ideology. Support for the Italians provides the framework upon which Swinburne can build his appeal to men to liberate themselves from their past and assert the integrity and supremacy of individual man; to join with his *Hymn of Man* in rejecting the stranglehold of repressive dogma and proclaiming,

> Thou art smitten, thou God, thou art smitten; thy death is upon thee, O Lord,
> And the love-song of earth as thou diest resounds through the wind of her wings –
> Glory to Man in the highest! for Man is the master of things.

In *Hertha*, which much later Swinburne selected as his best poem,[18] the life-spirit behind all creation lyrically appeals to men to live and be free, and no longer to be the captives of false moral and religious systems. In total contrast with the self-satisfied notions of liberty we have noted a century earlier, contemporary events in Italy merge in this volume into all-embracing statements on the human condition.

But, of course, there is really nothing new in all this. It is simply a narrower, more strident, and up-dated statement of things that Byron and Shelley had already, and more richly, said. Swinburne's thinness in comparison with the earlier writers is evident in a comparison of his *Marino Faliero* (1885) with Byron's. Swinburne's play is static – almost half of it consists of Faliero's exceedingly long monologues – and the scenes are very ineffectually chosen, with nothing of Byron's flair for the dramatic. There is none of the felt presence of Venice which occurs in Byron's play, and the characterisation is pale and the verse effete. The play is simply a tract to make the point about liberty quoted above; Swinburne's temerity in publishing so bloodless a play with the example of Byron's treatment of the same material before him is astounding. One interesting work does, however, open up a new dimension in writing about Italy, although it seems unfortunately to have had no influence on the development of subsequent works of a similar kind, since it remained unpublished and apparently unknown until 1942.

Lucrezia Borgia. The Chronicle of Tebaldeo Tebaldei. 'Renaissance Period' seems to have been written in the early 1860s. Swinburne's interest in his heroine had doubtless been stimulated, at least in part, by his enthusiasm for Victor Hugo, whose purely sensational play, *Lucrèce Borgia*, had been published in 1833. The novelty of Swinburne's unfinished work is its form, which remarkably anticipates the theory and practice of Corvo's historical writing. (Corvo seems not to have been aware of *Lucrezia Borgia* when he discussed the theory of the historical novel at the beginning of *Don Renato*.) Swinburne poses as the translator of an early sixteenth century manuscript written by one Tebaldeo Tebaldei, servant and lover of Lucrezia Borgia. It is effectively a development, parallel to Browning's *Dramatic Monologues*, of the kind of writing represented by Landor's *Imaginary Conversations*: Landor, one recalls, was always admired by Swinburne as a model of pagan-classical sanity, and it was to Landor that he offered, in Florence in 1864, the dedication of *Atalanta in Calydon*. But Swinburne evokes an aspect of Renaissance Italy rather different from that which Landor had treated in *The Pentameron*: indeed, he anticipates the whole tendency of the most significant part of English writing about Italy around the end of the nineteenth century. For he creates an essentially decadent Renaissance, a period whose colour, paganism, vitality, beauty and amorality he joyously celebrates in contrast to the very different public virtues of his own day. The book centres around a long and fine lascivious description of how Lucrezia receives her servant as her lover; it is the enjoyment of her love, and the memory of it when she is dead, which gives meaning and a certain distinction to Tebaldeo's life and on which he bases his (Swinburne's?) hedonist ethic:

> Beauty is the beginning of all things, and the end of them is pleasure . . . A beautiful soft line drawn is more than a life saved; and a pleasant perfume smelt is better than a soul redeemed. For all spiritual and lofty good comes to us only by perception and conception; which things by their very names are naturally of the flesh and the senses. Therefore though we do much good and though we become very virtuous, notwithstanding, to take pleasure and to give it again is better than all our good deeds. For the excellence of wellbeing includes and involves the excellence of welldoing; and if one enjoy greatly he is good after the fashion of the gods, but if he act greatly he is good only after the fashion of men. So that if one think to make himself godlike by mere action and abstinence, he is a fool. To refrain from evil and to labour in doing good are as it were the two feet and hands of a man wherewith he walks and climbs; but to enjoy the supreme and

sovereign pleasure is to have the wings and eyes of the angels of God.[19]

The poems assert that man and not God is the master, and the prose work suggests to man the way in which he may become godlike, by living according to what Swinburne represents as the ethos of the Renaissance. Had the work been published soon after its composition, the subsequent history of our subject might have been rather different. As it is, much of the rest of our study will be concerned with tracing the process by which later writers moved towards a view of Renaissance Italy which, unknown to them, had been anticipated in all its essentials in Swinburne's hedonistic manuscript.

10 The Victorians and the Renaissance

Throughout the first half of the nineteenth century studies of Italian Renaissance art and history had flowed increasingly from the press. Not only in England, but all over Europe, a massive effort had been devoted to the elucidation and evaluation of the achievement of Italy between the thirteenth and sixteenth centuries: the footnotes to Symonds' *Renaissance in Italy* provide an extensive bibliography. It was on the Continent that the really significant work had been done. In Paris Michelet had excitingly discovered the very concept of the Renaissance as a coherent historical phenomenon of the first importance,[1] and in Basel Burckhardt had laid the foundation for all subsequent work on that period of Italian history with his *Die Kultur der Renaissance in Italien* (1860; translated into English in 1878). But in England works on the Renaissance period had characteristically been either of specialist or of purely journalistic interest, with neither pretension nor title to literary esteem; rare indeed among their pages are those qualities which give a piece of writing a distinctive lasting value independent of changes of attitude towards its subject. One of the features of the last four decades of the century, however, was the appearance of a succession of studies of Italian cultural history of considerable literary quality and importance.

JOHN ADDINGTON SYMONDS (1840–93)

John Addington Symonds devoted his adult life, from his Oxford Prize Essay on *The Renaissance* in 1863 until his death in Rome thirty years later, to literary work built around a central concern with the Renaissance in Italy. His seven volume work on the subject, *The Renaissance in Italy* (1876–86), though lacking the intellectual calibre and seminal importance of Burckhardt's study, which was one of his sources, was a significant literary achievement, clearly marking a stage in the development of English attitudes to Italy.

The obvious comparison, sketched out by a contemporary reviewer in *The Times*,[2] is with Gibbon. He, as we have seen, was one of the last major figures in that humanist tradition whose awakening had been one of the features of Renaissance Italy. His book ends with Poggio's meditations on the ruins of Rome, meditations which helped arouse that desire to emulate in modern Europe the greatest achievements of ancient civilisation, which lasted as a major cultural force until the eruptions of the late eighteenth century left the world in fragments. From his works, and particularly his letters, it is clear that Symonds was familiar with all those treatments of Italian material we have considered above, and was aware of his own relation to them. Between his own day and that of Gibbon was a chasm; the humanist tradition was broken and the Romantic trauma and the increasing collapse of every kind of faith seemed to have plunged Europe into a new dark age requiring a new Renaissance to re-establish sound values and a purposeful sense of direction. An obvious approach was to analyse the experience of the earlier Renaissance. The Romantic treatment of the subject was vitiated by its sensationalism: the sufferings of Tasso and the violence of the Cenci had to be treated historically, not dramatically. Ruskin, though an invaluable stimulus, was limited by his rejection of the spirit of paganism: from the very beginning of his study of the subject the young Symonds observed that 'it is not necessary, with Mr Ruskin, to stigmatise the Renaissance as a monstrous growth of pride and infidelity',[3] and tended rather towards the ethos represented by Browning in his portrait of Andrea del Sarto.

For to Symonds it was precisely the stress on individualism and the pagan enjoyment of life which was attractive and vital in the Renaissance and which was the major theme running through all his work. Lacking Ruskin's earnestness, Symonds believed that the object of life is 'to live as much as possible; & if it may be at the close of life to feel that every year has passed almost unheeded from its fullness of occupation!'[4] There was nowhere better to look for guidance in pursuing this object than that age when 'How to make the best of human life, is substituted for the question how to ensure salvation in the world beyond the grave', the age whose motto had been 'Man made master of the world and of himself by spiritual freedom.'[5]

Such was the spirit in which Symonds took up the study of the Renaissance, attempting to connect the post-Romantic world with the sources of vitality which had sustained the greatest ages of the past. The main single result of this tudy, the seven volumes of *The Renaissance in Italy*, is open to attack on several fronts. It over-emphasises personalities, giving little attention to economic history. The personalities themselves are arbitrarily selected on the basis of Symonds' feelings of affinity, so that Giordano Bruno receives far more attention than Galileo, and Michelangelo than Leonardo, and they come mostly from the sixteenth century, at the expense of earlier periods of the Renaissance. There is a strong literary bias, the sections on music, painting, sculpture and architecture being markedly weaker than those on books and manuscripts. Even the best volumes, on literature, though based on first-hand knowledge of the subject, are unoriginal and rely heavily on previous historians;[6] and the style is often tedious and repetitive.

On the other hand, the style is equally often irreproachable; and Symonds' is still the only comprehensive study of the period originally written in English, and demands respect for having brought a broad picture of that age before a wide audience. It can still stimulate serious thought on the Renaissance,[7] and provides incomparably attractive introductions to those aspects of the subject which do enjoy Symonds' sympathy. Though the third volume, on the fine arts, is inadequate, the first is still fascinating and illuminating in its wealth of documentation on *The Age of Despots*, the second, despite its awkward and dated theory of intellectual evolution, is contagious with the excitement of *The Revival of Learning*, and the fourth and fifth remain unchallenged in English as a general non-technical account of Italian Renaissance literature.[8]

Throughout the volumes runs Symonds' concern with seizing the vital creative spirit which could reconnect his own time with the great ages of the past. The identifiable manifestations of civilisation, which had been the source of the tradition culminating in Gibbon, were less important than the intangible play of free and joyous vitality which could be detected behind them. A crucial and brilliant passage is Symonds' discussion of Tasso's frequent use of the phrase 'un non so che.'[9] Its vagueness, says Symonds, is something new in poetry, quite unlike the concrete, sculptural images of classical literature, the precise, mathematical art of Dante, or the painterly clarity of Petrarch, Boccaccio and Ariosto; a feeling for the ineffable and incomprehensible was the new dominant characteristic of art, and it was no accident, he argues, that the age of Tasso should have seen the creation of modern music, whose strength is precisely in its ability to render those feelings which cannot be put into words or stone or paint. The passage is the equivalent in Symonds to Pater's more famous 'All art constantly aspires towards the condition of music' in the *School of Giorgione* essay; both men sought less to analyse the great art of the past than to establish a tremulous relationship with the creative impulse which had made that art great, a relationship which had something of the intangibility of music.

In Symonds this effort produced both more prolific writing and a broader response to the experience of Italy than Pater did. But his works on the Italian Renaissance are unfortunately repetitive and show strikingly little intellectual development. The volumes which precede *The Renaissance in Italy* are an introduction to it, while those that follow are effectively appendices. (The relevant books, between 1863 and 1895, are listed in the bibliography.) Symonds' other works, on the English poets, Whitman, and Greek literature, and his poems, are all linked to this central interest in the spirit of the Renaissance; one sees clearly the connection in his writing about contemporary Italy.

From his first enthralment with Venice during the long vacation of 1862 until his death in Rome in 1893, Symonds visited Italy, first from England and after 1877 from his home in Davos, as often as his precarious health permitted. He was intimately familiar with the country, as well as with its history and literature. One of the features of *The Renaissance in Italy* is its frequent references to the small towns of Italy, especially Tuscany; and one of the most attractive offshoots of work on the book was his three collections of *Sketches in Italy and Greece* (1874), *Sketches and Studies in Italy* (1879) and *Italian Byways* (1883). These travel sketches, most of which appeared originally as magazine articles, are a major contribution to the genre. Ranging throughout Italy, both geographically and historically, Symonds' subjects vary from contemporary Venice through Medicean Florence to the Capri of Tiberius and Antinous. Everywhere he seeks to evoke the spirit of the place, to reveal those magical dimensions in which all the most vivid feelings which men have felt there in the past seem to flood back into a place and to pulse inspiritingly through the imagination of the attuned observer. With Symonds, who makes explicit in prose what had permeated Browning's Italian poems, the Italian past becomes life-enhancing;

it is no longer a question of meditating over decay, or of comparing the state of modern England with that of ancient Rome or medieval Italy; rather, the traveller must seek to charge his spiritual batteries by making contact with the plenitude of the finest qualities of life which wells up from the great creative spots of Italy. At Taormina, for example,

> Every spot on which the eye can rest is rife with reminiscences. It was there, we say, looking northward to the Straits, that Ulysses tossed between Scylla and Charybdis; there, turning towards the flank of Etna, that he met with Polyphemus and defied the giant from his galley. From yonder snow-capped eyrie, Α᾿ίτγας σκοπία, the rocks were hurled on Acis. And all along that shore, after Persephone was lost, went Demeter, torch in hand, wailing for the daughter she could no more find among Sicilian villages.[10]

All over Italy the sensitive traveller could find places which would stock his mind with images of this kind of resonance of association. Symonds is explicit about the value, the necessity, of such experience. Writing of the debt of English to Italian literature, he comments,

> As poets in the truest sense of the word, we English live and breathe through sympathy with the Italians. The magnetic touch which is required to inflame the imagination of the North, is derived from Italy. The nightingales of English song who make our oak and beech copses resonant in spring with purest melody, are migratory birds, who have charged their souls in the South with the spirit of beauty, and who return to warble native woodnotes in a tongue which is their own.[11]

He is talking, of course, of purely literary debt, as well as of the fruits of actual experience of the south. What is significant is the extremely high importance that Symonds assigns to the debt to Italy, a debt which is not to its civilisation, nor to the moral qualities of its early Christian art, but simply to the amorally inspiring effect of its atmosphere. In making this kind of stress, Symonds is creating the new, decadent attitude to Italy. His lines on Capri are characteristic:

> Capri, the perfect island – boys and girls
>   Free as spring-flowers, straight, fair, and musical

Of movement; in whose eyes and clustering curls
  The youth of Greece still lingers; whose feet fall
  Like kisses on green turf by cypress tall
And pine-tree shadowed; who, unknowing care,
Draw love and laughter from the innocent air.[12]

It is, of course, well known that what really attracted Symonds to
the feeling of the 'youth of Greece' in Italy was the beauty of Italian
boys and young men, and he introduces to writing about Italy that
atmosphere of homosexuality which then pervades the literary
treatment of Italians, at least until Lawrence (and in more recent
novels, like Donald Windham's *Two People* (1966) and Francis
King's *A Domestic Animal* (1969)). In passages like the following, one
is struck by the new note, and perhaps particularly by the contrast
with the vigour with which Byron had celebrated the eyes of Italian
peasant girls; Symonds, however, becomes ecstatic about the men:

  O the beautiful eyes of the contadini!
  O the ring of their voices on the hill-sides!
  O their gravity, grace of antique movement –
  Driving furrows athwart the autumnal cornland,
  Poised like statues above the laden axles
  Drawn by tardy majestic oxen homewards!
  What large melody fills you, ye divine youths,
Meet companions of old Homeric heroes?[13]

Some positive advances resulted from the introduction of the
homosexual theme. In a particular case, his own propensities
allowed Symonds to be fairly explicit, in his biography, about
Michelangelo's homosexuality, a subject about which earlier
biographers[14] had been either ignorant or silent. It was also a
considerable force in drawing sympathetic attention to the common
life of Italy: lines like those above are obviously utterly unlike the
eighteenth century's blanket contempt for all living Italians, while
an essay in *Italian Byways* on *The Gondolier's Wedding* celebrates the
happiness and amusement of an event in the domestic life of the
ordinary people of Venice in a way which clearly owes something to
George Sand.[15]

  But against these positive aspects of the work, one must weigh a
sense of a certain thinness in the achievement. In Symonds' Venice
one feels painfully the lack of a Byronic toughness and openness to

experience. Paradoxically, Byron, who stressed the melancholy and decay of the city, conveys far more vitality in his pictures of Venice than does Symonds, who ostensibly sets out to ignore the decay and extract the lasting genius of the city; there is always the danger that in seeking the aethereal one will become vapid; or that, Clough-like, one will find oneself tormented by the strength of the unbeautiful in the world, as is the case of the hero of Symonds' Venetian sonnet sequence, *Vagabunduli Libellus* (1884), which echoes, though adds nothing to, Clough's treatment of Venice. (Symonds wrote articles on Clough in 1866 and in 1868 helped his widow with her edition of the poems.) And in his account of the Renaissance, though his sympathies are much wider than Ruskin's, the effect of his work is much narrower, since he lacks the intensity and intellectual rigour with which Ruskin raises fundamental questions and stimulates the reader to thought far beyond the immediate significance of the particular work of art or architecture that happens to be under discussion.

However, the place of Symonds' work in the history of English attitudes to Italy is considerable. We have already considered Browning as originating the typical modern attitudes to Italy; Symonds we may regard as filling out and popularising these attitudes, providing his readers with the example and the information which would give them a feeling of the frisson of the past whenever they went to Italy. Gibbon's volumes on Rome had marked the end of an epoch; when Symonds' seven volumes on the Renaissance took their place on the bookshelves of the upper middle classes they marked the opening of a new age of touristic values. Put beside any of the major works on Italy we have so far considered, Symonds' books, despite their bulk, seem rather lightweight and superficial; but doubtless these very qualities contributed to his popularity and importance.

WALTER PATER (1839–94)

Almost exact contemporaries, Pater and Symonds each reluctantly admired the other's work while disdaining his attitude to life.[16] Essentially, Pater, working on a much narrower range of material than Symonds, develops to its extreme the kind of attitude that we have found in Symonds' work; so great, however, was the difference of degree that Symonds' response to the publication of *The*

Renaissance in 1873 could be taken as representative of the outraged reception the volume met with, especially in Oxford:

> His view of life gives me the creeps, as old women say. I am sure it is a ghastly sham; & that live by it or not as he may do, his utterance of the theory to the world has in it a wormy hollow-voiced seductiveness of a fiend.[17]

Evidently, there was a wide gap between these two men, both of whom are associated primarily with Renaissance studies, to which they had been stimulated largely by their reading of Ruskin (Pater read *Modern Painters* at school), whose beliefs they then went on to undermine quite thoroughly.

Very little is known of Pater's experience of Italy. If he wrote any letters from Italy, none appear to survive, and we do not even know how many times he went there. It is clear that his first visit in 1865 was important in acquainting him with many of the works which form the subjects of his essays, and we know that he first visited Rome in December, 1882 and stayed for several weeks, apparently working on *Marius The Epicurean*; but beyond the indirect evidence provided by these works we know nothing of his impressions of the country.

On one level this is unimportant; on another it is symptomatic: unimportant because, unlike Symonds, Pater is interested not in conveying the pleasures of Italy to a fairly wide audience but with selecting artistic examples with which to initiate a sensitive élite into a system of ethics; symptomatic, because its narrow inability to respond vigorously to life is one of the most obvious criticisms of the system. As Lord David Cecil put it,

> It is absurd to rhapsodize about Leonardo da Vinci to the extent that Pater does, when in life one would have avoided him as just another dreadful foreigner.[18]

Rather like the Grand Tourists of an earlier age, Pater seeks moral and intellectual stimulus in Italy, while disdaining any contact with the everyday life of the country. Unlike Symonds, who tried to place the life-giving spirit of the Renaissance within the context of Italian life and history, Pater is interested, in his critical essays on Italian art, only in the quintessence of that spirit. But if his attitude in some ways recalls that of the eighteenth century, it is in other, more significant, ways totally different. The Grand Tourists found their positive values in the massive remains of the grandeur of Rome; Pater in the relatively fragile canvasses of the Renaissance. The eighteenth century found social values, readily accessible to all educated observers, and the self-confidence of Empire; Pater found the most attenuated aesthetic pleasures, revealed only to the gifted few, for whom they were the refuge from the ugliness and anguish of a world which had discovered that there were no absolutes for society to rely on. No contemporary observer had earlier or more accurately analysed the change from a world of absolute values to one of relativity than Pater in his 1866 essay on Coleridge, and his essays on the Italian Renaissance are one of the major symptoms of the change.

If there are no absolutes, no stability of past or future, the sound thing to do, says Pater, is to live intensely in and for the present, extracting from the passing moment every last drop of spiritual nourishment it has to offer. 'To burn always with this hard, gemlike flame, to maintain this ecstacy, is success in life'; and art offers the principal means of attaining this success, for, 'Art comes to you proposing frankly to give nothing but the highest quality to your moments as they pass, and simply for those moments' sake.'[19] All his studies of Italian Renaissance art are directed to showing how, for example, Giorgione knows better than any other painter the art of embodying in his work the

> brief and wholly concrete moment into which . . . all the motives, all the interests and effects of a long history, have condensed themselves, and which seem to absorb past and future in an intense consciousness of the present.[19]

But the intensity, surely, is stifling. Since classical times readers had repeatedly been exhorted to live for the present moment, but in a liberating, invigorating way; Pater's narrow insistence suggests rather the drowning man clutching at straws than the emancipated man magnificently facing the possibilities of living. In treating the Italian art-works in this way, Pater may gain some narrow insights, but only at the expense of violating their fuller life and nature, of replacing their serene and joyous demonstration of man's profound creative instinct and ability by a stridently earnest assertion of only one constricted part of that broad vitality. One feels that Pater is treating in too purely cerebral a manner works that demand a much more visceral response.

But Pater, of course, developed beyond the aesthetic poise of these essays, and in doing so presents another interesting use of Italian material. He spent five years working on *Marius The Epicurean* (1885), including the winter of 1882–3 in Rome absorbing the feeling of the city and the Campagna. Set in the final years of Roman greatness, the novel inevitably recalls *The Last Days of Pompeii*. Bulwer's sensationalism is replaced by a wonderfully calm atmosphere of reflection; philosophical wrestling replaces physical violence, and the crude, unquestioned triumph of Christianity in the earlier novel here becomes a subtle, problematic matter. Romanticism has been replaced by a more modern struggle to come to terms with man's position in an alien universe; or, as Pater puts it, with 'man's radically hopeless condition in the world.'[20] The development of the novel is existential. Marius is brought up according to the doctrine of the notorious *Conclusion* to *The Renaissance*:

> He was acquiring what it is the chief function of all higher education to impart, the art, namely, of so relieving the ideal or poetic traits, the elements of distinction, in our everyday life–of so exclusively living in them–that the unadorned remainder of it, the mere drift or *débris* of our days, comes to be as though it were not.[21]

Such selective aestheticism, however, comes to seem inadequate to Marius's experience of life, and he searches all the philosophies available to him for a more satisfactory ethic. Christianity comes nearest to providing a convincing system, but, characteristically of Pater and his time, the novel does not fully endorse its validity. It is almost accidentally that Marius becomes a Christian martyr; the success of his search has been not to find philosophical revelation in the teaching of Christianity but to commit himself to responsible action. His act of identification with the persecuted Christians is existential rather than religious. Unfortunately, it is an act which entails his death: Pater has magnificently conducted his analysis of the rôle of the intellectual in a relativistic world through aesthe- ticism to a noble artistic statement of the necessity and difficulties of moral commitment; but, himself uncertain of his own allegiances, he is unable to go on to explore the problems of the continuous living process of such commitment, and his hero has to die.

VERNON LEE (1856–1935)

Together with Symonds and Pater we must mention their younger friend Vernon Lee, who spent most of her life in Italy, the country she loved above all others, and whose influence permeates almost half a century of her prolific writing.

Although she had been largely brought up in Italy, with the streets of Rome for her university,[22] Vernon Lee was as deeply aware as Symonds and Pater were, when they discovered Italy through their reading in England, of the immense influence of Ruskin, whose writings had revealed

> Not merely the aesthetic loveliness, but also the imaginative fascination, of Venice and Verona. Think how even Goethe saw these towns, and how *we* see them. Well, the difference is due, two-thirds, to Ruskin. Similarly with the Alps . . .
>
> He has shown us art, history, nature, enlarged, transformed and glorified through the loving energy of his spirit. He has shown us a scheme of life in which great justice for all would result merely from greater happiness of endowment of every one. He has given us an example of contemplative union with all living things, and in this contemplative ecstacy made all noble things alive. The most larklike soul of our times, he sings at heaven's gates, and his song makes heaven's gates be everywhere above us.[23]

Nevertheless, she shared with Symonds and Pater their feeling of the inadequacy of Ruskin's simple equation of artistic quality with the values of a rather narrow morality; but she was not so enthusiastic as them about the vitality of the Renaissance, being troubled by the amorality of an age which apparently felt no contradiction between the enjoyment of civilised pleasure and the vicious pursuit of power.[24] She preferred Ruskin's fundamental faith in humanity to the ethos of aestheticism, beneath whose glowing surface she detected a morbid festering, which she exposed in her novel *Miss Brown* (1884), where she writes of 'the pessimism which is at the bottom of all aestheticism, the belief in the fatal supremacy of evil and ugliness.' (Vol. 2, pp. 223–4)

Vernon Lee found the antithesis of both pessimism and amorality in the eighteenth century, and she first attracted attention with her *Studies of The Eighteenth Century in Italy* (1880), a collection of essays which bring the artistic atmosphere of eighteenth century Italy more fully alive than probably any other book, earlier or later. Even Dr Burney, who of all English travellers of his century had been the most responsive to the creative activity of contemporary Italy, seems more memorable in her pages than in his own. Her essays combine enthusiasm and sympathy with authority and great descriptive verve to demonstrate that the Italian eighteenth century, far from being a sterile gap between Renaissance and Romanticism, had been a period of considerable significance and immense fascination. The history of the Arcadian Academy is narrated with a delightful and appreciative mixture of admiration and amusement; she gives an attractive brief biography of Metastasio and surveys the musical life of the century; and she considers the pleasures of the Venetian comedy of Gozzi and Goldoni. She not only conveys something of the enthusiasm with which she responds more vividly to the creative Italians of the eighteenth century than to those of the Renaissance, but also makes a strong case for her novel contention that those men who, with a few exceptions like Piranesi and Canaletto, had been ignored by the English had been the most culturally alive artistic community of the century.

This novel case had not only the quality of arguing for the revaluation of a particular period; it is a splendidly argued protest against the tendency of fashionable taste to ignore those arts or works which it cannot readily assimilate. If she could persuade her reader to enjoy and esteem eighteenth century Venetian comedy and opera, she had helped to prevent him from being stultifyingly confined to the repertoire of works approved by the cultural pundits of his day. In *Studies of The Eighteenth Century* such an aim is merely implicit; but in a later essay on *Botticelli at The Villa Lemmi* in *Juvenilia* (1887) she protests against 'the modern gallery-and-concert tendency' (Vol. 1, p. 117) in a way which strikingly anticipates part of the argument of Malraux's *Musée sans murs*. The essay is a sensitive analysis of her feeling of regret that a Botticelli fresco should be removed from a fairly inaccessible and decaying farm near Florence to the Louvre. In Paris the painting will be seen by far more people than would ever see it in its original site; it will in some ways be more available to the writer herself, even though she lives near Florence; and it will certainly be much better preserved in the museum. Yet she cannot persuade herself that her regret is selfish, when she describes looking at the fresco on the wall on which Botticelli had put it, in the architectural and lighting conditions for which he planned it, and turning from it to the landscape from which he drew material, and to a sunset such as he may have relaxed in at the end of a day's work. From being the focus of that kind of rich experience, when the painting is in the Louvre, though many will see it, few will ever really look at it, and those who do will see merely a document in the history of painting, rather than a vibrant work of art. Though theoretically she believes that the benefit of contact with beauty (which she later said leads to 'higher complexities of vitalisation, to a more complete and harmonious rhythm of individual existence'[25]) should be available to as many people as possible, she cannot but feel that the painting will be terribly debased in a gallery, while left where it is it would remain a moving place of pilgrimage for those who appreciate art enough to want to go there. Her description of a visit to a little Tuscan farmyard has become a stimulating protest against the application of the Benthamite calculus to art.

The rest of her Italian writing developed in two main directions, both related to this Botticelli essay. One was a series of short travel sketches evoking the spirit of place, following the pattern established by Symonds; the other, a growing concern with aesthetics, both on a theoretical and on a social level. The significance of these works can be stated simply: the travel pieces form a link between the tradition we have considered of literary involvement with the Italian landscape and the proliferation of travel books of little or no literary merit in this century; while the aesthetical works are the point of contact between the brief period when art criticism in English was a literary matter and the age of the specialist critic: she had known Pater and she knew Berenson.

But English literature's creative involvement in the exploration of Italy was not yet over; we must consider how the novelists were responding to Italy, and for that we must go back to take up the novel where we left it, in mid-century.

11 Italy and the English Novel in the Mid-Century

Though many novels continued to appear with Italian characters or Italian settings very few of them around the middle of the century were sufficiently interesting to demand our attention individually; but in order to provide a background for those few, and generally to carry our subject forward, we must briefly characterise the main developments in the fictional convention of Italy which were taking place at this period.

Although the Oxford Movement itself does not directly concern us, the atmosphere of religious polemic which it engendered was reflected in the treatment of Italy in the English novel. The sensational resources of the Gothic novel were readily adaptable to the specific purposes of Protestant propaganda, as Mrs Sherwood demonstrated in *The Nun* (1833), the ostensible autobiography of a Piedmontese woman who as an orphan had been sent to a convent, whose horrors and miseries she describes at considerable length, from which she is eventually released as a minor result of the French Revolution. She then marries an Englishman and becomes an Anglican, writing the narrative of her sufferings,

> that those things respecting the Roman Catholic Church, which I have faithfully recorded, may tend to fill the inhabitants of this Protestant land with a sense of gratitude to that God, who has liberated their country from the slave of that great apostacy whose name is Mystery. (p. 326)

This novel provided the model for a series of equally crude novelistic tracts, such as Mrs Sherwood's own *The Monk of Cimiés* (1837), Julia Waddington's *The Monk and The Married Woman* (1840), and William Sewell's *Hawkstone: A Tale of and For England in 184-* (1845), where, in one scene which epitomises the process of harnessing Gothic device to Protestant polemic, a disillusioned Jesuit in Rome scarcely begins to warn the hero against the wicked machinations of his Order before he is leapt upon and stabbed through the heart.

As improving communications made the Continent more accessible, however, and as the number of converts to Roman Catholicism grew in England, such an outrageous picture of the Church began to lose its credibility, as the English became more realistic in their attitudes towards it.

> Monks are no longer to us the mere illustrations of old stories of romance, but we know them of families among whom we have grown up, – we count among them our friends; the cowl and tonsure are familiar to us in fact, as they used to be in pictures. And a Nun no more seems to us the creation of a poet's fancy, some fair idol of the past. They who have moved in our drawing-rooms, and made the mirth of our fire-sides, are Nuns; those whom we have sat side by side with in the churches of our land, whom we have met in the streets, with whom we have walked in the fields, are Nuns.

The passage is from Elizabeth Harris's *From Oxford to Rome* (1847, p. 272), a novel whose hero is an exemplary Anglican curate who becomes increasingly attracted to Catholicism, especially when he visits Rome, and eventually enters a monastery as a novice, but soon regrets his decision, realises that he should have remained to fulfil his rôle where Providence had placed him, and dies young and unhappy. Abandoning Gothic sensationalism, Mrs Harris tries to enlist for her polemic purposes the other novelistic convention of the association of Italy with frustration and death. As an argument for the rejection of Catholism it is quite unconvincing; but it is at least less insulting than the earlier novels.

The most interesting of those novels which use Italian settings for religious purposes is Froude's *Nemesis of Faith* (1848). Froude gives a moving and acute analysis of the religious crisis of his hero, Markham Sutherland, a young clergyman increasingly unable to accept the tenets and practices of the Anglican Church; but the subtlety and sensitivity of the first part of the novel are abandoned when Sutherland goes off to convalesce from his problems on the shores of Lake Como, where he becomes involved in an affair with an unhappily married Englishwoman, contrived to provoke the nemesis of faith of the novel's title. When her young daughter dies the woman sees it as a divine punishment for her having married without love, a view which only increases the anguish of Sutherland, who sees the death rather as a punishment for their guilty liaison. Although coaxed away from suicide by an English Catholic priest (a thinly disguised Newman), he soon wastes away and dies. The Italian section of the novel is disappointing; there is, indeed, no crude assertion, as in the earlier novels, of the evils of Catholicism, but the hero's death is an evasion of the important issues of the painful difficulties of religious belief or disbelief for an intelligent Englishman in the middle of the nineteenth century, abandoned at the point where their complexity has developed beyond the writer's skill to handle. It is characteristic of the Italian convention that in seeking an easy and dramatic solution to the difficulties of his material, Froude should have sent his hero off to Italy.

Though, of course, there continued to be other kinds of treatment of Italian material, especially historical romances, like J. R. Beste's *The Pope* (1840) and *Isidora: or, The Adventure of A Neapolitan* (1841), and Emma Robinson's *Caesar Borgia* (1846), it was works like these, developing older conventions within a specifically religious context, which constituted the growth-point in 'Italian' fiction in the years before the middle of the century. In the 'fifties and 'sixties such novels continued to appear. C. Sinclair's *Beatrice* (1852), Wiseman's *Fabiola; or, The Church of The Catacombs* (1855), G. Fullerton's *Rose Leblanc* (1862) and *Mrs Gerald's Niece* (1869), and W. Bramley-Moore's *The Six Sisters of The Valleys* (1864) argued both pro- and anti-Catholic cases between them. But now the main development of fictional interest in Italy went forward in other directions. The new element influencing the novelists was the series of political events following the establishment of the short-lived Roman Republic in 1848. Carbonarist activities had briefly attracted fictional attention in the late 'twenties,[1] but after the middle of the century the novelists' interest in Italian revolutionary and reactionary politics, running parallel to that we have already noticed in the poets, became almost obsessive, and was accompanied by a favourable revaluation of the Italian character, based partly on George Sand.

Charles Lever settled in Florence in 1847 and for the rest of his life made his home in Italy, becoming British Vice-Consul at La Spezia in 1859, and later Consul at Trieste, where he died in 1872. Most of his novels written in Italy have some reference to that country, but they are mostly quite trivial, and only three concern us here. Lever ardently supported the Italian movement, and was aware of a complexity of which he warned his readers: namely, that apparently admirable insurrectionary activities in the smaller states might, in fact, be provoked and manipulated by the reactionary powers in order to oblige the ruler of the state to appeal for military assistance, thus enabling them to effect a de facto occupation of his country. In his novel *The Daltons* (1852) the Abbé d' Esmonde is at the centre of a clerical conspiracy to re-establish the political authority of the Church by this method, which is described in action in the 1848 events in Lombardy, while in *The Fortunes of Glencore* (1857) the Austrians scheme to take over Massa and Carrara in this way: these novels developed his attack on the power of tyranny in Italy in three articles in the *Dublin University Magazine* for 1852. His novels, however, also contain one other minor development which we may mention here before going on to consider other treatments of political affairs.

Lever was a popular figure in the English colony at Florence, but the picture which his novels present of such expatriate societies is distinctly unattractive. In *Horace Templeton* (1848) his hero observes, à propos of Florence, that 'envy, hatred, malice, and all uncharitableness [are] prime features in an English colony on the Continent,' (ed. 1878, p. 317) and in *The Daltons*, particularly, Lever sets out to re-create this society for his reader. He produced perhaps his most entirely successful study of character in his portrait of the Ricketts family, with their astonishing and nauseating faculty for worming their way into whatever ball, excursion, discussion, or other social group they felt it desirable to be seen in. Their convincing presence in the novel seems to justify Lever's interesting assertion that, rather as the most successful employees of the prison service were those recruited from the criminal classes, the English society of foreign capitals recruited its most eminent members from among those who dared not show their face in England. The suggestion of criminality is pressed further in *The Daltons* by occasional references to the basis of the wealth of the English residents in morally dubious financial speculation to exploit for their own profit the manpower and natural resources of Italy. Lever, however, does not explore the matter very far; but we shall see presently how other novelists took the theme up where he left off.[2]

Giovanni Ruffini's *Dr Antonio* (1855) was central to the novelistic treatment of political events in Italy. Ruffini was an Italian exile who wrote novels in English, and this, his most successful work, 'in which he depicted so feelingly and so truthfully the wrongs of his country, did no small service to the Italian cause.'[3] The novel follows the conventional pattern in so far as the love it traces between an aristocratic English girl and an Italian doctor is inevitably doomed to failure, but it has important new elements as well. The doctor is handsome, skilful, a master of the English language, a perfect gentleman, with immense tact and thought for others, and the nobility of cherishing a lofty patriotic cause – quite a different picture, in fact, from that of the stock Italian villain of romance. He tends the English girl, Lucy, back to health after an accident near Bordighera, but though they fall, of course, in love, there is no prospect of her being allowed to marry him, and she returns to England and accepts a conventionally suitable husband, while Antonio devotes himself entirely to Italy. In 1848 Lucy, now a widow, returns to Italy in search of him, and finds him involved in revolutionary activity in the south. In Naples he is made a political prisoner, and for a time the novel develops into a powerful documentary exposure of the evils of the tyrannical régime in Naples, reminiscent of Gladstone's famous *Letters to The Earl of Aberdeen* (1851), which Ruffini mentions in the text. Returning again to the fiction, Antonio is sent as a prisoner to Ischia, where he refuses to desert his comrades and use an escape route Lucy has prepared for him, and she dies on the island, gazing at the castle where he is imprisoned.

After *Dr Antonio*, where Poerio and Settembrini had been mentioned in the Neapolitan section, it became commonplace for the personalities of contemporary Italian politics to appear as characters in English novels. Mazzini had appeared in Ruffini's *Lorenzo Benoni* in 1853, and Pius the Ninth, for example, appears in J. R. Beste's *Modern Society in Rome: A Novel* (1856), which re-creates the events of 1848–9, as do the anonymous *Angelo. A Romance of Modern Rome* (1854) and Margaret Roberts' *Mademoiselle Mori. A Tale of Modern Rome* (1860), while Mrs Hamilton's *The Exiles of Italy* (1857) asserts the accuracy of her depiction of events through frequent documentary footnotes, and describes with questionable taste scenes such as Garibaldi's burial of his wife and Ugo Bassi's mother's reception of the news of her son's death. Garibaldi re-appears in the anonymous *Angelo San Martino. A Tale of Lombardy in*

1859 (1860), and Orsini features in Anne Manning's *Selvaggio. A Tale of Italian Country Life* (1865).

So great was the attraction of contemporary Italian events and the new-found nobility of the Italian character that even Meredith attempted an epic novel on the country 'where I would live, if I had the choice',[4] although his literary gifts lay in quite another direction. Meredith first introduced the Italian theme into *Emilia in England* (1864; later renamed *Sandra Belloni*). The novel emphasises the ruthless cruelty of the Austrians and the long-suffering gallantry of the Italians, and very attractively represents the quality of British support for the Italians in the person of Merthyr Powys, while pouring scorn, particularly in the final chapter, on the conventional English middle-class contempt for the Italian character. The presentation of the heroine, Emilia Sandra Belloni, daughter of an exiled Italian violinist and his English wife, gives an alternative view of the Latin temperament. Emilia has three characteristics which are quite lacking in the upper-middle-class Englishwomen who patronise her and in whose company we see her: she has artistic sensibility, a noble devotion to a great cause (Italy), and a naif sincerity which contrasts utterly with the social hypocrisy of the Englishwomen. It is in the portrayal of this last, however, that the real strength of the novel lies. Meredith is at his best when he shows the subtle and bitter battles by which the children of the Pole family fight their way rung by rung up the ladder of social success; the ideals represented by Emilia's character and the Italian cause are artistically pale and unconvincing beside the destructive satire on the egoism of English society. When a few years later Meredith devotes the whole of the sequel, *Vittoria* (1867), to following the involvement of his characters with the north Italian uprisings of 1848–9 the result is a noble failure. Noble, because he wanted to put into powerful fictional form the admiration and enthusiasm for the Italian fighters which he had felt while following events as war correspondent of the *Morning Post* in 1866[5]; but a failure because his skill is for the delicate, yet penetrating and devastating, exposition of the motives of social behaviour, and not at all for the sustained epic tone, the large and colourful canvas and massive action which he attempts here. Meredith's involvement with Italy in these two novels is sympathetic, but artistically unfortunate.

But if Italy was only peripheral to Meredith's work as a novelist, it was the stock in trade of Thomas Adolphus Trollope, Anthony's elder brother, who spent more of his life in Italy than anywhere else, and made a fortune out of the facile exploitation of Italian 'local colour'. He himself claimed a serious function for his work, a function representative of the growing interest, in the mid-century, in the more out of the way parts of the Italian countryside and Italian history. Trollope frequently comments on the general English ignorance of Italy beyond the narrow limits of the tourist corridors through the country:

> No land was ever visited by nearly so great a number of foreign travellers as Italy; yet no European country, not even Spain, has remained so unknown and neglected in certain parts.

> Never, perhaps, was any country so travelled over for so long a series of years, as Italy has been by Englishmen, with so small a resulting knowledge of the people visited.[6]

In the middle of the nineteenth century, however, English interest in all aspects of Italy was growing rapidly; and nothing testifies to the fact more eloquently than the astonishing number of books on Italian subjects which Trollope could market as readily as he could produce them. Between 1850 and 1881 he wrote twenty books on Italy: historical works, travelogues, accounts of the progress of the Risorgimento and the politics of the Vatican, and novels.

The main influence on the novels was George Sand, whom Trollope met in Paris in the 1830s and whom he championed enthusiastically in the *Foreign Quarterly Review* in 1844, claiming to express 'convictions formed slowly through the course of five years' very intimate acquaintance with her works.'[7] From her he learnt the sympathetic portrayal of the Italian character and the colourful evocation of the Italian environment. But whereas George Sand presents these in a way that is fresh and stimulating and related to a concern with serious issues, in Trollope's novels one feels that it is more a question of meretricious padding. His novels are characteristically love stories whose utter emptiness and superficiality are to an extent masked by the profusion of picturesque Italian detail; and when he boasts of having composed the entire manuscript of his two volume novel *Beppo The Conscript* (1864), a tale of love among the peasantry of the Romagna, in only twenty-three days,[8] one might be forgiven the reflection that, indeed, the writing of his novels was more a physical than an intellectual or imaginative achievement.

To Trollope, as to other novelists of the period, Italy was

essentially an easy option: material which could be stretched out over only a few pages in a familiar English setting could, with a modicum of skill, be spun out almost indefinitely by the insertion of commonplace observations on Italian character and landscape, detailed accounts of picturesque Italian customs, and a liberal sprinkling of Italian words and supposedly Italian turns of phrase. Happily, we are spared the necessity of going into any detailed consideration of novels of this sort, since Henry James has authoritatively and incomparably described the state of 'Italian' fiction, perfectly represented by Thomas Adolphus Trollope, in the years leading up to 1875:

> There has come to be a not unfounded mistrust of the Italian element in light literature. Italy has been made to supply so much of the easy picturesqueness, the crude local colour of poetry and the drama, that a use of this expedient is vaguely regarded as a sort of unlawful short-cut to success, – one of those coarsely mechanical moves at chess which, if you will, are strictly within the rules of the game, but which offer an antagonist strong provocation to fold up the board. Italians have been, from Mrs Radcliffe down, among the stock-properties of romance; their associations are melodramatic, their very names are supposed to go a great way toward getting you into a credulous humor, and they are treated, as we may say, as bits of coloring-matter, which if placed in solution in the clear water of uninspired prose are warranted to suffuse it instantaneously with the most delectable hues. The growing refinement of the romancer's art has led this to be considered a rather gross device, calculated only to delude the simplest imaginations, and we may say that the presumption is now directly against an Italian in a novel, until he has pulled off his slouched hat and mantle and shown us features and limbs that an Anglo-Saxon would acknowledge.[9]

There were, however, exceptions; and notably Dickens and George Eliot, who showed themselves as far superior to their contemporaries in their treatments of Italy as in any other aspect of the art of fiction.

CHARLES DICKENS (1812-70)

Dickens' *Pictures From Italy* (1846), the fruit of almost a year's visit, largely spent at Genoa but travelling as far as Venice and Naples, is quite unlike any other English book on Italy. To an extent one can plot its position on the chart of developing attitudes to Italy, in so far as its responses to the common life of the Italian people build on the work of George Sand, and are in total contrast to the interests of the Grand Tourists. (The old attitudes to Italy are represented in *Little Dorrit* by Mrs General, who goes around 'scratching up the driest little bones of antiquity, and bolting them whole without any human visitings – like a Ghoule in gloves.' (p. 612)[10]) But *Pictures from Italy* is made unique by Dickens' ability to throw off a seemingly endless series of portraits whose precision and insight are only surpassed by their hilarity – or, sometimes, their pathos. The book is full of the street life of Italy, from the riotous gaiety of the Corso during the Roman Carnival to the house of the Capulets in Verona where 'there was a grim-visaged dog, viciously panting in a doorway, who would certainly have had Romeo by the leg, the moment he had put it over the wall, if he had existed and been at large in those times.' (p. 337) It is the people who give the book its life – the slow-driving postilion who, asked to go a little faster, 'brandished his whip about his head (such a whip! it was more like a home-made bow); flung up his heels, much higher than the horses, and disappeared, in a paroxysm, somewhere in the neighbourhood of the axle-tree' (p. 328); 'old Shylock passing to and fro upon a bridge' in Venice (p. 336); the vertiginous Pope being carried around St Peter's, 'his eyes shut and a great mitre on his head, and his head itself wagging to and fro as they shook him in carrying' (p. 370); the moving scene of an execution in Rome; the audience at a Marionetti theatre; or the cicerone at Mantua, so shabby and pathetic that 'I would as soon have trodden on him as dismissed him' (p. 341). The reflective, pathetic note of this last comment is important; for Dickens' Italy is not merely vividly amusing, it is humanely educative.

There is nothing patronising or superior in Dickens' humour; the Italians are not simply useful padding. The characters of his vignettes emerge so strongly because he respects them; and, light as the book appears to be, it is unequalled as a plea to the English to abandon their insularity and treat their European neighbours frankly and openly on terms of equality as fellow human beings.

Dickens rejects, for example, the frequently repeated complaint of tourists that Italian inns are notable only for their filth and wretchedness and that every Italian innkeeper is an arrant rogue, and asserts that, on the contrary,

> If you are good-humoured to the people about you, and speak pleasantly, and look cheerful, take my word for it you may be well entertained in the very worst Italian Inn, and always in the most obliging manner, and you may go from one end of the country to the other (despite all stories to the contrary) without any great trial of your patience anywhere. Especially, when you get such wine in flasks, as the Orvieto, and the Monte Pulciano. (pp. 361–2)

It is the tourists, and not the innkeepers, who are ill-mannered and despicable; and in their attitudes to the poor, also, Dickens objects to the customary touristic delight in poverty so long as it is picturesque, for 'it is not well to find St Giles's [in London] so repulsive, and the Porta Capuana [in Naples] so attractive.' (p. 413)

Unfortunately, *Pictures From Italy* has always been one of Dickens' lesser-known works, and it can scarcely be said to have had any visible effect in improving the behaviour of Britons on the Continent. It remains, however, a magnificent product of Dickens' contact with a country which he came to love to the extent of feeling 'an attachment for the very stones in the streets of Genoa' (p. 283), and to which he bids farewell by gracefully summing up the relation between his feeling of delight in Italy and his general belief that the world was gradually becoming a more humane place to live in:

> Let us part from Italy, with all its miseries and wrongs, affectionately, in our admiration of the beauties, natural and artificial, of which it is full to overflowing, and in our tenderness towards a people, naturally well-disposed, and patient, and sweet-tempered. Years of neglect, oppression, and misrule, have been at work, to change their nature and reduce their spirit; miserable jealousies, fomented by petty Princes to whom union was destruction, and division strength, have been a canker at the root of their nationality, and have barbarized their language; but the good that was in them ever, is in them yet, and a noble people may be, one day, raised up from these ashes. Let us entertain that hope! And let us not remember Italy the less regardfully, because,

in every fragment of her fallen Temples, and every stone of her deserted palaces and prisons, she helps to inculcate the lesson that the wheel of Time is rolling for an end, and that the world is, in all great essentials, better, gentler, more forbearing, and more hopeful, as it rolls. (p. 433)

Awareness of this enthusiasm for Italy allows one to appreciate the tact and restraint of Dickens' later treatment of Italy in *Little Dorrit* (1857). Superficially, the novel continues the well-established conventional use of Italy as the country where English characters go seeking health and happiness and find sorrow and death. Dorrit sets off to parade his new-found wealth and social eminence on a Grand Tour of Europe, but ends by dying in Rome under the pathetic illusion that he is still in the Marshalsea. The important new feature of the novel's treatment of Italy, however, is the way in which this is integrated into the pattern of imagery running through the whole work, to become not simply a convenient setting for the death of Dorrit but also a means of exploring the state of mind of his daughter. For Italy is constantly seen through the eyes of Little Dorrit. Dickens himself was enchanted by the beauty of Venice, which he describes as a wonderful dream in *Pictures From Italy*, and which he told Forster was the first thing he had encountered which seemed too stupendous to be handled in prose.[11] But Little Dorrit's Venice is very different. There is little evocation of the beauty of the city, because to Little Dorrit it is worse than a prison. The shimmering light and wonderful open spaces of Venice ironically emphasise her loneliness away from the familiar confines of the Marshalsea prison; and the much vaunted elegance and excitement of the life of Anglo-Venetian society appears to her superficial, perverted in its values, and no less stifling of the full development of human potentiality than the physical confinement of a prison. Dickens brilliantly combines the relation of the girl's feelings with the dominant prison image of the novel and a biting satire on the purposelessness of what George Eliot later (in Chapter 20 of *Middlemarch*) called 'the brilliant picnic of Anglo-foreign society':

It appeared on the whole, to Little Dorrit herself, that this same society in which they lived, greatly resembled a superior sort of Marshalsea. Numbers of people seemed to come abroad, pretty much as people had come into prison; through debt, through idleness, relationship, curiosity, and general unfitness for getting on at home. They were brought into these foreign towns in the custody of couriers and local followers, just as the debtors had been brought into the prison. They prowled about the churches and picture-galleries, much in the old, dreary, prison-yard manner. They were usually going away again tomorrow or next week, and rarely knew their own minds, and seldom did what they said they would do, or went when they said they would go: in all this again, very like the prison debtors. They paid high for poor accommodation, and disparaged a place while they pretended to like it: which was exactly the Marshalsea custom. They were envied when they went away, by people left behind feigning not to want to go: and that again was the Marshalsea habit invariably. A certain set of words and phrases, as much belonging to tourists as the College and the Snuggery belonged to the jail, was always in their mouths. They had precisely the same incapacity for settling down to anything, as the prisoners used to have; they rather deteriorated one another, as the prisoners used to do; and they were untidy dresses, and fell into a slouching way of life: still, always like the people in the Marshalsea. (p. 55)

Dickens may have had in mind Lever's suggestion in *The Daltons*, of a parallel between prison hierarchies and expatriate British colonies; if he did, he develops it in a way incomparably beyond anything Lever was capable of.

Throughout her stay there, sadness and disillusion pervade Little Dorrit's experience of Italy. At Rome, she would often go alone to explore the ruins:

> The ruins of the vast old Amphitheatre, of the old Temples, of the old commemorative Arches, of the old trodden highways, of the old tombs, besides being what they were, to her, were ruins of her own old life – ruins of the faces and forms that of old peopled it – ruins of its loves, hopes, cares, and joys. Two ruined spheres of action and suffering were before the solitary girl often sitting on some broken fragment; and in the lonely places, under the blue sky, she saw them both together. (p. 612)

Dickens puts into prose that analogy between a state of mind and the physical reality of the ruins which Byron had created in poetry; and this is his great contribution to the fictional treatment of Italy, which becomes no longer background but a country whose rich environment could be used in an artistically subtle and creative way to bring out the qualities and states of mind of a character exposed to contact with it. The novel opened up possibilities for the fictional use of Italy which no serious novelist could afterwards afford to ignore; and the first, in England, to take up and consolidate Dickens' achievement was George Eliot.

GEORGE ELIOT (1819–90)

As early as *Mr Gilfil's Love Story*, the second of the *Scenes of Clerical Life* (1858), George Eliot had used one of the literary stereotypes of the Italian character: requiring a heroine whose nature should be marked by 'intense love and fierce jealousy' (Vol. 1, p. 206) and whose love should be pathetically disastrous, she almost inevitably chooses an Italian, the orphan Caterina; and in her last novel, *Daniel Deronda* (1876), she again follows convention by taking an Italian setting, in Genoa, for the painful events of Deronda's meeting with his mother and the drowning of Grandcourt. But these are trivial cases in comparison with her treatment of Italy in *Romola* and *Middlemarch*.

We have noted that the typical use of Italy in the minor fiction of the mid-century was to pad out a story which in an English setting would rapidly collapse through lack of impetus or interest. *Romola* (1863) is a curiously different case: a story dealing seriously with nineteenth century English problems incongruously dressed up in unconvincing Italian Renaissance clothes. The basic concern of the novel is with the moral responsibility of the person who suddenly finds himself a free agent, having lost the guidance of any immediately obvious loyalties or duties based on religious belief. It is essentially a problem of that period of crisis of belief which crystallises around the publication of *The Origin of Species* in 1859, when there seemed to many to be 'no longer any God or any hereafter or anything in particular to aim at.'[12]

In the novel Tito Melema makes the wrong choice when faced with the responsibility of an important decision. Instead of employing the jewels of his supposed father, Baldassare, to try to rescue him from slavery in the East, he uses them as the first step towards making his fortune in Florence, a decision which launches him on a course of action where he frequently has to choose between duty and self-interest, and always prefers the latter. To Tito the decision had seemed reasonable and if necessary reversible, but he was unaware of the nature of responsibility, whereby

> Our deeds are like children that are born to us; they live and act apart from our own will. Nay, children may be strangled, but deeds never: they have an indestructible life both in and out of our consciousness; and that dreadful vitality of deeds was pressing hard on Tito for the first time. (*Romola* ed. 1863, vol. 1, p. 270)

The pressure forces Tito into a life of sordid dishonour. For emphasis, the process of a wrong decision rapidly assuming unmanageable proportions is repeated when, for fun, he makes a peasant girl believe she has been married to him by a carnival showman, then finds it increasingly difficult to undeceive her, until he has two illegitimate children by her and is planning to run away with her from his wife and his responsibilities in Florence. But his deeds catch up with him and he is killed by Baldassare.

Tito's wife, Romala, lives through an opposite process. Disillusioned with the falsity and evil of her husband, she flees Florence, but does not get very far before she is rebuked by Savonarola, who commands her to return to her duties as a Florentine citizen. When pestilence strikes the city she finds a temporary vocation in selfless devotion to tending the sick and needy, until, herself mentally sickened by the evil both of her husband and of the state of Florence, which has unjustly executed her godfather for treason, she again flees, buys a boat at the coast, and attempts to drift away into oblivion, hoping 'to be freed from the burden of choice when all motive was bruised', 'from that burden of choice which presses with heavier and heavier weight when claims have loosed their guiding hold.' (Vol. 3, pp. 161, 163) Providentially, she drifts ashore at a village suffering from the plague, devotes herself to helping the inhabitants, realises that such social commitment is the only thing that can give a sense of purpose to her life, and returns to Florence to care for Tito's mistress and his illegitimate children. The moral is evident: self-interest is fatal, while devotion to others leads to happiness and the justification of one's existence. The problem is that this issue seems to have been grafted on to the evocation of an historical period where it scarcely seems to belong.

Fifteenth century Italy had continued to be a perennial source of material for historical novelists, whose treatments of the period had become increasingly sophisticated as time had gone on: G. P. R. James's *Leonora d' Orco* (1857) and Charles Reade's *The Cloister and The Hearth* (1861) are the most notable examples in the years immediately before *Romola*. But no fictional recreation of Renaissance Italy had been so painstakingly documented, so precisely detailed, as was *Romola*. With G. H. Lewes, who gave her the idea for the novel when they were in Florence in 1860, George Eliot spent a month gathering material in Florence in 1861, and they completed their researches at the British Museum in 1862. They minutely studied at least sixty books on the period, over half of which are quoted more or less verbatim in the novel.[13] Unfortunately, the weight of learning is all too apparent. One is constantly aware of reading a reconstruction of Florentine life which is a work of careful scholarship rather than of any spontaneous creative vitality, and the novel's atmosphere falls awkwardly between two stools. As an historical reconstruction it might have been more compelling had it been more purely historical, without its fictional elements: as in Landor's *Imaginary Conversations*, there is the crippling problem that Machiavelli and Savonarola are far more vivid and interesting in their own pages than in George Eliot's. While, on the other hand, the attempt at historical veracity deprives the novel of those qualities of spontaneity and vitality which are not only essential to any fiction if it is to grip its reader's attention, but which are particularly felt to be missing in an evocation of a period which is valued precisely because of the presence of those very qualities in every aspect of its activity. The novel, therefore, tends to split apart. One can extract the moral scheme of the story, and leave intact the framework of Renaissance Florence within which it is set, and which, if anything, only detracts from the central moral concern of the novel – for the alternative might have been to explore the same issues in an English setting, to which George Eliot could bring exactly those qualities of creative familiarity and insight which were stifled by the laborious process of research into the 'local colour' of *Romola*.

In the context of the development of the fictional treatment of Italy two points stand out about *Romola*. Firstly, the phenomenon of so fine a novelist devoting so much effort to creating an Italian atmosphere which by its very nature cut her off from her own most important sources of creativity is extremely suggestive of the power of attraction which Italy held over the English creative mind in the nineteenth century. Secondly, her failure to make any very exciting use of Italian Renaissance material contrasts interestingly with that major and enthusiastic treatment of the period which was beginning at the very time when she was working on *Romola*, with Swinburne's *Tebaldeo Tebaldei* and Symond's first Oxford lecture on *The Renaissance*. The Italian Renaissance came increasingly to represent the individualism, amoral enjoyment of life, and colourfulness which appeared to be repressed by the dominant ethos of the Victorian period. The curious position of *Romola* is that it attempts, following Ruskin and the teaching of Savonarola, to use Renaissance material to advocate just that Puritanical, and anti-Renaissance, ethos of duty and self-sacrifice.[14] In the end, the failure of *Romola* is not only that its Renaissance setting fails to come very fully alive, but that the more vivid it became, the more it would undercut the novel's clear moral intent. The very fact of this failure doubtless suggested to subsequent novelists that the true potential of the Renaissance lay in a moral direction quite opposite to that of *Romola*.

Middlemarch (1871–2), however, gave not a warning but a positive example to later writers of how the Italian setting could be fruitfully used in the novel. Building on Dickens' exploitation in *Little Dorrit* of the contrast between the immediately obvious attractions of Italy and the very different responses to the country felt by his heroine, George Eliot creates what Mrs Leavis has called '*the* example I should choose to illustrate what we mean by saying that in the 19th century the novel took over the function of poetic drama.'[15]

Chapters 19 to 22 of *Middlemarch* describe Dorothea and Casaubon's wedding journey to Rome. The shock of this first contact between the sensitive girl who has been brought up entirely within the confines of English provincial Protestantism and the wealth of sensuous impressions which constitute the unrivalled stimulus of Rome becomes an image of the shock, which occurs at the same time, of her realisation of the nature of her marriage. Rome confuses Dorothea by offering her too many new experiences, which she can scarcely begin to assimilate; while the marriage from which she had expected so much offers nothing but frustration.

To those who have looked at Rome with the quickening power of a knowledge which breathes a growing soul into all historic shapes, and traces out the suppressed transitions which unite all contrasts, Rome may still be the spiritual centre and interpreter of the world, but let them conceive one more historical contrast: the gigantic broken revelations of that Imperial and Papal city thrust abruptly on the notions of a girl who had been brought up in English and Swiss Puritanism, fed on meagre Protestant histories and on art chiefly of the hand-screen sort; a girl whose ardent nature turned all her small allowance of knowledge into principles, fusing her actions into their mould, and whose quick emotions gave the most abstract things the quality of a pleasure or a pain; a girl who had lately become a wife, and from the enthusiastic acceptance of untried duty found herself plunged in tumultuous preoccupation with her personal lot. The weight of unintelligible Rome might lie easily on bright nymphs to whom it formed a background for the brilliant picnic of Anglo-foreign society; but Dorothea had no such defence against deep impressions. Ruins and basilicas, palaces and colossi, set in the midst of a sordid present, where all that was living and warm-blooded seemed sunk in the deep degeneracy of a superstition divorced from reverence; the dimmer but yet eager Titanic life gazing and struggling on walls and ceilings; the long vistas of white forms whose marble eyes seemed to hold the monotonous light of an alien world: all this vast wreck of ambitious ideals, sensuous and spiritual, mixed confusedly with the signs of breathing forgetfulness and degradation, at first jarred her as with an electric shock, and then urged themselves on her with that ache belonging to a glut of confused ideas which check the flow of emotion. Forms both pale and glowing took possession of her young sense, and fixed themselves in her memory even when she was not thinking of them, preparing strange associations which remained through her after-years. Our moods are apt to bring with them images which succeed each other like the magic-lantern pictures of a doze; and in certain states of dull forlornness Dorothea all her life continued to see the vastness of St Peter's, the huge bronze canopy, the excited intention in the attitudes and garments of the prophets and evangelists in the mosaics above, and the red drapery which was being hung for Christmas spreading itself everywhere like a disease of the retina. (ed. 1871, vol. 1, pp. 349–51)

The emphasis on the vastness of the potential experience of Rome contrasts with Dorothea's growing sense of the awful narrowness of her husband's mind; and the gloom of the libraries where he goes to pursue his futile studies is contrasted with the sunlight of the sculpture galleries where Ladislaw and Naumann catch sight of the pensive Dorothea. In *Middlemarch* there is nothing gratuitous or merely conventional, as had typically been the case in earlier novels, about the use of an Italian setting for some of the scenes. For Rome itself is totally integrated into the overall development of the novel. No other city could have provided, or not so naturally, the wealth of contrasting experience which so adequately reinforces Dorothea's discovery of the nature of her marriage. As in *Little Dorrit*, Rome becomes a positive, creative presence in the novel, and not merely a piece of background. After 1872, *Middlemarch* provided a model which implicitly condemned all fictional pictures of Italy which were less genuinely creative, while at the same time providing an admirable point of departure for any subsequent novelist who wished seriously to explore the use of Italian imagery. Henry James, especially, was the heir of George Eliot in this as in other respects; and in order to approach him in his proper perspective we must consider the use which previous American novelists, rather differently from the English, had made of Italy.

12 The American Novelists in Italy

JAMES FENIMORE COOPER (1789-1851)

Cooper was the first American to produce a significant fictional treatment of Italy. In many ways Cooper, who spent two years in Italy, from 1828 to 1830, which he described in his *Excursions in Italy* (1838), might have been considered in the earlier chapter on the treatment of Italy by English novelists in the 1830s. The novels we shall mention were, in fact, first published in England and only subsequently in America; and it was from English literary models that Cooper built his own picture of Italy. His novel *The Bravo. A Venetian Story* (1831) developes the kind of literary material we have encountered in Lewis's *Bravo of Venice*, to become the most vivid example in prose of the Byronic attitude to Venice.

The novel follows the fortunes of the love of the Calabrian prince, Don Camillo Monforte, for the orphan Violetta, a rich ward of the Venetian state. Their love contrasts and conflicts with the greed of the state, which does not want to lose Violetta's vast inheritance through her marriage to a foreigner. After many difficulties and near disasters the couple manage to flee to safety and happiness, aided by the bravo Jacopo, who had innocently and nobly entered the service of the state in a vain effort to save his father from unjust and cruel imprisonment, acquired a terrible and quite unjustified reputation, vividly presented in the earlier part of the novel, as a ruthless murderer, and is eventually executed in the Piazza for the murder of an old fisherman which, far from having committed, he had been particularly disgusted by. The fisherman was, in fact, killed by agents of the state for the crime of asking that his young grandson should be released from unjust conscription in the galleys.

Throughout the novel the contrast is firmly established between the public gaiety of Venice – the social life of the Piazza, and the magnificence of the Regatta – and the sinister darkness and secrecy of the meetings of the Councils, the prison, the calm arrangements for political murder, and the sordid characters of Senators and Jews. Beneath the superficial brilliance is a state in which everyone who is not wilfully corrupt is corrupted, misled, manipulated or destroyed. It is the nature of his stress on this contrast which makes Cooper's the first distinctly American treatment of Italy, the link between Byron and an important tradition in the American novel, and which leaves us in no doubt that his place is in this chapter and not in an earlier one. For in *The Bravo* Cooper is consciously writing for an American audience. As well as telling an exciting adventure story, he sets out to explore the question, which he pursues in the two further volumes of his European trilogy, *The Heidenmauer* (1832) and *The Headsman* (1833), of what lessons for its future the New World can learn from a survey of the state of the Old. Hence the emphasis in *The Bravo* on the operations of the machinery of state; for if American republicanism is a fine liberal institution in comparison with the oppressiveness of the Venetian oligarchy, in order to remain so it must beware the dangers of corruption which could lead it to the wretched state of that government, whose public morality is lower than the decent standards of private morality, and which consequently corrupts or compromises even the most respectable men who become involved in its administration.

To Cooper the danger of this happening in America lies in the total commitment of so many Americans to purely materialistic activity; and not only the warning but an indication of the remedy is to be found in Italy. For what is needed is a stronger sense of the need to cultivate the emotional and intellectual pleasures, to enjoy life for its own sake, and nowhere is this to be learnt better than in Italy. In *The Water Witch* (1830), written at Florence and Sorrento, the magical beauty of Italy, and especially of the Bay of Naples, is symbolically used as a positive contrast to American commercialism, and in *The Wing and Wing* (1842) the Mediterranean coast is celebrated, in terms reminiscent of Disraeli, as 'the most delightful region of the known earth' and 'the centre of all that is delightful and soothing to both the mind and the senses.'[1] (The novel is simply a well-narrated yarn of the adventures of a French privateer cruising the Italian coast, through it deserves to be noted for its amusing satire on the absurd pomposity of petty Italian bureaucracy, in the figures of the podestà and vice-governatore of Elba.)

By stressing both the beauty of Italy and the corruption of

eighteenth century Venice, Cooper has marked out the lines within which the treatment of Italy in the American novel is to develop; and in that development his own work would soon become dated. For in his novels the evil and the beautiful aspects are easily identifiable and separable from one another; the problem for subsequent writers was to be whether the two were not more subtly inter-related than Cooper had supposed, and whether it was possible to gain self-fulfilment from the one without being blemished by the other.[2]

NATHANIEL HAWTHORNE (1804–64)

This became the particular concern of Hawthorne. Long before visiting Italy he had chosen an Italian setting, in Padua, for his story *Rappaccini's Daughter*, in *Mosses From An Old Manse* (1846), built on the symbol of the presence of evil in paradise, but his fullest treatment of Italian material came in *The Marble Faun* (1860), as a result of his seventeen months' experience of Italy in 1857–8. Following the example of Madame de Staël (whose *Corinne* is evoked in Chapter 16) in setting his action against travelogue descriptions of the tourist attractions of Rome, Hawthorne's novel became, in Henry James's words, 'part of the intellectual equipment of the Anglo-Saxon visitor to Rome', and in W. D. Howells's, 'our aesthetic handbook in Rome.'[3]

The Marble Faun is by no means a total success. There are disturbing inconsistencies in various aspects of its technique. While Hawthorne often depends, for example, on the convention of the omniscient narrator, he disingenuously claims ignorance about a character's motives or past history whenever it suits him. Thus he creates an awkward gap at the centre of his characterisation of Miriam, by frequently referring to some past evil in which she has been involved, but never allowing the reader to see and assess what the evil actually was; and, perhaps more seriously, as James observed, 'the element of the unreal is pushed too far'[4] and jars with the convincingly realistic Italian setting.

But within its limitations the novel does make a strikingly new use of Italy. For, far from being a mere colourful conventional backcloth, Italy – Rome, particularly – becomes problematic, and the problem is of the essence of the novel. Rome presents certain possible experiences and ways of life quite different from those familiar to someone from a background of New England Puritanism, and the central movement of the novel is to explore whether such an American should reject, or how much he should – or can – accept and assimilate such possibilities. While in England Dickens had used, and George Eliot would later use, a character's response to Italy as part of the pattern of imagery in a novel, Hawthorne makes the nature of this response the basic issue around which his novel is built.

Despite its superficial beauty, Rome appears as fundamentally a city of crime and corruption. In utter contrast with the youthful vigour of New England, the ancient streets of Rome seem to be weighed down with a massive burden of evil. The weight of the past, of the chaos of continuous human activity over two thousand years, lies on the city as it cannot lie on the young country of America; the streets and palaces seem sinister, the indolence of the aristocracy seems immoral to American dynamism, and to the Puritan mind the concentration of Catholic clergy must inevitably suggest unimaginable depths of iniquity. The most vigorous description of Rome in the novel comes when the sculptor Kenyon's fear for Hilda's safety brings his deepest feelings for the city rushing through his mind:

> It seemed to Kenyon, looking through the darkly coloured medium of his fears, that all modes of crime were crowded into the close intricacy of Roman streets, and that there was no redeeming element, such as exists in other dissolute and wicked cities.
> For here was a priesthood, pampered, sensual, with red and bloated cheeks, and carnal eyes. With apparently a grosser development of animal life than most men, they were placed in an unnatural relation with woman, and thereby lost the healthy, human conscience that pertains to other human beings, who own the sweet household ties connecting them with wife and daughter. And here was an indolent nobility, with no high aims or opportunities, but cultivating a vicious way of life as if it were an art, and the only one which they cared to learn. Here was a population, high and low, that had no genuine belief in virtue; and if they recognized any act as criminal, they might throw off all care, remorse, and memory of it, by kneeling a little while at the confessional, and rising unburthened, active, elastic, and incited by fresh appetite for the next ensuing sin. Here was a soldiery, who felt Rome to be their conquered city, and doubtless

considered themselves the legal inheritors of the foul license which Gaul, Goth and Vandal have here exercised in days gone by.

And what localities for new crime existed in those guilty sites, where the crime of departed ages used to be at home, and had its long, hereditary haunt! What street in Rome, what ancient ruin, what one place where man had standing room, what fallen stone was there, unstained with one or another kind of guilt! [5]

This is the Rome where Donatello loses his almost mythical innocence by the crime of throwing the mysterious persecutor of Miriam to his death from the Tarpeian Rock. But in losing his innocence he also becomes, much more than he can truly be said to have been before, a man. At the expense of his knowledge of guilt he has become far more fully open than before to the richness of human experience. The crucial question of the novel is whether this is not also true of Hilda, the slender, brown-haired New England girl. By accidentally witnessing Donatello's crime she too feels implicated in its guilt; but might this not also be a kind of initiation into the acceptance of a whole range of other kinds of experience, symbo-lised by Rome, which, like the prospect of feeling guilty of one's actions, are kept abhorrently at more than arm's length by her New England Puritan conscience?

It is less a limitation than a sign of integrity in the novel that it does not ultimately answer the question. Oppressed by feelings of guilty implication, Hilda's religious background and beliefs only make her anguish the greater; whereas in St Peter's, significantly referred to in a chapter heading as 'The World's Cathedral', she feels irresistibly the attraction of the solace which the Roman Church can offer to its faithful:

Who, in truth, that considers the matter, can resist a similar impression? In the hottest fever-fit of life, they can always find, ready for their need, a cool, quiet, beautiful place of worship. They may enter its sacred precincts at any hour, leaving the fret and trouble of the world behind them, and purifying themselves with a touch of holy-water at the threshold. In the calm interior, fragrant of rich and soothing incense, they may hold converse with some Saint, their awful, kindly friend. And, most precious privilege of all, whatever perplexity, sorrow, guilt, may weigh upon their souls, they can fling down the dark burthen at the foot of the Cross, and go forth – to sin no more, nor be any longer disquieted – but to live again in the freshness and elasticity of innocence![6]

The sympathetic authorial comment on the confessional contrasts with Kenyon's antagonistic Puritan view; and Hilda comes to share the former, being led even to criticise her own religion:

'Do not these inestimable advantages,' thought Hilda, 'or some of them at least, belong to Christianity itself? Are they not a part of the blessings which the System was meant to bestow upon mankind? Can the faith, in which I was born and bred, be perfect, if it leave a weak girl like me to wander, desolate, with this great trouble crushing me down?'[6]

Impulsively, she pours out her troubles to a kindly old priest in a confessional in St Peter's, and experiences a sense of relief and redemption which her own religion had never offered her. But there is never any question of her abandoning that religion; she has come to understand something of the quality of the Catholic Church, and lost her former prejudice against it, but she cannot envisage the possibility of being seriously attracted towards allegiance to it. Soon after the scene in St Peter's she becomes engaged to Kenyon and they return to America. Rome has immensely expanded her experience of living, and stretched her capacity for both suffering and serenity. But she has only made a first step, and after that step, instead of going further, instead of risking contamination from the corrupting elements in the Italian environment in the hope of living through to a fuller, profounder knowledge of life, she retires to the safer, narrower environment of America. But her adventures in Italy had sketched out a problem which was to become central in American intellectual life, and other fictional characters would follow her to Europe to continue the process of exploration.

THE EIGHTEEN SIXTIES

The decade after *The Marble Faun* appears rather as an expectant gap, as if the Italian theme in American literature were waiting for James to come and make it his own. Established American novelists did write about Italy, but produced nothing of great importance. Harriet Beecher Stowe's *Agnes of Sorrento* (1862) took up Cooper's emphasis on the beauty of the Bay of Naples and effectively evoked the landscape and sunlight of 'dreamy, voluptuous Southern Italy' (p. 156), but though her fifteenth century setting includes both the luscious south and the persecution of Savonarola in Florence, the substance of the novel is a love story of the most superficial kind, whose only value was escapist. While Mark Twain in *The Innocents Abroad* (1869) has little sympathy with Italy and is primarily interested in the opportunities that his tour offers him of being amusing, whether at the expense of the Italians or of his fellow tourists. The Italian section of the book is frequently entertaining, but can scarcely be said to have contributed anything to the serious literary process of American self-analysis through contact with Italy.

The 1860s did, however, see advances made in this direction, in the work of Story and especially of Howells. William Wetmore Story's contribution to the literary apprehension of Italy was made less in his own published work than through his social life. As the good friend and excellent host of most of the literary people of his day who visited or lived in Italy, his home at the Palazzo Barberini in Rome became an important centre for the exchange of anecdotes, feelings and ideas, a house where, for example, the young James could compare his own first impressions of Italy with the feelings of older writers and with memories of Romantic Italy transmitted through Story's friendship with the aged Landor in Siena: James's feeling of debt for this pervades his *William Wetmore Story and His Friends* (1903).

Story's most important book on Italy was his *Roba di Roma* (1863), which combines a considerable amount of historical information with an attractive emphasis on the evocation of the everyday life of the Roman people in the city and in the Campagna. It is part of the reaction of the mid-century against the stereotyped touristic attitudes to Italy:

> Every Englishman carries a Murray for information, and a Byron for sentiment, and finds out by them what he is to know and feel at every step . . . All the public life and history of the ancient Romans, from Romulus to Constantine and Julian the Apostle (as he is sometimes called,) is perfectly well known. But the common life of the modern Romans, the games, customs, and habits of the people, the every-day life of To-day, has only been touched upon here and there.[7]

Story attempts to correct the balance by describing at length these facets of contemporary Roman life, in which he is principally impressed by a feeling of deep continuity with the past:

> Would you like to know the modern rules for agriculture in Rome, read the *Georgics*: there is so little to alter, that it is not worth mentioning.[8]

The continual repetition of the same activities in the same place over thousands of years gives an underlying serenity and wisdom to life which contrast poignantly and valuably with the sense of uncertainty in societies where such continuity has been lost, whether it be in the young country of America or the new industrial society of Britain. Story's attitude to the thickness of the past is the precise opposite of Kenyon's in *The Marble Faun*. Story, however, developed the contrast between traditional and emergent societies less forcefully than did W. D. Howells.

The young Howells went to Venice in 1861 as American Consul, a post he filled for the next four years. What most impressed him in Venice, and throughout Italy as he came to know the country, was the way in which the ordinary events of everyday life expressed fundamental values altogether healthier and more attractive than those which appeared in the day to day contact of American life. American tourists had apparently already developed the habit of rushing into the great buildings and galleries of Europe and demanding, 'Show me all you can in five minutes,'[9] and Howells suggests that the wise Venetian cats easily recognise Americans,

> by the speed with which we pass from one thing to another, and by our national ignorance of all languages, but English. They must also hear us vaunt the superiority of our land in unpleasant comparisons, and I do not think they believe us, or like us, for our boastings.[10]

In Venetian life, on the other hand, there is less hurry and more grace:

> A Venetian who enters or leaves any place of public resort touches his hat to the company, and one day at the restaurant some ladies, who had been dining there, said 'Complimenti!' on going out with a grace that went near to make the beef-steak

tender. It is this uncostly gentleness of bearing which gives a winning impression of the whole Venetian people, whatever selfishness or real discourtesy lie beneath it. At home it sometimes seems that we are in such a haste to live and be done with it, we have no time to be polite. Or is popular politeness merely a vice of servile peoples? And is it altogether better to be rude? I wish it were not. If you are lost in this city (and you are pretty sure to be lost there, continually), a Venetian will go with you wherever you wish. If he is poor, he will take your gratuity; if he is not, you will not offer it. At any rate, he has done this amiable little service out of what one may say old civilisation has established in place of goodness of heart, and which is perhaps not so different from it.[11]

It is not that the Italians are any better or worse than the Americans, but simply that to conduct life in this manner is more attractive and more mentally healthy than to dehumanise personal contact by channelling it always through the cash nexus. When Howells bargains to buy firewood in Venice[12] he loses time and is, of course, cheated; but there has been a human encounter, not merely a cold commercial transaction, which has contributed something worthwhile to his feeling for life. It is not simply that Italian life is colourful – that observation, as we have seen, was as likely to be derogatory as appreciative – but that those things which give it colour have a genuine vitality which has been lost in drabber, more modern societies. Howells states the difference succinctly in a later work:

> Life, which has become to us like a book which we silently peruse in the closet, or at most read aloud with a few friends, is still a drama with them, to be more or less openly played.[13]

It is this which makes Italy 'above all lands the home of human nature.'[14]

Howells's feelings for Italy found a response in America. *Venetian Life*, when first published in book form in 1866, was widely acclaimed and sold well in several editions over the next fifty years. The success of the volume and its sequel, *Italian Journeys* (1867), established Howells as an authority on Italy in the United States, and formed the foundation of his friendship with Longfellow, who was at work on his translation of Dante. (Though this was, of course, an important element in the transmission of Italian culture to the

American audience, Longfellow's direct responses to Italy, in his poems and in *Outre-Mer* (1835), are too slight to detain us here.) More importantly, Howells's descriptions of everyday life in Italy marked a stage in his development as a writer. J. L. Woodress, Jr, has described in detail[15] how the experience of writing the earlier books, and his study of the presentation of Venetian life in Goldoni's comedies, formed the basis of the realistic style for which Howells's novels became famous. Some of these novels themselves result from Howells's years in Italy, and have sometimes been regarded as transitional between *The Marble Faun* and James's Italian novels. However, this is scarcely the case, despite James's known admiration for Howells's fiction,[16] for the American characters whom Howells sends to Italy are singularly little affected by the environment they find there and, except in a very negative way, the international theme hardly appears; and James had, anyway, begun to treat this theme in his short stories and was writing *Roderick Hudson* by the time of Howells's *A Foregone Conclusion* (1874). In this novel a Venetian priest falls in love with an American girl who is visiting Venice with her mother. The girl enthusiastically encourages his absurd idea of renouncing the priesthood – a spiritual and psychological crisis to which the novel's lightweight touch is quite inadequate – and earning a living in America as an inventor, until, horrifiedly, she at last realises that he is in love with her. She, in fact, loves the American Consul, who loves her, and they are later married, back in America. Neither of them appears to have been appreciably affected by the events which have devastated the poor Italian priest. Again, in *The Lady of The 'Aroostook'* (1878), when a New England girl is sent to stay for a while with her aunt in Venice, although she experiences a sense of shock at the social conventions of life there, she has no real contact with the city, and the novel entirely concerns her relations with other Americans. The contrast is obviously with James's *Daisy Miller*, published in the same year; and since Howells's later novels continue to use Italy merely as a kind of holiday background for American characters (in *A Fearful Responsibility*, 1881; *Indian Summer*, 1885; and *The Ragged Lady*, 1899), it will be as well to turn immediately to the more important case of James.

HENRY JAMES (1843–1916)

> The world has nothing better to offer a man of sensibility than a first visit to Italy during those years of life when perception is at its keenest, when knowledge has arrived, and yet youth has not departed.[17]

This eminently high estimation of the value of Italy which James makes in a fictional context is irresistibly applicable to his own personal experience. The initial contact with Italy in 1869 seems suddenly to have awakened in James a dormant feeling for the finest things of life and a consequent pre-occupation with the difficulty of attaining them, which was to become of the essence of his work. For something quite new, and fundamentally important, enters his life and work with his first experience of Italy, a change whose dimensions are suggested by his assessment of the value of a first visit there.

James went to Italy familiar with the work of those literary precursors we have looked at, and particularly with the conflicting presentations of the weight of the Italian past as oppressive in Hawthorne and invigorating in Story and Howells. None of these writers, however, seemed adequate to the strength of feeling which Italy called out in him. Only one author came near to this, an author whom James first discovered in Italy in that autumn of 1869: Stendhal. We have not yet had occasion to mention Stendhal, since although the present century has come to value his treatment of Italy much more highly then George Sand's, the Victorian opinion was quite the reverse and his work was very little known in England.[18] In the 1820s he had, indeed, contributed a considerable amount of journalism, often on Italian subjects, to the British reviews,[19] but this was insignificant since it contained little of his later, fuller response to Italy, and was in any case not known to be by Stendhal. The important work came in the late 1830s, with the *Chroniques Italiennes* (1837–9) and *La Chartreuse de Parme* (1839), celebrating both Renaissance and modern Italy as the country where, by contrast with France, men (and women) were directly motivated by passion, uncorrupted by considerations of money or the fear of appearing ridiculous. The contrast with New England was likely to be even stronger, and it was fully felt by James as he travelled through Italy reading Stendhal:

In these dead cities of Verona, Mantua, Padua, how life had revelled and postured in its strength! How sentiment and passion had blossomed and flowered! How much of history had been performed! What a wealth of mortality had ripened and decayed! I have never elsewhere got so deep an impression of the social secrets of mankind. In England, even, in those verdure-stifled haunts of domestic peace which muffle the sounding chords of British civilisation, one had a fainter sense of the possible movement and fruition of individual character. Beyond a certain point you fancy it merged in the general medium of duty, business, and politics. In Italy, in spite of your knowledge of the strenuous public conscience which once inflamed these compact little states, the unapplied, spontaneous moral life of society seems to have been more active and more subtle. I walked about with a volume of Stendhal in my pocket; at every step I gathered some lingering testimony to the exquisite vanity of ambition.[20]

The 'I' of this passage is not, indeed, James, but the hero of one of his early tales. The passage, however, is clearly closely autobiographical. The problem for James was how – if – he could fruitfully integrate a response to this passion which was felt to be everywhere in Italy, and which was so obviously a vital part of a full response to life, with the life of the sensitive, sophisticated intellectual, whose delicate stability the dark eruptive force of passion seemed to threaten. As James felt this tension most strongly in Italy, so he most frequently and most importantly explores the problem in an Italian setting.[21] Particularly, this exploration is a major phenomenon of his early work, and what principally concerns us here is this early working out of the attitude to Italy which thereafter recurs frequently throughout James's fiction.

In the first two Italian tales, *Travelling Companions* (1870) and *At Isella* (1871), the hero feels the immense attraction of Italy, though without being drawn into any significant contact with the country. This begins to appear in *The Madonna of The Future* (1873). An American artist has spent over twenty years in Florence contemplating the production of an ideal painting of the Madonna, but quite blind to the fact that the woman who seems to him the ideal model is every day becoming older and uglier, so that 'one by one, the noiseless years had ebbed away, and left him brooding in charmed inaction, forever preparing for a work forever deferred.'[22] When the deterioration of his model is eventually pointed out to him he frantically tries to get his idea of the portrait down on canvas, but can do nothing, dies of a fever, and is buried in the Protestant cemetery at Fiesole. Italy has revealed to him the possibility of attaining the highest artistic ambition, but at the same time enervated him so that he cannot achieve it, and held him in tantalising and ultimately destructive frustration. Is there some fundamental incompatibility between the American desire to create and the potential sources of vitality in Italy? The short stories of the next couple of years suggest increasingly that there may be.

The Last of The Valerii (1874) contains a Roman Count who evidently owes something to Hawthorne's Donatello. Like him, he is utterly unsophisticated and innocent of all moral problems, a man 'fundamentally unfurnished with ideas. He had no beliefs nor hopes nor fears, – nothing but senses, appetites, and serenely luxurious tastes.'[23] An American girl marries the Count: she is, therefore, probing much more deeply into the fibre of Italian life than had ever been the case with Hilda in *The Marble Faun*. There might be some hope of a fruitful interaction of American wealth and Italian culture when she devotes some of her fortune to archaeological excavations on her husband's estates; but when a Greek figure of Juno is dug up the Count is irresistibly drawn to worship the goddess and neglect his wife. Even when she has apparently regained his affection by the drastic step of having the statue buried again, his deepest feelings remain directed to one of its hands which he has secretly preserved.

In another story of the same year, *Adina*, a young American in Italy with his fiancée loses her through his attachment to an ancient topaz intaglio of Tiberius. The Italian peasant from whom he bought it for an absurdly low price avenges himself for having been cheated by winning away the fiancée and marrying her himself: scarcely a promising marriage. The abandoned lover flings the intaglio into the Tiber: in both stories the suggestion is that the extreme beauty represented by the Italian past is not merely alien to the American mentality, but destructive of its chances of happiness. Yet without some genuine contact with the past, such a mentality is cripplingly limited: in James's only allegory, *Benvolio* (1875), an American poet has to choose between the inspiration of a Countess, representing Europe, and Scholastica, who represents America. He chooses Scholastica; and his poetry becomes intolerably dull.

This is the predicament which James sets out to explore more fully in his first serious novel, *Roderick Hudson* (1875). The sculptor

Hudson does manage to relate to the artistic heritage he finds in Rome. The sculptural genius which had only been latent in New England blossoms in response to the stimulus of Italy. It is as though the artistic temperament needs to take nourishment from an atmosphere more richly charged with the creative activity of the past than is the case in America, and which it finds to perfection in Italy. But as the richness of the texture of life increases, so does its moral and psychological complexity. Before leaving America Hudson had become engaged to the very pure New England girl, Mary Garland. In Rome he falls madly in love with the cosmopolitan beauty, Christine Light. But his passion for Christine is doomed to failure. The illegitimate daughter of an American mother and an Italian Cavaliere, she is effectively the property of her mother, who has brought her up with the express intention of marrying her to the highest bidder. Torn by anguish at his infidelity to Mary and the unattainability of Christine, Hudson languishes, his genius fails, and he goes off to seek, and find, death in the mountains. Rome has been his Mephistopheles, giving him a period of fulfilment at the expense of premature and painful destruction. Had he stayed at home the assumption is that he would have been deprived of the full development of his art, but spared the suffering he meets in Italy. Rome, in *Roderick Hudson*, is the symbol of the tragic dilemma which characteristically confronts the Jamesian hero: the predicament that the delicate sensitivity which enables a man to appreciate the finest achievements of civilisation renders him also peculiarly vulnerable to the less delicate emotional blows of life. James's early fictional explorations of Italy had established the paradox which was to be at the centre of his work as a novelist.

When subsequent Jamesian characters go to Italy it is to suffer. Daisy Miller tries to enjoy Rome in her own flirtacious way, only to take a fatal fever at the Colosseum. Isabel Archer, in Italy, falls into the trap of her appalling marriage. The sequence of events leading to Paul Muniment's suicide in *The Princess Casamassima* (1886) begins with his realisation in Venice that there are rich dimensions to life which his comrades' revolutionary programme would wilfully destroy. The narrator of *The Aspern Papers* (1888) is frustrated in his hopes of obtaining the precious Aspern manuscripts in Venice, and in *The Wings of The Dove* (1902) Milly Theale goes to Venice to die. But their suffering in Italy has a significance beyond that of earlier fictional heroes. For James in his early work has made a convention self-conscious: the fatal inability of the Anglo-Saxons to attain a fruitful relationship with the potential wealth of the Italian atmosphere has become one of the most poignant and central images of his dominant concern with man's inability ever to achieve a totally satisfactory relationship with the conditions of life. James's repeated demonstrations that as man reaches to attain the finest experiences of life he only exposes himself, ever more perilously the more he reaches, to the shocks and buffets of life are perhaps the nearest the novel has approached to tragedy. In attempting to formulate this view of life in his fiction James found a major stimulus in Italy. His treatment of Italy renders explicit and sophisticated the attitudes which had confusedly underlain the earlier novelists' feeling of the malignancy of Italy; and in doing so he challenges the superficiality and futility of any attempt, such as we have reviewed above, to relate Anglo-Saxon life creatively to one or another aspect of Italian life and culture. James's work draws together many of the strands which have so far threaded themselves through our study. In many ways his work is the counter-balance to Byron's: Byron had used Italy to demonstrate the nature and possibility of the full life; James uses it to argue that such possibilities are tragically chimerical. James is the antithesis of Byron; and the synthesis of the two we shall find in the development of Lawrence's Italian work, the keystone of the pattern we are attempting to uncover.

13 Italy and the English Novel, 1870–1917

OUIDA (1839–1908)

The most significant English novelist to write on Italy in the 1870s was Ouida. After occasionally using purely conventional Italian scenery in a very minor way in some of her earlier novels (*Chandos*, 1866; *Idalia*, 1867; and *Puck*, 1870), she fell in love with the country on her first visit there in 1871, settled in Florence, and thereafter looked constantly to Italy for her literary material.

Ouida takes up the fictional potential of Italy where T. A. Trollope left off; the more so since she shared with him a common model for the treatment of Italy in her deep admiration of George Sand.[1] Like Trollope's, Ouida's Italian novels were for the most part thoroughly sentimental love stories narrated with a minimum of psychological insight and prose quality and a maximum of local colour for padding. But despite the general superficiality of her work she does at times respond to Italy more deeply than Trollope's novels had done, and can offer her reader two new kinds of feeling towards the country, both of which, after she had introduced them, go on to culminate in important aspects of Lawrence's Italian work.

The first is a particular stress in her treatment of the attraction of Italy to the northener, the attraction which has meant that 'the atmosphere of Italy has been the greatest fertiliser of English poetic genius.'[2] England seems to Ouida to be stultifying to the creative imagination. 'All lands are soulless where the olive does not lift its consecrated boughs to heaven;'[3] and they are soulless because they have lost contact with any roots they may have had in the past in a sensuous, pagan enjoyment of life. The olive is the symbolic point of contact between modern man and the ancient pagan civilisations which flourished in the 'dryad-haunted groves' of the Mediterranean; and it is this contact which particularly delights Ouida in Italy. Her favourite city, Florence, is always half a pagan at heart – she, the daughter of Hercules, who saw the flying feet of Atalanta shine upon her silvery hills, and heard the arrows of Apollo cleave her rosy air.

The past is so close to you in Florence. You touch it at every step. It is not the dead past that men bury and then forget. It is an unquenchable thing; beautiful, and full of lustre, even in the tomb, like the gold from the sepulchres of the Aetruscan kings that shines on the breast of some fair living woman, undimmed by the dust and the length of the ages.[4]

Throughout the novels references to the Etruscan past abound whenever Ouida wishes to evoke the graceful and joyous response to life which seems to her to be the most valuable thing that Italy has to offer the visitor from the north. Most of the novels are set in that part of Tuscany which is redolent of the ancient civilisation; and in *In Maremma* (1882) there are even scenes set in an Etruscan tomb on the Tuscan coast. The constant assertion and reminder of the continuity of a joyous celebration of life going on in the Italian countryside over thousands of years is an attempt to give depth and significance to an admiring attitude towards Italian peasant life which nevertheless remains, like Trollope's, purely sentimental. Ouida relies too simply on the use of the word 'Etruscan' as a magic charm without ever making any serious attempt to explore and portray, for example, what precisely these 'Etruscan' qualities are and how they can relate to the lives of her readers. Her uncritical enthusiasm contrasts painfully with the pre-occupations of the work which James was producing at the same time as her own. But she does have the distinction of having first rendered explicitly in the novel that connection between modern Italian life and the attractions of pagan antiquity which was implicit in contemporary work on the Renaissance, and was to become a substantial theme of the English novel during the next forty years.

However, there was another side of modern Italian life which was distinctly not derived from the Etruscans and was, indeed, threateningly antagonistic to all that was best in the Italian character. Hitherto, English writers had often expressed their support and admiration of the Italian people in their struggle against the Austrians and the temporal power of the Church; and Ouida's own first Italian novel, *Pascarèl* (1873), concerns a hero of the fight against Austria. But living in Italy during the first years of unification, Ouida became the first English writer to chronicle the sense of growing disillusion with the actual achievement. For the end of the political and military struggle had not produced the expected flowering of the magnificent potential of Italy, but a sadder and more devastating series of attacks on that potential than had ever been seen under the old régime.

Ouida identified two major factors contributing to this attack. We have noted how Lever, in *The Daltons*, had suggested that English residents in Florence were involved in dubious financial speculation in Italian affairs. In the 1870s, with the new nationalistic government, Italy offered unprecedented opportunities to such speculators to launch schemes which would ostensibly bring benefit and glory to Italy, but in reality merely bring profit to their own pockets; and it is against this that the first part of Ouida's attack is directed. *Friendship* (1878) takes up Lever's criticisms of English society abroad in a sustained and strident attack on all Ouida's real or imagined enemies in Florence, the chief of whom, Lady Joan (based on Janet Ross), is accused of many kinds of dishonesty, but denounced for nothing so bitterly as for her constant involvement in fraudulent speculation.

Such activities were made all the easier by the second factor to which Ouida attributes Italy's sorry plight in the early years of independence: the creation of a bureaucracy invested with tyrannical powers and utterly devoid of moral principle and of any sense either of duty or compassion. Throughout the country brutal men had been able suddenly to seize dominating positions in the local political and administrative structures, whence they could bully and exploit their neighbours. A central event in the short story *The Marriage Plate*, in *Pipistrello & Other Stories* (1880), which Ouida presents as characterising the new state of affairs in Italy, is the shock of a poor peasant on discovering that his beloved dog, which he has left guarding his pony and trap in Florence, has been viciously dragged away by the police because of a new law against leaving dogs unchained in the streets of the city. The people who had been promised freedom through independence find, bewilderingly, that there is only a worse tyranny than before.

Ouida combines both these elements of contemporary Italy in her finest novel, *A Village Commune* (1881). The village of Santa Rosalia is described as representative of the autonomous petty tyrannies which the Risorgimento has created all over Italy. The system is personified by the Syndic's brutal secretary, Nellemane.

He himself has written the by-laws of the community, which are carefully designed to line his own pocket by making every inhabitant constantly liable to be fined, since even the most ordinary and inevitable events of daily life can be found to contravene one or other of the provisions of the wretched man's personal criminal code. By a combination of brute force and manipulation of the law, he and his henchmen terrorise the village and create an atmosphere of fear and hatred; while at the same time the whole countryside is being laid waste by the speculative building of railways, tramways and steam-mills. The villain Nellemane naturally has an interest in such profitable enterprises, and is in a position to give full scope to their development in the area under his control. His own pet scheme is a plan to convert the Roman catacombs into an underground railway, a plan whose palpable absurdity is only a striking exaggeration, and not a mis-representation, of the scandalous nature of many such projects which were actually in the air at the time. (Ouida provides an appendix guaranteeing the authenticity of her material.) Eventually, Nellemane is rewarded for his administrative zeal by being made a Deputy.

All this was new food for thought for the English reader interested in Italy. If what was needed to rejuvenate industrial society was a return to the essence of paganism, then Italy was evidently the place to establish contact; and if contact was to be made, it must be made quickly, for the Italian people and the Italian country seemed daily to be losing some of their charm and beauty in the face, precisely, of the encroaching industrialisation and brutalisation of modern life. Despite the prevalent sentimentality and superficiality of her work, Ouida had indicated the area in which much subsequent literary interest in Italy was to lie, and had contributed one significant novel to the tradition of English writing about Italy.

FRANCIS MARION CRAWFORD (1854–1909)

Ouida was succeeded as the most popular 'Italian' novelist of the day by Francis Marion Crawford. The son of an American sculptor, Crawford was born at Bagni di Lucca in 1854 and brought up principally at Rome. After travelling extensively, he settled at Sorrento in 1884, and for the next quarter of a century poured out a stream of Italian fiction and occasional minor historical works on

Italy. Fundamental to his work was his oft-repeated belief that only he was qualified to interpret Italy to the English-speaking world:

> Without a single exception, every foreigner, poet or prose-writer, who has treated of these people has more or less grossly misunderstood them . . . To understand Italians a man must have been born and bred among them.[5]

The work itself, however, can hardly be said to live up to Crawford's pretension. The novels are distinguished neither for literary power nor psychological insight; indeed, in view of the number of times he returned to Italian themes, they are remarkable for the absence of both. Crawford's feeling about the Italians was quite straightforward, and is more noteworthy for being consistent with the trend of English thought about Italy at this time than for any astonishing originality:

> The Italian habitually expresses what he feels, while it is the chief pride of Northern men that whatever they may feel they express nothing. The chief object of most Italians is to make life agreeable; the chief object of the Teutonic races is to make it profitable.[6]

The novels are largely set in Rome during the last years of Papal government, a period of Roman history for which Crawford, like most people who had known it (as one sees throughout Henry James's *William Wetmore Story and His Friends*), was deeply nostalgic. Implicitly, there is a contrast with the feeling of Roman life in more recent years, but though he does sometimes discuss this, as in the first chapter of *Saracinesca* (1887), and does present one of his villains as a massive speculator in *Don Orsino* (1893), there is nothing of the force of Ouida's concern with the spreading malaise of Italy. Crawford's are thoroughly optimistic novels where the forces of good – true love and the Roman Catholic Church – always triumph in the end. Apart from his Catholicism and the greater sophistication of his style, Crawford recalls the Gothic novelists of the beginning of the century, sharing their crudely simple moral pattern of unfailing retribution and reward. Some of his villains, indeed, could almost have come straight out of those earlier novels: to such an extent that – as also in Marie Corelli's grippingly sensational Italian novel, *Vendetta!* (1886) – one is struck by a curious sense of anachronism whenever one of them lights a cigarette or travels by train. Such novels do not develop the literary exploration of Italy; but their very feeling of old-fashionedness emphasises the changes in the literary treatment of Italy since the days when the Gothic image had been the normal convention.

GEORGE GISSING (1857 –1903)

The more serious, and less popular, English novelists who were interested in Italy around the turn of the century were not concerned with these trite and trivial versions of life in the south, but effectively – though never explicitly – with trying to disprove James's theory that the inspiration of the Italian past was tragically unattainable for the modern Anglo-Saxon, by constructively relating their own feelings of discontent with contemporary English life to the profound sources of vitality which were undoubtedly to be found in Italy. Looking back at their work, one may feel that what they produced was a series of admirable, but painful, demonstrations of the truth of James's assertion.

As we shall see, the novelists in question approached the problem of Italy in a number of ways, but the common factor they shared was a debt to the writers on the Renaissance considered earlier, and particularly to Symonds. With him they tended to share an admiration for just those qualities of the Renaissance which had led Ruskin to denounce it, and a delight in the frequent sense of contact in Italy with the ancient sources of pagan feeling for life, a feeling which seemed invigoratingly and sanely wholesome by comparison with the inhibitions and hypocrisy of Victorian England. Whereas for one reason or another they each felt outsiders in England, Italy seemed to offer societies, whether actual or historical, where they could feel more happily at home and more readily able to develop their own lives to the full.

A case in point, which we must note in passing, was Samuel Butler, who fell in love with Italy during early visits with his parents in 1843 and 1853 and revisited the country as often as possible throughout his life, coming to regard it as 'my second country.'[7] What he found, above all, in Italy, was the warmth of human contact; it was a country where he could much more easily make friends, where he more frequently received gratifying attention as a man of letters, than in England, and where he felt surrounded by affection and esteem which helped to compensate for the emotional starvation of his loveless upbringing in England. As well as occasional references in his two novels, Butler's attachment to Italy led to his famous theory that the *Odyssey* was written by a woman from Trapani, and his two books on the curious art-works of the Val di Sésia, *Alps and Sanctuaries* (1882) and *Ex Voto* (1888). These, however, are minor works, and their contribution to our subject is negligible; Gissing is much more important.

Like Butler, Gissing, when he first went to Italy in 1888, found a society whose human warmth and joyful acceptance of living offered precisely those qualities which seemed to be lacking in the colder and more circumspect English way of life. In his fiction this contrast became embodied in the development of the character of Miriam Baske in *The Emancipated* (1890). She and her brother have been brought up in an atmosphere of English Puritanism, and the novel attacks its emotionally evil effects upon them. Her brother reacts against his background and leads a dissolute life of increasing degeneracy until he dies in a sordid brawl in Paris. Miriam, however, remains true to her family faith until, as the wealthy young widow of a Lancashire industrialist, she goes to stay with cousins in Naples. There, she is at first quite insensible to the beauty of her environment, maintains a solitary English Sunday in her room, and works on her plans to use her wealth to build a fine new chapel for the dissenting congregation back in Bartles. But she comes gradually to lose her Puritanism and abandon her English preoccupations, as she begins to appreciate the beauty of the Bay of Naples, of Dante, and of art, her responses brought out by the sympathetic figure of Mallard, a landscape painter who adores the south. The congregation in Bartles, angered at seeing the plans for their chapel abandoned, regard her as having fallen into the clutches of a Roman Catholicism which they conceive in much the same horrific terms as the novelists of the beginning of the century; in fact, she is losing all religious belief, and finding happiness and fulfilment which England could not offer her, in a purely pagan apprehension of the enjoyment of life. She and Mallard become happily married; and at his suggestion the money which she had promised for the chapel is devoted to building public baths, an appropriately pagan symbol of her emancipation.

In this novel, at least, an English character is led to happiness through the influence of Italy. Unfortunately, the presentation of so attractive a procedure is much less convincing than James's fictional warnings of the insuperable difficulties involved in seeking fulfilment in Italy. There is a strong feeling of wish-fulfilment about *The Emancipated*. Everything is too carefully arranged so as to throw into relief the blossoming of Miriam's sensibility – the contrast with the opposite process in her brother, for example, or with the Bradshaws, English visitors who fail even to begin to understand Italy – and she never encounters any serious difficulties which might test the resilience of her new-found paganism. Above all, she has no real contact with Italy, only with the cultivated English view of it: there are no Italian characters in the novel. Gissing, one feels, has been too selective in subjecting his heroine only to those influences which will educate her out of Englishness, while sheltering her from the full force of the impact of Italy which is necessary to test the validity of her escape.

Indeed, Gissing himself, in his personal relationship with Italy, is a more interesting figure than his heroine. Although when he went there he found himself attracted by the everyday life of the Italians, his primary interest in Italy was classical. From his school days he had laid a foundation of classical reading whose extent is evident from his early prize poem *Ravenna* (1873). Throughout his years of poverty in London the vision of his ideal image of the classical south sustained him with a sense of something far finer in life than the grim, foggy city around him, to the extent that, like Goethe before him, his longing to travel south began to afflict him as a physical anguish:

> I dare not read a book about Rome, it gives me a sort of *angina pectoris*, a physical pain, so extreme is my desire to go there.[8]

When he first realised his dream of going to Italy, in 1888, visiting Naples, Rome, Florence and Venice, it was the classical sites, especially Rome and Paestum, which most enthralled him:

> To be sure Florence does not appeal to me as much as Rome, or even as Naples. Christian art has not the unspeakable charm that I find in the Pagan relics and memories. Florence is the city of the Renaissance, but after all the Renaissance was only a shadow of the great times, and like a shadow it has passed away. There is nothing here that impresses me like the poorest of Rome's antiquities.[9]

Gissing's interest in the ancient associations of Italy was quite different from that of the eighteenth century; where they had been chiefly attracted by the great civic and imperial achievements of the Romans, he was more interested in the charm and grace of ancient culture, the aethereal rather than the monumental aspects of the pagan past. After 'glorious Rome'[10] he longed to visit Greece and the far south of Italy, where the way of life had changed least since ancient days and he could feel most closely in contact with the beautiful spirit which had suffused the work of the classical writers:

> Every man has his intellectual desire; mine is to escape life as I know it and dream myself into that old world which was the imaginative delight of my boyhood. . . The world of the Greeks and Romans is my land of romance; a quotation in either language thrills me strangely, and there are passages of Greek and Latin verse which I cannot read without a dimming of the eyes, which I cannot repeat aloud because my voice fails me. In Magna Graecia the waters of the two fountains mingle and flow together; how exquisite will be the draught![11]

But *By The Ionian Sea* (1901), which records Gissing's visit to this land of his dreams in 1897–8, though it is a very delightful, and often a very amusing, little book, is in the end a very sad document. There is everywhere so deep a sense of loss; the great city of Croton, 'bounded with a wall of twelve miles circumference', has completely vanished, and left not even a ruin in the 'squalid little town'[12] of modern Cotrone. 'Squalid' is probably the commonest epithet in the volume: all over the south there is a squalor which jars harshly with Gissing's search for the beauty of ancient culture. The ancient Croton had been famed as the healthiest city in the world: 'beauty and strength distinguished its inhabitants.' 'Today there was scarce a healthy man in Cotrone: no one had the strength to resist a serious illness,'[13] and Gissing himself fell ill there.

Not all is lost, however. There was still some contact with the past. He could imagine Pythagoras musing on the hillside at Cotrone, and at Taranto the sight of the half-naked fisherman carried him back through the centuries:

> When Plato visited the Schools of Taras, he saw the same brown-legged figures, in much the same garb, gathering their sea-harvest. When Hannibal, beset by the Romans, drew his ships

across the peninsula and so escaped from the inner sea, fishermen of Tarentum went forth as ever, seeking their daily food.[14]

But such idyllic day-dreams are short-lived, and destined to become memories to be recalled in the sadly different circumstances of daily life back in drab England. Despite the dirt and disappointments of the south, Gissing would love to stay and live out his days in the sun. In the last sentence of the book he bids farewell to the south as he sits in Reggio about to begin his journey back towards England:

> Alone and quiet, I heard the washing of the waves; I saw the evening fall on cloud-wreathed Etna, the twinkling lights come forth upon Scylla and Charybdis; and, as I looked my last towards the Ionian Sea, I wished it were mine to wander endlessly amid the silence of the ancient world, to-day and all its sounds forgotten.[15]

Gissing is, as it were, his own hero in this book, caught in the dilemma which he had over-simplified in *The Emancipated*. He takes away from Italy memories which will sustain him in what he feels to be the hostile environment of the modern world, but this nostalgia is only a palliative. It provides a dream-world in which to gain from time to time the illusion of escape from the harsh world of reality, but whose very elusiveness is likely simply to intensify one's feeling of the abrasive frustration of that world. Once again, Italy has revealed something of her charms to an adorer only so that he will miss her the more painfully when he has to leave her.

(As if to underline this frustration, Gissing's historical novel, *Veranilda*, published in 1904, inspired by his last visit to Italy, remained unfinished at his death. It is a complex and insignificant fragment of a story set in sixth century Rome.)

FREDERICK ROLFE 'BARON CORVO' (1860–1913)

No-one's work illustrates more harrowingly than Corvo's the recurrent Italian theme of Italy giving her admirers privileged and exalted moments only in order to be able the more viciously to strike them down afterwards.

Corvo's first Italian works were the idyllic Toto stories, which began to appear in *The Yellow Book* in 1895 and were collected as

Stories Toto Told Me (1898) and *In His Own Image* (1901). These offered a delightful new version of Italian life. Most of the characters are religious, either priests or saints in heaven, and Toto tells of their amusing little quarrels: the rivalry of the Jesuits (who always come off worse) with the other Orders, and the squabbles of the saints, which are frequently settled by the intervention of a benign, paternal figure of God. The stories are narrated in a naïf, childish manner, with abundant monosyllables, and the English occasionally retains an attractive Italian turn of phrase to give a pleasant impression of spontaneous translation:

> Last night, when he had held her in his arms, he told her that he knew she wished him well.[16]

The effect is altogether charming, recalling somewhat the primitive representation of religious legend in the early Italian painters, and giving a very different, and more sympathetic, view of Italian attitudes to religion than had usually been the case before.

Toto himself was,

> sixteen years old, a splendid, wild (*discolo*) creature, from the Abruzzi, a figure like Cellini's Perseus, skin brown, with real red blood under it, smooth as a peach, and noble as a god.[17]

The description recalls Symonds' admiration of the Italian peasant; and Corvo is, of course, with Oscar Wilde (whose letters from Rome in 1900 are explicitly pederastic), the most notorious of Symonds' homosexual successors in Italy. In the next stage of his Italian work, more colourful and less serene than the Toto period, Corvo entered Symonds' own province, the Renaissance. Like Butler and Gissing, Corvo had suffered in England, and looked for some sort of compensation in Italy. In Britain he felt persecuted by the Roman Catholic Church's treatment of him, particularly by its refusal to recognise his vocation, and was obviously made something of a social outsider by his homosexuality. He felt that contemporary England stifled his personal development, which would have been encouraged and flourished in Renaissance Italy.

His first Renaissance writing was the incomplete *Chronicles of The House of Borgia* (1901), abandoned and disowned by Corvo after disagreements with his publisher. Its best chapter, on *The Legend of The Borgia Venom*, displays not only an intimate knowledge of the period, but an immense fascination with the intricacies of the Renaissance search for a super-poison: the constant implication is that an age which could devote so much effort and ingenuity to such immoral and exhilarating activity offered a scope to the individual talent which made it a far more worthwhile time in which to live than later centuries had become. This feeling led to Corvo's two major attempts at recreating the atmosphere of so eminently attractive a period, in *Don Renato. An Ideal Content*, written about 1902 though not published until 1963, and *Don Tarquinio. A Kataleptic, Phantasmatic Romance* (1905). Though it had remained unpublished, and Corvo was apparently unaware of it, these books are effectively sophisticated developments of Swinburne's *Tebaldeo Tebaldei*. Like that work, their major literary debt seems to be to Browning[18]: they are extended dramatic monologues in prose. They are supposedly translations, into a deliciously rich English style, of two sixteenth century macaronic manuscripts: *Don Renato* is presented as the diary of a priest-cum-tutor-cum-apothecary in a princely Roman household in 1528–30, while *Don Tarquinio* poses as a manuscript written in 1523–7 to describe a crucial day in the author's life in 1495, so that his son shall know what life was really like at Rome at that time, and not be deceived by the ignorant calumnies of the Florentines, Guicciardini and Giovio. Corvo's constant emphasis in manufacturing these documents is on the beauty of the age – in its art, its literary style, the beauty of its women and young men, and of their clothes, and the fascination of its science, its occult arts, and of the intricacies of its religious ritual and Machiavellian statecraft. It is, of course, a violent age, but the element of danger, in the luscious day-dream that these two works constitute, only adds to its excitement: and at the very worst it is only a small price to pay for the freedom and exhilaration of living in an age where individual excellence was the supreme virtue, allowed to shine untarnished by the corrosive mediocrity which seemed to Corvo responsible for the drabness of his own day.

It was, however, only a dream. Corvo was inevitably condemned to live in his own century, and no-one was really going to come along and offer him the chance of becoming Pope Hadrian the Seventh: and even in that other day-dream, his fictitious Pope's attempt at splendid individualism in the modern world ends in the defeat of assassination. The beauty of Renaissance Italy offered Corvo his most powerful image of how magnificent life could be in the right conditions; and his experiences in Venice were to give him his most violent image of the horror of having to carry this vision of earthly paradise through an inferno of suffering.

Corvo went to Venice in 1908, and apparently in the following year wrote most of *The Desire and Pursuit of The Whole. A Romance of Modern Venice.* The hero of the strongly autobiographical novel is the unrecognised genius, Nicholas Crabbe. Very short of money as a result of having had manuscripts stolen from him by 'friends' in England, he is appalled by the hideous and patronising nature of the English colony at Venice; at first, he cannot believe that 'such specimens actually survived outside Ouida's *Friendship* and *In A Winter City.*'[19] When he becomes quite penniless he does everything possible to keep up appearances so that these awful people cannot gloat over his misery. He sleeps in a little open boat on the lagoon, or wanders the back alleys of Venice, hiding away as much as he can, and then putting in an appearance at the Bucintoro Boat Club, or in full pomp on the Grand Canal, in order to mystify his enemies. The atmosphere of Venice is totally integrated into the texture of the novel. The city is the perfect setting for Crabbe's sufferings. Others might provide the contrast between the superficial glamour of cosmopolitan society and the squalor to which Crabbe retreats to hide his anguish and his hunger, but no other city offers also the potent image of his pulling away in his little boat to suffer his lonely days and nights amid the desolation of the most deserted parts of the lagoon. No image of the artist starving in his garret is as moving as that of Crabbe drifting on the lagoon, refusing to accept defeat; it is the profoundest cri de coeur of neglected genius and the most harrowing, and most powerfully creative, of all pictures of Venice.

There is a redeeming life-principle in the novel, however. After an earthquake in Calabria Crabbe had rescued a young orphaned girl, Zilda, who, dressed as a boy, becomes his gondolier in Venice. Crabbe tries to prevent himself from falling in love with her, because of his guardian–like relationship with her. But when he finally collapses she tends him back to health and he discovers that she has always been watching over him in his wanderings. They declare their mutual love, and go off to be married; and so, ends the novel, 'So the Desire and Pursuit of The Whole was crowned and rewarded by Love.'[20] It is a fine ending to the novel: it would have been so easy to end in utter pathos, or in a Rastignac–like defiance of the world; by contrast, the serenity of the ending is somehow deeply satisfying.

The termination of Corvo's own life in Venice was rather less serene. In abject poverty and isolation, he lived out Crabbe's worst sufferings. In March, 1910 he was living on the beach at the Lido; in October, 1911 he lived in an old boat on the lagoon, until it began to sink:

> If I stay out on the lagoon, the boat will sink, I shall swim perhaps for a few hours, and then I shall be eaten alive by crabs. At low water every mudbank swarms with them. If I stay anchored near an island, I must keep continually awake: for, the moment I cease moving, I am invaded by swarms of swimming rats, who in the winter are so voracious that they attack even man who is motionless. I have tried it. And have been bitten.[21]

Corvo had no Zilda, and, penniless, could find no human contact beyond the extreme fringes of the sordid world of Venetian homosexual prostitution, which has given notoriety to his *Venice Letters*.[22] Their pederastic descriptions should be read in conjunction with passages like that quoted above, and with his *Blackwood's* article *On Cascading Into The Canal*,[23] an hilarious account of how he delighted a quayside audience by behaving with the most exaggerated English sang froid when he fell into a canal and came to the surface again still smoking his pipe. If the letters are to be regarded as shocking, it should not be for any intrinsic qualities, but for the cruelty of a life which reduces a man of Corvo's sensitivity and creativity to so abysmal an existence. The humour of the magazine article, evidence that his spirit was not shattered by such suffering, seems only to make the cruelty more hideous.

In the last year of his life Corvo became a little better off, and could afford the luxury of an hotel room, where he was found dead in October, 1913. The previous year, Thomas Mann had published *Death In Venice*; for the real, as for the fictional, death, Venice provided an incomparably moving setting, the magnificence of the city contrasting poignantly with the suffering of the individual, while its inexorable decay and its fragile position between sea and sky provide suggestive analogues of the human condition.

E. M. FORSTER (1879–1970)

Corvo's creative response to Italy was very little known by his contemporaries. Far better known were the 'Italian' works of E. M. Forster and Norman Douglas.

Forster found in Italy ideal material for his recurrent theme of the confrontation of the civilised, sophisticated northener and the enduring presence in more elemental ways of life (whether in the Mediterranean or in India makes no substantial difference) of deep and passionate forces which are an essential part of the total experience of life, but which are not only lacking in the advanced and self-conscious society, but threaten, whenever given the chance, to devastate its very fabric. It is basically the same problem that had concerned James, but Forster approaches it in a different way. Where James had analysed the acute and subtle pain felt in facing this dilemma by the highly developed sensibilities of his heroes, Forster looks at the effects which Italy can have on the social attitudes of the English upper-middle classes.

Forster's two earliest stories, *The Story of A Panic*, written in 1902, and *Albergo Empedocle* (1903), are both set in southern Italy. In each the major set of characters is a group of English tourists, amusingly satirised for the conventional superficiality of their attitudes to Italy, and their general ignorance of what they are seeing and inability to take anything of very deep value from their experience of the south. But in each party there is one member who does respond deeply to the spirit of place: the boy Eustace in *The Story of A Panic*, who, on the hillside above Ravello, becomes a worshipper of Pan, unable any longer to endure the stifling confines of social life and behaviour; and in *Albergo Empedocle* the young man who, at Girgenti, becomes seized by the idea that he has formerly been a citizen of the ancient Greek city, and has to be repatriated to a lunatic asylum. In both cases, although the people involved, by the violence of their feelings, are made exiles from society, there is something in their new-found passion which is presented as healthy and attractive. The problem, which Forster's two Italian novels investigate, is how to create a fruitful, and not a destructive, relationship between these deep passions and the existing conditions of English life.

The central movement of *A Room With A View*, the first written of the novels (published 1908), is Lucy Honeychurch's escape from the confinement of her English upper-middle class upbringing into a freer and fuller life, represented by her eventual marriage to the unconventional figure of George Emerson. Italy plays a major role in bringing this about. On her first arrival there, as a tourist in Florence, Lucy's total dependence on the standards of social convention is splendidly presented when she finds herself alone in

Santa Croce, without either guide or guide-book:

> Of course, it must be a wonderful building. But how like a barn!
> And how very cold! Of course, it contained frescoes by Giotto, in
> the presence of whose tactile values she was capable of feeling
> what was proper. But who was to tell her which they were? She
> walked about disdainfully, unwilling to be enthusiastic over
> monuments of uncertain authorship or date. There was no one
> even to tell her which, of all the sepulchral slabs that paved the
> nave and transepts, was the one that was really beautiful, the one
> that had been most praised by Mr Ruskin. (ed. 1908, p. 30)

But as she comes to respond ever more spontaneously to the
stimulus of the Italian environment she discovers another Italy,
which lies beyond the banalities of the guide-books, and in
discovering which she begins to discover herself. Italy gives her
intuitions of the vigour of the pulse of life such as she, in her sheltered
existence, has never suspected before. Even more, Italy seems
almost in a personal way to be pushing her into closer relationship
with George Emerson: in the crucial scene where he first kisses her as
she suddenly and radiantly appears before him on a Tuscan hillside,
it is through the inspired misunderstanding of an Italian coachman
that she has been brought to the spot, a spot which seemed 'the well-
head, the primal source whence beauty gushed out to water the
earth.' (p. 104) The genius loci has an effect on Lucy's life similar in
kind to those in the two short stories, though less intense and thus
capable of more constructive integration into her life. Although at
first the break from her background is too great for her to make, and
she returns to England and becomes engaged to a conventionally
suitable fiancé, when she realises that by contrast with her
experiences in Italy life with him would be terribly restricted she
ends the engagement, marries Emerson, and returns with him to
Florence. The beauty and vitality of Italy have provided the
essential catalyst in her escape to a fuller life. It is one of those rare
occasions when the influence of Italy on the lives of fictional
characters appears to be entirely beneficent. But the novel has the
same limitation as Gissing's *The Emancipated*. Lucy's experience of
Italy, though sufficient to liberate her from her narrow prejudices, is
still only superficial. It is an almost mystical affair, based on
occasional privileged moments of insight, and not on any real
contact with Italian life, which is where the real contrast with the

English bourgeois way of life was to be found. This was the problem which Forster went on to study in *Where Angels Fear To Tread* (1905).

The contrast is between the well-off English suburban life of Sawston and the Tuscan hill-town of Monteriano. In Monteriano there is an atmosphere of beauty, while Sawston is drab; its inhabitants act spontaneously out of warm passion, while in Sawston actions are dictated not by feeling, but by an elaborate system of considerations as to what becomes one's social standing. In Monteriano, in a way that is not true of Sawston, 'so many things have happened. . . people have lived so hard and splendidly.' (ed. 1905, p. 167) In fact, in Monteriano one seems constantly in touch with an elemental life which has been etiolated to the point of disappearance in the process of elaborating the sophisticated social code of Sawston.

Lilia Herriton, who feels her own vitality being whittled away by the frustrating enforced pettiness of Sawston, believes that she has found a way of escaping into a fuller life when she falls in love with Gino, the son of the Monteriano dentist. But the story of her marriage seriously questions whether such escape is possible. She is appalled at being treated as an Italian wife: at not being allowed to take walks alone, and not being able to give little English-style tea-parties in her home. Her dreams are all shattered, and she is far more unhappy in Monteriano than she had ever been in Sawston. She learns too late that she cannot attain that apparent sensual fulfilment which she admires in Italian life and desires for herself, without making the psychologically impossible total sacrifice of her Englishness. The impossibility of successfully bridging the rift between north and south is underlined by her death in childbirth and the death of her baby in an accident when her English relatives try to take him from his father to be brought up in Sawston. Nothing fruitful, it would seem, can come out of the interaction of England and Italy.

The other two English characters most involved with Gino are Lilia's brother-in-law Philip and her friend Caroline. Philip is at first presented as an enthusiastic Italophile, but the prospect of being in any way related to an inhabitant of Monteriano is intolerable to him. Gino appears to him as a vile seducer, and Italy loses all her charm:

Italy, the land of beauty, was ruined for him. She had no power to change men and things who dwelt in her. She, too, could produce avarice, brutality, stupidity – and, what was worse, vulgarity. It was on her soil and through her influence that a silly woman had married a cad. (pp. 118–9)

The extreme superficiality of his previous enthusiasm for Italy is evident from the terms in which he revolts against the country; so that when he is won back to admiration for Italy through the experience of Gino's animal-like reaction to the death of his son, one has no reason to hope that Philip will get anything more profoundly important out of Italy than he had in the past. He is essentially a dilettante; and when Caroline Abbott, the do-gooding English spinster, falls in love with Gino, one may admire the characteristic Forsterian imitation of reality by having the utterly improbable erupt into his novel, but one can scarcely imagine that she will be the model to show English civilisation how it can successfully re-establish contact with elemental humanity.

Thus, as for James, the confrontation of the Anglo-Saxon with Italy is for Forster a re-enactment of the Romantic dilemma. Italy represents life-forces which are felt to be essential to a full flowering of the human potential, but which, by the time a sophisticated society has reached the point of yearning for them, have already been irretrievably lost in the very process of sophistication. The most that can be hoped for is to gain a degree of liberation through fortunate contact with the atmosphere of Italy, as in *A Room With A View*; any attempt to go deeper will be devastating, not liberating.

NORMAN DOUGLAS (1868–1952)

To Norman Douglas things seemed easier. He had, it is true, anticipated Forster's concern with the destructively violent effects of the primal forces of Italy, in his early short story *Nerinda*, in *Unprofessional Tales* (1901), whose hero falls in love with a plaster cast in the Pompeii museum of a girl whose body had been found preserved in the lava. His infatuated belief that he can bring her back to life leads him to madness, murder and suicide. This early story, however, is exceptional in Douglas's 'Italian' writing.

For the most part, Douglas, living on Capri and sensitively enjoying his surroundings, realised something of that existence which to Gissing had been an unattainable dream; and from this privileged existence in the south, the message which he constantly sent out to his readers in England was that Italy could have an immediate and vital relevance to their own lives, and that they should attempt to profit from it by opening themselves to the life-enhancing forces of the Mediterranean:

> Many of us would do well to *mediterraneanize* ourselves for a season, to quicken those ethic roots from which has sprung so much of what is best in our natures.[24]

What, he felt, the Mediterranean heritage offered above all to the Englishman was a ready acceptance and enjoyment of life: his characterisation of Santa Serafina represents the opposite attitude, which she shares with the English Protestant tradition:

> She is the very embodiment of what the Hellenic spirit was *not*: its very antithesis. Earthly existence she held to be an illusion; the world was death; the body a sinful load which must be tortured and vexed in preparation for the real life – the life beyond the grave. To those Greeks, the human frame was a subtle instrument to be kept lovingly in tune with the loud-voiced melodies of earth and sky and sea; these were the realities; as for a life beyond, let the gods see to it – a shadowy, half-hearted business, at best.[25]

Siren Land (1911) and *Old Calabria* (1915) set out to help the reader attain something of the wisdom of the Mediterranean view of life. Douglas's evocations of the extreme attractiveness of southern Italy, where 'an ancient world, our ancient world, lies spread out in rare charm of colour and outline, and every footstep is fraught with memories',[26] must surely make the reader long to be among the landscapes he is describing. The fact of such longing is a recognition of a lack in the English environment of something felt to be richly desirable; and Douglas, implicitly in the travel books and by demonstration in *South Wind* (1917), believes it to be possible for the Anglo-Saxon to take deeply valuable nourishment from the south. In *South Wind* the Anglican Bishop of Bampopo's fortnight on the island of Nepenthe (evidently, though ostensibly not, Capri) destroys all his narrow English prejudices, and constitutes an initiation into the pagan acceptance of the full richness of life. As in *The Marble Faun*, the development of the novel centres around the hero's accidentally witnessing a man's being pushed to his death; but in Douglas's novel there is no moral anguish or sense of incrimination. When the Bishop sees his cousin push her blackmailing first husband from a cliff his initial sense of shock, which a few days earlier would have been profoundly disturbing to his whole moral system, rapidly gives way to an appreciation of the eminent reasonableness of an action which quietly rids the world of an utter scoundrel. He goes to England to settle his affairs, determined no longer to be an active member of the Church of England, and to return to Nepenthe in the autumn for the vintage. The island has opened up new areas of human experience for him, unencumbered by the narrow conventional orthodoxy which has hitherto restricted his responses to life.

The problem, however, lies in the nature of the cosmopolitan society he intends to return to on Nepenthe. For Douglas has splendidly satirised the inhabitants of the island. (Satire which found an hilarious sequel in Compton Mackenzie's *Vestal Fire*, 1927.) They are, indeed, all released from any moral inhibitions, and most of them are basically good and attractive people. But their cynical, alcoholic, calculating, gossiping society is scarcely a good advertisement for the beneficent influence of the south; and it is the brilliance of their presentation, rather than the conversion of the Bishop, which forms the strength of the novel. In the company of such people one can hardly believe that the Bishop's future on the island will not be one of degeneration, rather than of fulfilment. Much as with *The Emancipated* and *A Room With A View*, however much one might wish that the novel's optimism were justified, one cannot but feel that James's account of the problem comes much nearer the truth.

However, if readers of the novel when it appeared during the first world war had any such doubts about the validity of Douglas's message, they were currently offered a more vigorous and questioning response to the vitalising potential of Italy in the work of D. H. Lawrence.

14 D. H. Lawrence

Lawrence first went to Italy in September, 1912, to Lake Garda, where he and Frieda stayed until April of the following year. As soon as he arrives there, his letters are full of enthusiasm for the beauty of the landscape and the sympathetic ambiance of the peasants. It is the beginning of an attachment to Italy which lasted throughout his life, surviving his annoyance with the Italian habit after the first world war of blaming every Englishman personally for the problems of the exchange rate, and taking him back to Italy again and again, even despite his dislike of Italian food. It was to Italy that Lawrence went as soon as he could get away from England after the war, and of the last ten years of his life four were spent in Italy – a remarkable amount when one considers that those ten years included his journeys to Ceylon, Australia and North America. Of the same period he spent something less than six months in England.

Lawrence's experience of Italy was deeply important to his thought and writing. It was his first contact with the south, during the stay on Lake Garda, which brought him consciously to realise and fully work out what was to become his central belief in the concept of blood consciousness, of the need for men to escape from the domination of mind and of ideas and to put their mental faculties into healthy relation with the full force of the deep feelings and movements of their bodies. Such ideas had been nascent in Lawrence's mind before he left England. W. E. Hopkins recalls his his having talked of 'dark powers' at the time of writing *The Peacock*.[1] In the novel itself the passage on the warm contact of Cyril and George's flesh is related to this feeling; and in Chapter 4 of *The Trespasser* he describes Siegmund's blood as being 'alive and conscious'. But the first developed statement of the belief is in a letter written from Gargnano, the village on Lake Garda where he and Frieda were staying, on January 17th, 1913. Its first sentence is well known; but a more extensive quotation is revealing:

My great religion is a belief in the blood, the flesh, as being wiser than the intellect. We can go wrong in our minds. But what our blood feels and believes and says, is always true. The intellect is only a bit and a bridle. What do I care about knowledge. All I want is to answer to my blood, direct, without fribbling intervention of mind, or moral, or what-not. I conceive a man's body as a kind of flame, like a candle flame, forever upright and yet flowing: and the intellect is just the light that is shed on to the things around – which is really mind – but with the mystery of the flame forever flowing, coming God knows how from out of practically nowhere, and being *itself*, whatever there is around it, that it lights up. We have got so ridiculously mindful, that we never know that we ourselves are anything – we think there are only the objects which we shine upon. And there the poor flame goes on burning ignored, to produce this light. And instead of chasing the mystery in the fugitive, half-lighted things outside us, we ought to look at ourselves, and say 'My God, I am myself!' That's why I like to live in Italy. The people are so unconscious. They only feel and want, they don't know. We know too much. No, we only *think* we know such a lot.[2]

In this first recorded exposition of his fundamental belief Lawrence explicitly relates it to the life of the Italian peasants, in contrast with the way people live in England. In contact with the life of Gargnano his earlier vague notions have grown into fully formulated ideas. The development is seen taking place in *Twilight In Italy*.

Twilight In Italy has received far less attention that it deserves. It seems generally to be regarded as merely an attractive travel book; and, indeed, it is extremely attractive in its descriptions of life in the Tyrol and on the shores of Lake Garda – which was at that time still part of Austria, but of whose Italianness Lawrence was in no doubt: 'Riva is still Austria, but as Italian as an ice-cream man,' he wrote to one of his friends.[3] But, more than that, *Twilight* is the first, and remains the clearest, extended argument of Lawrence's dominant beliefs. The book falls into two parts, the first four chapters being directed to this exposition of his credo, while the rest is on the lesser level of charmingly written anecdote.

Versions of the first four essays had appeared as journalism in 1913, and in these earlier versions they too are more simply descriptive, with little of the prophetic writing which characterises their final form. But there seems every reason to believe that they were essentially completed in this final form during the stay at Gargnano. That the ideas they expound were formed in Lawrence's mind at that time is clear from the letter quoted above; and his narration in *Twilight* of the way in which the forceful expression of these ideas is stimulated by things that strike him in the casual events of his life at Gargnano is so vivid that it is difficult not to believe that the events he describes did indeed provide the foci of his thinking. That he does not offer his deepest insights in the first published versions of the essays is hardly surprising, since they would have made, at that early stage of his career, much less suitable material for freelance journalism than the slighter sketches which he actually published; and in a comment in a letter of 1913 – 'Frieda abused my articles in the *English* but I think they are all right for magazine stuff'[4] – one senses a feeling that he had deliberately written his material down for journalistic purposes. He worked on the book in 1915 before submitting it for publication, but in the absence of any documentation of what he actually wrote then, internal evidence suggests that it was a matter of adding to the already completed argument of the first four essays a few lighter pieces to make it up to book length. The first of these, *San Gaudenzio*, is also the first in which he mentions the war; and it is noticeable that the war, which shocked him deeply, is not mentioned in his panoramic account of European history in the third essay, *The Lemon Gardens*, an omission which suggests that the essay was not very extensively retouched in 1915. Indeed, everything in the book indicates that the profoundly important ideas it contains are directly the result of his first visit to Italy, and that events between that visit and the book's publication in 1916 (his uneasy contact with the Cambridge-Bloomsbury group, and the shock of the war) had little effect on its writing. This emerges most clearly from the inter-action of narrative and argument in the first four essays.

In the first, *The Crucifix Across The Mountains*, Lawrence crosses the Tyrol from Bavaria to northern Italy. Amongst the Tyrolean peasants he recognises something he can take as an ideal. They do not suffer from the malaise of exalting the mind and denying their bodies. On the contrary,

Everything is of the blood, of the senses. There is no mind. The mind is a suffusion of physical heat, it is not separated, it is kept submerged. (p. 12)[5]

This earliest is also the clearest and most succinct of Lawrence's repeated formulations of the ideal relationship of mind and body. The strong pulse of life in these peasants is emphasised by the contrast with the stillness and coldness of the snow on the mountains above:

> Beneath is life, the hot jet of the blood playing elaborately. But above is the radiance of changeless not-being. (p. 12)

Into this stark red and white contrast between life and negation comes the dark, shadowy presence over the land of the crucifixes along the road, bringing a feeling of deep religious significance and tradition into the perennial struggle of man and the antagonistic elements. Lawrence does not explore at all deeply the nature of this religious significance – it is sufficient that he makes its presence so powerfully felt. Sufficient, that is, to make a vivid implicit contrast with the effeteness of English religion, which he frequently deplored in later writing. In the original version of the essay, *Christs in The Tyrol*, he makes the contrast explicit by wondering 'why in England one always sees this pale, pitiful Christ with no 'go' in him.'[6] As he approaches Italy he is already using the life he sees around him as an exhortation to his countrymen to open their lives to deeper levels of experience. The description of a fallen crucifix which ends the essay is a symbolic renunciation of Lawrence's past as he prepares to meet the influence of pagan Italy.

The Italian part of the book begins with *The Spinner and The Monks*, the most impressive of the essays. From the crucifixes of the first essay Lawrence goes on to discuss the difference between the two aspects of the Holy Spirit, represented by the two types of church – the shy and hidden churches of the Dove and the proud, imperious churches of the Eagle. ('There are, moreover, the Churches which do not belong to the Holy Spirit at all, but which are built to pure fancy and logic; such as the Wren Churches in London.' (p. 25)) In the essay the spinner is the embodiment of the spirit of the eagle:

> There was the slight motion of the eagle in her turning to look at me, a faint gleam of rapt light in her eyes (p. 30)

and the monks represent the dove.

Lawrence's meeting with the old woman spinning in front of San

Tommaso – a church of the Eagle – is beautifully described. He is fascinated by her eyes:

> Her eyes were clear as the sky, blue, empyrean, transcendent . . . like the visible heavens, unthinking, or like two flowers that are open in pure clear unconsciousness . . . like the first morning of the world, so ageless. (pp. 29–32)

What he sees in her eyes, in her attitude as she works, and chatters in incomprehensible dialect, is her utter self-sufficiency, the wholeness with which she is herself:

> Her world was clear and absolute, without consciousness of self. She was not self-conscious, because she was not aware that there was anything in the universe except *her* universe. In her universe I was a stranger, a foreign *signore*. That I had a world of my own, other than her own, was not conceived by her. She did not care . . . She knew that I was an inhabitant of lands which she had never seen. But what of that! There were parts of her own body which she had never seen, which physiologically she could never see. They were none the less her own because she had never seen them. The lands she had not seen were corporate parts of her own living body, the knowledge she had not attained was only the hidden knowledge of her own self. (pp. 30–1)

Her presence is so over-powering, so perfectly self-contained, that Lawrence runs away from it and goes to pick flowers. The gathering of primroses and evocation of the casual sights and sounds of the Saturday afternoon provide an effective and attractive transition to the contrast with the old woman, the two monks whom Lawrence sees walking in the twilight of a monastery garden below him. As the shadows of the mountains lengthen and the snow glows in the setting sun the monks walk and talk in their garden, 'backwards and forwards, backwards and forwards, in the neutral, shadowless light of shadow.' They are a feeble but dangerous neutrality, 'the flesh neutralizing the spirit, the spirit neutralizing the flesh.' In them spirit and flesh have cancelled each other out, instead of fusing into the ideal of vital wholeness, 'light fused in darkness and darkness fused in light, as in the rosy snow above the twilight.' (p. 36) Lawrence gathers a few more flowers and returns to the village in the early moonlit night. The old woman is gone. She is too entirely a creature of the sun of know anything about the moon. Now, in the moonlight, Lawrence can place her. She is limited by the entirety of her self-sufficiency:

> She did not know the yielding up of the senses and the possession of the unknown, through the senses, which happens under a superb moon. (p. 37)

The human fulfilment which Lawrence strives for is a fusion of apparent contrasts, a 'transcendent knowledge in our hearts, uniting sun and darkness, day and night, spirit and senses.' (p. 38) The old spinner is so completely herself, 'whole even in her partiality,' (p. 31) that she cannot surrender to, and fuse with, the not-herself. The monks abnegate, and do not fuse, the two within themselves. But what we must try to achieve, says Lawrence, is the consummation of the two, where both are perfect, and which is 'beyond the range of loneliness or solitude.' (p. 38)

To achieve this is, of course, a matter for individuals themselves. In the next essay, *The Lemon Gardens*, Lawrence expands the argument to show how the individual crisis has developed within the historical context and to examine the historical situation at the time when he was writing. He presents the argument in the way he masters so effectively in these essays: the generalisations are always developed from and kept closely related to particular events in his life at Gargnano, which are themselves presented with great vividness. He starts with an amusing account of his being called to the rescue of one of the local minor gentry, Signor di Paoli, whose American patent door-spring has been wrongly fixed to the door and causes it to fly open instead of to shut. This trivial incident, with its assumption that the northener would know how to make things work, leads smoothly into a finely written account of the different development of northern and southern Europe since the Renaissance. It is not meant to be a comprehensive historical survey, and leaves much out of account. But Lawrence seizes the outlines which interest him within the terms of the book's argument and develops them compellingly. He sees the Renaissance as a celebration of the flesh in contrast with the medieval striving for spirituality. The Italian attitude to life is still that of the Renaissance, regarding the flesh as divine and worshipping sensation. 'The mind, all the time, subserves the senses.' (p. 42) The dark force of the body triumphs over the light of the intellect, and becomes itself a shining light. Botticelli's Venus, 'queen of the senses' (p. 41), is its emblem. It is, he says, the spirit of Blake's tiger, 'burning bright'. To the Italian, his senses are arrogant, absolute; what is not himself is nothing: it is what we have seen vividly in the old spinning woman.

This is one way of achieving an infinite, but there is another. Since the Renaissance the south has worshipped the self, the flesh, but the north has renounced these associations of the Father and followed Christ the Son to a belief in selflessness. This has fostered science and technology – the analysis of the world outside the self, and the creation of power in that outside world.

> This selfless God is He who works for all alike, without consideration. And His image is the machine which dominates and cows us, we cower before it, we run to serve it. For it works for all humanity alike. (p. 48)

So now, when men of the north want to be tigers, they can't, for they are servants of the machine. The one cannot embrace the other. At this point Lawrence gives his reader a pause for breath after this remarkable tour de force. But though the tone changes from exhilaration to humour the argument is still being pursued. His account of his adjustment of the door-spring and the joy with which di Paoli and his wife greet his success in making the door shut with a bang provides both a delightfully funny picture of the contrast between north and south which Lawrence has just been talking about in such large terms and a smooth transition to the next stage in the argument.

Lawrence describes di Paoli's shame at being childless when he sees his wife playing with her young nephew. This suggests to Lawrence that the fascination of Italy for the English is that

> To the Italian the phallus is the symbol of individual creative immortality, to each man his own Godhead. (p. 51)

That is why, he says, an Englishman always feels physically inferior beside an Italian; but he also feels superior, because we have used science to try to seek out the real Godhead and try to perfect humanity.

But we have exhausted ourselves in the process. We have found great treasures, and we are now impotent to use them . . . Continuing in the old, splendid will for a perfect selfless humanity, we have become inhuman and unable to help ourselves, we are but attributes of the great mechanized society we have created on our way to perfection. (pp, 52–3)

Through his contact with the south, Lawrence is able to articulate in terms of an historical vision the sense of loss in modern England which lay behind the English interest in Italy which we have been studying. There are two infinites, and a man must know them both – physical fulfilment and spiritual ecstacy. These are Father and Son; man must be the Holy Ghost, fusing them together in himself, assuming the power of each without becoming the slave of either. The re-introduction of the image of the Holy Ghost, referring back to the first paragraph of *The Spinner and The Monks*, neatly marks the completion of this stage of the argument.

Fittingly, the tone of the essay is again relaxed at this point, and Lawrence gives an attractive account of a conducted tour of Signor di Paoli's lemon gardens. But still the argument is being pursued. The English, Lawrence claims, have lost contact with both infinites. The Italians, at least, still have one, represented by the spinner, and they still have not spoilt the humanised beauty of their landscape. But now these too are threatened. Di Paoli wants to introduce machinery, both so as to make more money and for the superficial exhilaration of the ego which comes from controlling machines. 'But he is too old. It remains for the young Italian to embrace his mistress, the machine.' (p. 60) The essay ends with Lawrence sitting amid the peace and beauty of Lake Garda, unchanged since the days of Goethe, who had described the scene in terms almost identical to Lawrence's, now itself threatened by the modern industrial blight, seeing an apocalyptic vision of the squalor of an England destroying itself by its industry and infecting and destroying the whole world, unless – and the possibility is seen as slight – the English might stop in time and find a saner way forward.

The next essay, *The Theatre*, though it is vivid and amusing, is less significant than these two. It mostly repeats the same ideas, apart from a brief pasage on Lawrence's concept of marriage as a sex-duel, which had already been expounded in the novels, and an account of *Hamlet* as a representative tragedy of its time, a tragedy of the convulsed reaction of mind away from flesh, an argument which he took up much more successfully in his *Introduction* to his paintings in 1929. The rest of *Twilight* is more simply anecdotal and descriptive than the first part and, though always interesting, cannot command the same amount of attention here. The book ends fittingly in Milan, the most 'advanced' industrial city in Italy, where, because of the vitality Lawrence sees in the Italian tradition, there is something vigorous in the industrialism,

> But always there was the same purpose stinking in it all, the mechanizing, the perfect mechanizing of human life. (p. 175)

In *Twilight in Italy*, one sees how much Lawrence's characteristic beliefs owed to his initial contact with rural Italian life and his contrasting of it with the life he knew in England. As one would expect, these developments are also evident in the fiction of the period. At Gargnano Lawrence finished *Sons and Lovers* and began *The Rainbow*. That is, he changes from writing about things he has lived through and mastered to using the novel as a means of exploring the possibilities of experience. In *The Rainbow* he begins to use the imagery of blood and darkness he has forged in *Twilight*. The Brangwen men have a 'blood-intimacy' with their work on the land. The tiger image referred to above recurs in the novel:

> He burned up, he caught fire and became splendid, royal, something like a tiger. (p. 444)

The aspirations of the Brangwen women for their children are remarkably similar to those of Maria Fiori in *Twilight*:[8]

> She did not want her sons to be peasants, fixed and static as posts driven in the earth. She wanted them to be in the great flux of life in the midst of all possibilities. (*Twilight*, p. 94)

> Why must they remain obscured and stifled all their lives, why should they suffer from lack of freedom to move? How should they learn the entry into the finer, more vivid circle of life? (*Rainbow*, p. 10)

The Rainbow has a strong new emphasis on the ugliness of industrial England: Lawrence is beginning to put into fiction the vision of squalor he had conceived in the lemon garden. In *Women in Love*, for the first time in the novels, England is seen from abroad, in one of the conversations in the Tyrol, and the general feeling is that unless the country soon sees the Lawrentian light it is doomed to eternal morbidity. In the face of the horrors of industrialism both these novels are largely concerned with the possibilities and difficulties of achieving satisfactory human relationships within the terms worked out in *Twilight in Italy*. They are an imaginative testing against the realities of English life of the values that have matured in his mind through living in the less complex and less sophisticated society of Gargnano.

In the next two novels, Lawrence works with characters who find some kind of redemption from English life by escaping to Italy. Unfortunately, neither is a great and convincing novel, but both have details which illustrate Lawrence's feelings about Italy at the beginning of the 'twenties, by which time he was living in Sicily. In *The Lost Girl*, Alvina Houghton tries to achieve sexual fulfilment by escaping the industrial grimness of Woodhouse with the Italian showman Cicio, who eventually takes her to Italy. As they leave England they watch the corpse-grey cliffs disappearing, 'like a long ash-grey coffin slowly submerging' (p. 347). This became Lawrence's standard image for the English coast, which recurs in *Kangaroo*, *The Virgin and The Gipsy* and *On Coming Home*. The contrast here is with the beauty of the south; for example, as the train runs in the darkness down the Ligurian coast,

> tripping on the edge of the Mediterranean, round bays and between dark rocks and under castles, a night-time fairy-land, for hours. She watched spellbound by the magic of the world itself. And she thought to herself: 'Whatever life may be, and whatever horror men may have made of it, the world is a lovely place, a magic place, something to marvel over. The world is an amazing place. (p. 353)

Disillusion soon comes, however, when she meets the reality of life in Cicio's village in the Abruzzi and discovers the savage bitterness of personal relationships beneath the apparently idyllic surface of peasant life, and realises that Cicio has nothing of the English sense of domesticity; the centre of his life is not the home but the Piazza. Remembering the lesson of Forster's Lilia Herriton, there seems little hope of Alvina's achieving the fulfilment she had sought when, at the end of the novel, she is left alone and pregnant in this alien environment when Cicio goes off to the war.

In fact, having suggested in his earlier work that some hope, however slight, for England lay in Italy, by the early 'twenties Lawrence had become thoroughly pessimistic. He felt that the war had destroyed something in the Italians, had made them mean: the prediction of *The Lemon Gardens* was coming true. In *Aaron's Rod* (1922), Aaron feels that Italy has become 'as idea-bound and as automatic as England: just a business proposition,' (p. 184) and although, indeed, Aaron attains a Lawrentian philosophy through his experience in Italy, the Lawrence-figure Lilly who guides him to it feels a need to get away:

> I would very much like to try life in another continent, among another race. I feel Europe becoming like a cage to me. (p. 337)

In *Sea and Sardinia* (1921), the most straightforward and least interesting of his Italian travel books, Lawrence feels that only in Sardinia does there remain something of the fine manliness, the 'fierce singleness,' (p. 69) which he had earlier admired in the mainland Italian peasants, but which he thought they had now lost; and in his school text-book, *Movements in European History* (1921), he contrasts Italy even in the eighteenth century, when 'men were men, and on the whole, rich and poor alike, they were perhaps more human in Italy than in the progressive countries,' with modern Italy where this vigour has been replaced by 'fretfulness, irritation, and nothing in life except money.'[9]

These are the feelings which lead Lawrence to abandon Italy and seek for hope in other continents – for if even Italy has fallen to the false god of mechanism there can be no hope left in Europe. A final impetus is given to the feeling by his experience of the wildness of Sardinia, stimulating him to seek out other savage lands, remote from the depressing sameness of industrial civilisation. In *Sea and Sardinia* there is a moving valedictory passage summing up his gratitude to Italy and his need nevertheless to go away:

> Wherever one is in Italy, either one is conscious of the present, or of the medieval influences, or of the far, mysterious gods of the early Mediterranean. Wherever one is, the place has its conscious genius. Man has lived there and brought forth his consciousness there and in some way brought that place to consciousness, given it its expression, and, really, finished it. The expression may be Proserpine, or Pan, or even the strange 'shrouded gods' of the

Etruscans or the Sikels, none the less it is an expression. The land has been humanized, through and through: and we in our own tissued consciousness bear the results of this humanization. So that for us to go to Italy and to *penetrate* into Italy is like a most fascinating act of self-discovery – back, back down the old ways of time. Strange and wonderful chords awake in us, and vibrate again after many hundreds of years of complete forgetfulness. And then – and then – there is a final feeling of sterility. It is all worked out. It is all known: *connu, connu!* . . .
Italy has given me back I know not what of myself, but a very, very great deal. She has found for me so much that was lost: like a restored Osiris. But this morning in the omnibus I realize that, apart from the great rediscovery backwards, which one *must* make before one can be whole at all, there is a move forwards. There are unknown, unworked lands where the salt has not lost its savour. But one must have perfected oneself in the great past first. (p. 131)

So Lawrence went away, to Ceylon, to Australia, to North America. But eventually he came back again to Italy. Having tested other parts of the world, he was irresistibly drawn back to Italy as the place where, if anywhere, he could find the fullest inspiration for his effort to achieve a spiritually healthy life in the difficult conditions of the modern world. The immediate contrast is with Mexico, whence he returned to Italy. For though the Mexican landscape can be immensely beautiful and the masterpieces of Indian art have a superlative grace redolent of the qualities Lawrence tried to embody in his own life and work, both also have a harshness and violence alien to his vision, whereas in Italy, and particularly in Tuscany, he found these values in a purer form; the very landscape of Tuscany proved that the life he aspired to could be achieved:

Thousands of square miles of Italy have been lifted in human hands, piled and laid back in tiny little flats, held up by the drystone walls, whose stones came from the lifted earth. It is a work of many, many centuries. It is the gentle sensitive sculpture of all the landscape. And it is the achieving of the peculiar Italian beauty which is so exquisitely natural, because man, feeling his way sensitively to the fruitfulness of the earth, has moulded the earth to his necessity without violating it.

Which shows that it *can* be done. Man *can* live on the earth and by the earth without disfiguring the earth. It has been done here, on all these sculptured hills and softly, sensitively terraced slopes.[10]

It was against this sort of physical background that Lawrence wrote *Lady Chatterley's Lover*, which was first published in Florence in 1928. Much of the final version of the novel was written sitting under an old olive tree at his last home at Scandicci, near Florence. There is nothing self-evidently Italian about the book: firmly set in the English Midlands, the only Italian reference is to Lady Chatterley's visit to Venice in the last chapter, which could equally well have been to any other city. But a large part of the stimulus of the novel flowed out of Lawrence's Tuscan environment. Frieda believed that the life of the Tuscan peasants 'gave the impetus to his work',[11] and Lawrence wrote at the time,

I find, here in Italy, for example, that I live in a certain silent contact with the peasants who work the land of this villa. I am not intimate with them . . . and they are not working for me; I am not their padrone.

Yet it is they, really, who form my *ambiente* . . . I don't expect them to make any millennium here on earth, neither now nor in the future. But I want to live near them, because their life still flows.[12]

But the relationship of this environment to *Lady Chatterley's Lover* is paradoxical. The Tuscan atmosphere was conducive to the writing of the novel since its everyday life contained so much of what Lawrence was appealing for in his work. The countryside was a profoundly beautiful product of man's working in harmony with nature, in contrast with the ugliness of Tevershall; and the people seemed perfectly open and frank about their enjoyment of sex and admiration of physical beauty. Lawrence's paintings which were destroyed as obscene by the British authorities had seemed completely natural to the peasants of Scandicci. When the nature of the sexual passages in the novel was explained to the Florentine printer he could see no objection to printing them since, he said, 'we do that everyday.' Implicit in the life of Tuscany was the criticism of the dangerous hypocrisy of English attitudes to sex which is made explicitly in the novel. But as he does so, Lawrence's tone becomes st lent, obsessive, almost neurotic. The tender and life-giving qualities which he advocates can only have real value when they become spontaneous: to feel the need to appeal for them so strenuously is effectively an admission of defeat. At the end of *Lady Chatterley's Lover* one can scarcely hope for a future of any great mutual fulfilment for Connie and Mellors; the values which survive uncontaminated in Tuscany cannot take root again in the poisoned earth of England. The progress from *Twilight in Italy to Lady Chatterley's Lover* is a sad one, from the discovery that Italy seemed still to possess the qualities of life which Lawrence felt to have been disastrously lost in England, to the acceptance of the insuperable difficulties of establishing any revitalising link between the Italian experience and the atrophied life of the senses in industrial England.

In some ways this internal development in Lawrence epitomises the overall pattern of our subject – from Byron's revelation, largely through his response to Italy, of the means of achieving a full and satisfying life in a world where relativity of values had replaced the stable absolutes of the past, through successive attempts to fertilise modern England with qualities which were felt to have been lost there but still to be available in Italy, to the increasing realisation of the tragic impossibility of such an aim. Only one step remained to be taken to complete the symmetry of the pattern; and this step Lawrence took in his last work on Italy, *Etruscan Places*.

As early as 1920 Lawrence had evoked something of the mystery and attractiveness of 'the long-nosed, sensitive-footed, subtly-smiling Etruscans' in the poem *Cypresses*, and in 1927 he spent a few days touring the principal Etruscan sites. The book records his impressions of the tour. The notes of a few days cannot, of course, constitute a serious archaeological work, but Lawrence's little book, which is quoted approvingly by at least one modern authority,[13] is remarkable for its anticipation of modern views of the Etruscans, in contrast to the works available at the time,[14] which he frequently criticises for their insensitivity. His fascination with the Etruscans is that their civilisation seemed to come much closer than any other to realising the spontaneous fulness of living which was all-important to Lawrence. Through their vivid religious belief in the vitality of the cosmos they were able to achieve 'the natural flowering of life' (p. 146): the imagery of flowers constantly recurs throughout the book. It is related, for example, to the Etruscan custom of building in wood and other non-durable materials so that, like the flower, they and their buildings would have their day and then pass away, not, like the Romans, leaving great carcasses of buildings to immortalise their grandeur. (The Romans, who destroyed the Etruscan way of life, are the villains of the book; no longer the admired ancestors whom we found at the beginning of our study, their heirs are now seen to be Mussolini's Fascists and, by extension, all those forces of modern society which oppress the qualities represented by Etruscan life.) The greatness of Etruscan life is in the vividness of its living moment. Etruscan art is a celebration of the exhilaration of living. It has

> The naturalness verging on the commonplace, but usually missing it, and often achieving an originality so free and bold, and so fresh, that we, who love convention and things 'reduced to a norm,' call it a bastard art, and commonplace. (p. 130)

Lawrence's attack on the then orthodox views of Etruscan art anticipates the attitudes of modern authorities, who see it as an art 'realized on the instant, not meditated upon in advance and worked out rationally.'[15]

For Lawrence, the great thing about the Etruscans was that they had their priorities right:

> There seems to have been in the Etruscan instinct a real desire to preserve the natural humour of life. And that is a task surely more worthy, and even much more difficult in the long run, than conquering the world or sacrificing the self or saving the immortal soul. (p. 123)

> It is as if the current of some strong different life swept through them, different from our shallow current today: as if they drew their vitality from different depths that we are denied. (p. 146)

Because they were so fully devoted to living, the Etruscans did not see death as oppressive or tragic. To Lawrence tragedy was superficial; he writes in the story *Sun* of the eyes of a Sicilian house-keeper,

> dark grey eyes that had the experience of thousands of years in them, with the laugh that underlies all long experience. Tragedy is lack of experience. (p. 32)

To the Etruscans death was no terror. Their tombs, the only buildings they made to last, are gaily decorated with scenes of enjoyment. The modern theory is that they believed that when the tomb was sealed the dead carried on living inside it a life similar to that they had known above the ground. Lawrence again anticipates the modern view. He says the Etruscan underworld was so gay, 'for the life on earth was so good, the life below could but be a continuance of it.' (p. 134)

> The Etruscans, at least before the Romans smashed them, do not seem to have been tangled up in tragedy, as the Greeks were from the first. There seems to have been a peculiar large carelessness about them, very human and non-moral. As far as one can judge, they never said: certain acts are immoral, just because we say so! They seem to have had a strong feeling for taking life sincerely as a pleasant thing. Even death was a gay and lively affair.[16]

Etruscan Places is a quiet book. Following the example of his heroes, Lawrence here refuses to make a fuss about life. It is a personal book in a way that most English writing about Italy in the two centuries preceding it had not been. The sharpest contrast, of course, is with the very public writing of the eighteenth century, based in attitudes towards Italy and especially towards ancient Roman civilisation which Lawrence has now totally reversed. But there is also the contrast with the nineteenth century's efforts to relate what it found in Italy – the attractions of pagan life, early Christian art, the high Renaissance, peasant life, or the struggle for liberty – to the problems of its own massive civilisation, which was indeed the heir of the Romans, though not in the glorious way the Enlightenment had apprehended, but in sharing their nature of being destructive of the essence of the fully developed life. In describing the qualities of what he conceives to be the finest flowering of the human spirit, in an age when it could flourish unimpeded by the weight of civilisation, Lawrence seems to be returning to a fountain-head of wisdom; and from it he drinks a draught of serenity. No longer seeking to relate two apparently irreconcilable ways of life, he is content to work out his own personal redemption from the modern world by following the model of the graceful and joyful Etruscans. After writing *Etruscan Places* the approach of death becomes an increasing theme in his work; he prepares for death with an Etruscan acceptance, taking their funerary emblem of the ship of death, mentioned in the first chapter of *Etruscan Places*, as his image:

> We are dying, we are dying, so all we can do
> is now to be willing to die, and to build the ship
> of death to carry the soul on the longest journey.
>
> A little ship, with oars and food
> and little dishes, and all accoutrements
> fitting and ready for the departing soul.[17]

After two centuries of efforts to find some kind of valid, fruitful relation between English life and all aspects of Italian life from pagan antiquity to the present day, some kind of fulfilment had been found by Lawrence in his contemplation of the Etruscans. But it was a sad fulfilment. It is almost symbolic that the book was published posthumously: an epitaph on the whole search we have been following. As one ponders its significance, it is difficult, if fruitless, not to wonder how different our story might have been if the Victorians had been more responsive to the example of Byron.

Notes

CHAPTER I

1. See J. Arthos, *Milton and The Italian Cities* (London, 1968).

2. See R. Marshall, *Italy in English Literature, 1755–1815* (New York, 1934).

3. See C. Campbell, *Preface* to *Vitruvius Britannicus*, vol. i (London, 1715).

4. Cf. Virgil, *Georgics*, ii, 136–76; *Aeneid*, vi, 756–853.

5. O. Goldsmith, *The Traveller*, 339–48.

6. T. Green, *Extracts From The Diary of A Lover of Literature* (Ipswich, 1810) p. 26; entry for 24 February 1797.

7. E. Gibbon, *Memoir of My Life*, ed. G. A. Bonnard (London, 1966) p. 80.

8. See G. A. Bonnard (ed.), *Gibbon's Journey From Geneva To Rome: His Journal From 20 April To 2 October, 1764* (London, 1961) pp. 130–86; G. M. Young, *Gibbon* (London, 1932) p. 58; and *Nomina Gentesque Antiquae Italiae*, in Gibbon, *Miscellaneous Works*, vol. iv (London, 1814) pp. 155–326.

9. J. E. Norton (ed.), *Letters*, vol. i (London, 1956) pp 197–8; letter of 21 July 1765.

10. E. Gibbon, *Memoir*, op. cit., p. 136, n. 7.

11. I.e. AD 98–180; E. Gibbon, *Decline and Fall*, ch. 3.

CHAPTER 2

1. See W. N. Hargreaves-Mawdsley, *The English Della Cruscans and Their Time* (The Hague, 1967); B. Moloney, *Florence and England: Essays on Cultural Relations in The Second Half of The Eighteenth Century* (Firenze, 1969); and J. L. Clifford, 'Robert Merry – A Pre-Byronic Hero', *Bulletin of The John Rylands Library*, xxvii (1942) 74–96.

2. W. Parsons, The *Elegy Written At Florence*, in *A Poetical Tour, In The Years 1784, 1785 & 1786, By A Member Of The Arcadian Society At Rome* (London, 1787).

3. W. Parsons, *Elegy, Written At Rome, On Visiting The Colosseo or Amphitheatre By Moonlight*, in his *Poetical Tour* (London, 1787).

4. *Inferno*, Canto 33 and *Purgatorio*, Canto 5; Reynolds exhibited a painting of Ugolino in 1773: see Marshall, op. cit., p. 109.

200   *Italy and English Literature 1764–1930*

5. G. Chapman (ed.), *Travel Diaries of William Beckford of Fonthill*, vol. i (London, 1928) p. 98.

6. Ibid, pp. 128–9.

7. J. Moore, *View of Society and Manners in Italy*, vol. ii (London, 1781) pp 372–3.

8. In the *Addition to The Preface* to *Childe Harold's Pilgrimage*.

9. Compare E. Wright, *Some Observations Made in Travelling Through France, Italy, etc*, vol. i (London, 1730) pp 173–4 with H. Matthews, *Diary of An Invalid*, 2nd ed. (London, 1820) pp 204–5, 269.

10. J. C. Eustace, *A Classical Tour Through Italy*, vol. iv (London, 1815) pp 293–4.

11. M. Summers, *Introduction* to C. Dacre, *Zofloya* (London, 1928) p. xiv.

12. Mario Praz did mention the work in this context in *The Romantic Agony*, 2nd ed. (London, 1951) pp 61, 78; but his lead has been ignored by later writers: P. L. Thorslev, *The Byronic Hero- Types and Prototypes* (Minneapolis, 1962); M. K. Joseph, *Byron The Poet* (London, 1964); E. J. Lovell, Jr, *Byron: The Record of A Quest* (Connecticut, 1966).

13. J. C. Eustace, op. cit., vol. i, pp 30–1.

14. Anna Jameson, *Diary of An Ennuyée* (London, 1826) p. 110.

15. G. S. Hillard, *Six Months in Italy*, vol. ii (London, 1853) p. 319.

16. Madame de Staël, *Corinne*, Bk. 1, ch. 2. London edition (1809) vol. i, pp. 7–8.

17. Ibid. Bk. 1, ch. 2. ed. cit., vol. i, p. 11.

18. Finden, *Illustrations of The Life & Works of Lord Byron*, vol. i (London, 1833: pages un-numbered).

19. Madame de Staël, op. cit., ch. 3. Ed. cit., vol. i, p. 364.

20. S. Rogers, *Italian Journal*, ed. J. R. Hale (London, 1956) p. 170; see also B. Melchiori, 'A Light-Fingered English Visitor To Italy', *English Miscellany*, xviii (1967) 260.

21. Goethe, *Italian Journey*, tr. W. H. Auden & E. Meyer (London, 1962) p. 91; see also F. Avventi, *Il Servitore di Piazza, Guida Per Ferrara* (Ferrara, 1838) pp. 99–105 and G. Gruyer, *L' art ferrarais à l' époque des Princes d' Este*, vol. i (1897; repr. Bologna, 1969) p. 354.

22. Madame de Staël, op. cit., ch. 6. Ed. cit., vol. iii, p. 62.

23. J. Moore, op. cit., vol. i, pp. 39–40.

24. R. Ascham, *The Scholemaster* (London, 1570) p. 83.

25. For the 17th century, see T. Coryat, *Coryat's Crudities*, vol. i (1611; repr. Glasgow, 1905) pp. 401–9, and F. Henriques, *Prostitution and Society*, vol. ii (London, 1963) ch. 3. For the 18th century, see T. Nugent, *The Grand Tour*, 2nd ed., vol. iii (London, 1756) p. 87; J. Northall, *Travels Through Italy* (London, 1766) pp. 443–4.

26. C. von Klenze, *The Interpretation of Italy During The Last Two Centuries* (Chicago, 1907) p. 52.

27. Don Juan Andres, *Cartas Familiares*, vol. iii (Madrid, 1790–3) p. 23. (Written 1785).

28. H. Piozzi, *Observations and Reflections*, vol. i (London, 1789) pp. 166–7.

29. Madame de Staël, op. cit., Bk. 15, ch. 9. Ed. cit., vol. iii, p. 85.

30. Ibid., Bk. 15, ch. 7. Ed. cit., vol. iii, p. 66.

31. See F. S. Frank, 'The Demon and The Thunderstorm: Byron and Madame de Staël', *Revue de Littérature Comparée*, xliii (1969) 320–43, and J. C. Collins, *Studies in Poetry and Criticism* (London, 1905) p. 93.

CHAPTER 3

1. H. C. Robinson, *Diary*, ed. D. Hudson (London, 1967) p. 176.

2. See M. H. Shackford, 'Wordsworth's Italy', *PMLA*, xxxviii (1923) 236–52.

3. See D. Sultana, *Samuel Taylor Coleridge in Malta and Italy* (Oxford, 1969).

4. *Byron's Letters and Journals*, ed. L. A. Marchand, vol. vi (London, 1976) pp. 193–4. Letter of 1 August 1819.

5. Eg. Lady Morgan, *Italy*, vol. ii (London, 1821) p. 454.

6. H. Matthews, *Diary of An Invalid*, 2nd ed. (London, 1820) p. 282.

7. See I. Origo, *The Last Attachment* (London, 1949).

8. For a detailed argument of this view, see R. Gleckner, *Byron and The Ruins of Paradise* (Baltimore, 1967).

9. P. B. Shelley, *Letters*, ed. F. L. Jones, vol. i (Oxford, 1964) p. 504. Letter of 8 September 1816.

10. W. Wordsworth, *The Prelude*, II, 77.

11. E. J. Lovell, Jr, *Byron: The Record of A Quest* (Connecticut, 1969) p. 229.

12. G. Mazzini, *Scritti*, vol. xxi (Imola, 1915) p. 238.

13. *Letters and Journals*, ed. cit., vol. v (1976) p. 126.

14. Ibid, pp. 129, 131. *Childe Harold*, IV, 18. (All references to Byron's poetry are to the *Poetical Works*, ed. F. Page, new ed., corrected by J. Jump, OUP, 1970).

15. *Marino Faliero*, IV, i and III, ii.

16. Byron, *Childe Harold*, IV, 55.

17. *Letters and Journals*, ed. cit., vol. v, p. 129.

18. *Letters and Journals*, ed. cit., vol. ii (1973) p. 63.

19. The best account of these literary debts is still that of C. M. Fuess, *Lord Byron As A Satirist In Verse* (New York, 1912) ch. 7.

20. Countess of Blessington, *Conversations of Lord Byron* (London, 1834) p. 38.

CHAPTER 4

1. P. B. Shelley, *Julian & Maddalo*, l. 57.

2. *Letters*, ed. cit., vol. ii, p. 504. Letter of 17 or 18 December 1818.

3. Ibid, vol. ii, p. 339. Letter of 16 August 1821.

4. Ibid, vol. ii, pp. 54, 94; *Preface to The Cenci*.

5. See Shelley's note to the poem.

6. See F. H. Ludlam, 'The Metereology of Shelley's Ode', TLS, 1 September 1972, pp. 1015–6.

7. Shelley, *Lines Written Among The Euganean Hills*, ll. 100–14.

8. Mary Shelley's note to *Hellas*.

9. Eg. J. R. Hale's Introduction to his ed. of Rogers' *Italian Journal* (London, 1956); & E. Giddey, *Samuel Rogers et son poème 'Italie'* (Genève, 1959).

10. *Italian Journal*, op. cit., p. 198.

11. Note on p. 243 of the 1830 ed. of *Italy*.

12. Eg. J. Waldie, *Sketches Descriptive of Italy in The Years 1816 & 1817*, vol. iii (London, 1820) pp. 264–9; C. Eaton, *Rome in The Nineteenth Century*, vol. iii (Edinburgh, 1820) pp. 180–8; J. Bell, *Observations on Italy* (London, 1828) pp. 247–53; S. Martin, *Narrative of A Three Years' Residence in Italy* (London, 1828) pp. 207–8; A. W. Power, 'Notes on Italy Written Immediately on My Return to Scotland in 1829', *English Miscellany*, iii (1952) 275–6; C. Bury, *Diary of A Lady in Waiting*, vol. ii (London, 1908) pp. 122–3. For a non-pathetic account, see L. Simond, *A Tour in Italy & Sicily* (London, 1828) pp. 263–4.

13. *Italian Journal*, op. cit., pp. 238–40.

14. L. Hunt, *Stories From The Italian Poets: With Lives of The Writers*, vol. i (London, 1846) p. 79.

15. Another exception to the morbid obsession with the pathetic was the anonymous *Spirit of Boccaccio's 'Decameron'* (London, 1812), which has been convincingly attributed to Thomas Moore by H. G. Wright, 'Thomas Moore as The Author of "Spirit of Boccaccio's 'Decameron'"', *Review of English Studies*, xxiii (1947) 337–48.

16. See *The Liberal*, vol. 1, 1822; more conveniently available, in an improved text, in L. Hunt, *Autobiography*, ed. J. E. Morpurgo (London, 1949) pp. 333–47.

CHAPTER 5

1. See G. M. C. Cullum & F. C. Macauley, *Inscriptions in The Old British Cemetery of Leghorn* (Leghorn, 1906).

2. W. F. Monypenny, *Life of Benjamin Disraeli*, vol. i (London, 1910) p. 109.

3. See B. R. Jerman, *The Young Disraeli* (Princeton, 1960) pp. 77–8; J. A. Lovat-Fraser, 'With Disraeli in Italy', *Contemporary Review*, cxxxviii (1930) 192–9.

4. L. Stephen, *Hours In A Library*, 2nd series (London, 1876) pp. 389–90.

5. See Monypenny, op. cit., vol. i, p. 106.

6. Bulwer Lytton, *England and The English*, vol. ii (London, 1833) p. 211. Martin's painting was destroyed in the Tate Gallery flood of 1928. It is reproduced in M. Pendered, *John Martin, Painter, His Life & Times* (London, 1923) and discussed in T. Balston, *John Martin, 1789–1854, His Life & Works* (London, 1947) ch. 8. Martin was also part of Gautier's response to Italy; see J. Seznec, *John Martin en France* (London, 1964) p. 26.

7. Phrase used by Macaulay in his poem and by Walter Scott; see W. Gell, *Reminiscences of Sir Walter Scott's Residence in Italy, 1832*, ed. J. C. Corson (London, 1957) p. 8. Mary Shelley's description is in her *Rambles in Germany and Italy*, vol. ii (London, 1844) p. 279.

8. Lytton also used purely conventional Italian settings in two later novels: *Ernest Maltravers* (1837) has the Italy of the hopeless love affair, and *Zanoni* (1842) is Italy à la Radcliffe. *Zicci* (1838) is an unfinished sketch of *Zanoni*.

CHAPTER 6

1. Both R. H. Super, *Walter Savage Landor* (London, 1957) p. 39 and M. Elwin, *Landor: A Replevin* (London, 1958) p. 79 mention this connection with Greatheed, but neither seems aware of *The Florence Miscellany* and they offer no suggestions on whether Greatheed may have helped arouse Landor's interest in Italy.

2. See T. S. Eliot's Introduction to M. Wardle's translation of Valéry's *Le Serpent* (London, 1924) p. 12, and F. R. Leavis in *Scrutiny*, xi (1942–3) 150. For Stephen see *Hours In A Library*, 3rd series (London, 1879) pp. 230–78.

3. T. E. Whelby & S. Wheeler (ed.), *The Complete Works of Walter Savage Landor* (London, 1927–36) vol. xi, p. 50.

4. *Works*, ed. cit., vol. ix, pp. 206–7.

5. E. T. Cook & A. Wedderburn, *Works of John Ruskin* (London, 1903–12) vol. xxv, p. 295. (All references to Ruskin are to this edition).

6. G. Reynolds, *Turner* (London, 1969) p. 110.

7. Ibid, p. 161.

8. Ibid, pp. 158–60.

9. See A. Dubuisson, *Richard Parkes Bonington: His Life & Work*, tr. C. E. Hughes (London, 1924) Ch. 8.

10. A. J. Finberg, *In Venice With Turner* (London, 1930) pp. 79–80; for the 1832 visit, see Reynolds, op. cit., p. 160.

11. *La Daniella*, vol. i (Paris, 1857) p. 63. Cf. 'L' homme . . . va méditer sur les ruines des empires, il oublie qu' il est lui-même une ruine encore plus chancelante, et qu' il sera tombé avant ces débris': Chateaubriand, *Voyage en Italie*, ed. J.–M. Gautier (Genève, 1968) p. 133.

12. *L' Histoire de ma Vie*, vol. ix (Paris, 1856) pp. 95–6.

13. *Correspondance*, ed. G. Lubin, vol. ii (Paris, 1966) p. 527. Letter of 6 March 1834.

14. See A. Poli, *L' Italie dans la vie et dans l' oeuvre de George Sand* (Paris, 1960) passim.

15. See C. P. Brand, *Torquato Tasso; A Study of The Poet & of His Contribution to English Literature* (Cambridge, 1965) ch. 8.

16. Published in *Memoirs & Essays* (London, 1846); all the quotations are from this essay.

17. Later visitors who followed her there were warned that the modern inhabitants of the house were not hospitable: see W. D. Howells, *Venetian Life* (London, 1866) p. 220.

18. Ruskin, *Works*, ed. cit., vol. xxxv, p. 374.

CHAPTER 7

1. Letter of 23 June 1878; *Works*, ed. cit., vol. xxxvii, p. 249; see also vol. xxxiv, p. 586.

2. Letter of 31 December, 1840; *Works*, vol. i, p. 381.

3. E. Gibbon, *Memoir of My Life*, ed. cit., p. 135; *The Diaries of John Ruskin*, ed. J. Evans & J. H. Whitehouse, vol. i (Oxford, 1956), p. 183.

4. *Praeterita*; *Works*, vol. xxxv, pp. 117, 151, 295.

5. *Essay on Literature*, 1836; *Works*, vol. i, p. 363.

6. *Velasquez, The Novice*, 1835–6; *Works*, vol. i, p. 542.

7. *Praeterita*; *Works*, vol. xxxv, p. 267.

8. *Stones of Venice*; *Works*, vol. x, p. 8; see also vol. ix, p. 18.

9. *Ruskin's Letters From Venice, 1851–1852*, ed. J. L. Bradley (Yale, 1955) p. 207.

10. *Works*, vol. xxxv, p. 295.

11. *Works*, vol. xi, p. 233.

12. Byron, *Childe Harold*, IV, 14, 17.

13. *Essay on Literature*, 1836; *Works*, vol. i, p. 373.

14. *Fors Clavigera*; *Works*, vol. xxviii, p. 146; see also vol. xxxv, pp. 347–51.

15. *Praeterita*; *Works*, vol. xxxv, p. 351.

16. *Works*, vol. ix, p. 38.

17. *Letters From Venice*, ed. cit., p. 128.

18. *Works*, vol. x, pp. 81–2.

19. See J. S. Dearden (ed.), *The Professor. Arthur Severn's Memoir of John Ruskin* (London, 1967) pp. 57–8.

20. *Works*, vol. xvi, p. 186. For denunciations of Murray's *Handbooks*, see vol. xxix, pp. 305, 315. Ruskin's notes are printed in vol. xxxviii, pp. 326–30.

21. *Works*, vol. xvi, p. 66.

22. *Works*, vol. xi, p. 254.

CHAPTER 8

1. Ruskin, *Works*, ed. cit., vol. vi, p. 449.

2. Though he 'could agree with him only by snatches', Browning admired *Modern Painters* on reading the first two volumes in 1848: see *Letters of E. B. Browning*, ed. F. G. Kenyon, vol. i (London, 1897) p. 384; for their friendship see vol. ii, p. 87.

3. A. Benedetti, 'Impressioni d' Italia nella poesia di Roberto Browning', *Nuova Antologia*, cclxxiii (1930) 351.

4. I. Jack, *Browning's Major Poetry* (Oxford, 1973) p. 272.

5. W. H. Griffin & H. C. Minchin, *The Life of Robert Browning*, 3rd ed. (London, 1938) p. 200; and E. B. Browning, *Letters*, ed. cit., vol. ii, p. 354.

6. Griffin & Minchin, op. cit., p. 96.

7. For the curious fact that it is actually not St Praxed's, see B. Melchiori, *Browning's Poetry of Reticence* (Edinburgh, 1968) pp. 20–1.

8. L. S. Friedland, 'Ferrara and "My Last Duchess"', *Studies in Philology*, vol. xxxiii (1936) pp. 656–84.

9. P. & L. Murray, *Dictionary of Art & Artists* (London, 1965) p. 20.

10. D. H. Lawrence, *Twilight in Italy*, Penguin ed. (London, 1960) pp. 26, 41.

11. Nor do the later volumes, *Pacchiarotto* (1876) and *Asolando* (1889) have anything significant to add.

CHAPTER 9

1. Letter of W. W. Story, quoting Browning, in H. James, *William Wetmore Story & His Friends*, vol. i (London, 1903) p. 270.

2. G. W. E. Russell (ed.), *Letters of Matthew Arnold*, vol. i (London, 1895) p. 277.

3. Ruskin, for example, thought *Aurora Leigh* 'the greatest *poem* in the English language': *Works*, ed. cit., vol. xxxvi, p. 247.

4. *Letters*, ed. cit., vol. ii, p. 8. Armida is the enchantress in Tasso's *Gerusalemme Liberata*.

5. Quoted in G. B. Taplin, *Life of E. B. Browning* (London, 1957) p. 452, n. 27.

6. See H. W. Rudman, *Italian Nationalism & English Letters* (London, 1940); E. Miller, *Prince of Librarians; The Life and Times of Antonio Panizzi of The British Museum* (London, 1967); and J. Morley, *Life of Gladstone*, vol. i (London, 1903) pp. 389–404.

7. *Casa Guidi Windows*, part 2, ll. 399–414.

8. *Aurbra Leigh*, Book 1, ll. 287–301: the quotations in the next sentence are all from book 1.

9. V. Woolf, *The Common Reader*, 2nd series (London, 1932) pp. 202–13.

10. See E. Greenberger, *Arthur Hugh Clough: The Growth of A Poet's Mind* (Cambridge, Mass, 1970). For the events of 1849, see E. E. Y. Hales, *Pio Nono* (London, 1954), especially pp. 115–33.

11. A. H. Clough, *Correspondance*, ed. F. L. Mulhauser (Oxford, 1957) vol. i, p. 252.

12. I. Armstrong (ed.), *The Major Victorian Poets: Reconsiderations* (London, 1969), pp. 275–98.

13. *Epilogue* to *Dipsychus*.

14. The quotations are from *Lovesight*, in *House of Love*, IV and Dante's *Donne, ch' avete intelletto d' amore*. Cf. H. Dupré, *Un Italien d' Angleterre. Le Poète-Peintre Dante Gabriel Rossetti* (Paris, 1921) p. 119.

15. A. C. Swinburne, *Works*, ed. E. Gosse & T. J. Wise (London, 1925–7) vol. xiv, p. 165. The passage was first published in *Nineteenth Century* in 1884.

16. Letter of 1872, in *Letters*, ed. C. Y. Lang, vol. ii (Yale, 1959) p. 176.

17. G. Lafourcade, *Swinburne* (London, 1932) p. 147.

18. In a letter of 1912; see *Works*, ed. cit., vol. xx, p. 104.

19. *Lucrezia Borgia*, ed. R. Hughes (London, 1942) pp. 57–8.

CHAPTER 10

1. See L. Fèbvre, 'Comment Jules Michelet inventa la Renaissance', in *Studi in Onore di Gino Luzzatto*, vol. iii (Milano, 1950) pp. 1–11.

2. F. Hueffer in *The Times*, 7 April 1882; collected in his *Italian & Other Studies* (London, 1883) pp. 62–82.

3. J. A. Symonds, *The Renaissance* (Oxford, 1863) p. 34.

4. Letter of 1863, quoted in P. Grosskurth, *John Addington Symonds* (London, 1964) p. 85.

5. J. A. Symonds, *Renaissance in Italy*, vol. v (ed. 1902) p. 400 and *The Renaissance of Modern Europe* (London, 1872) p. 32.

6. See G. N. G. Orsini, 'Symonds & De Sanctis: A Study in The Historiography of The Renaissance', *Studies in The Renaissance*, xi (1964) 151–87.

7. See D. Hay, *The Italian Renaissance in Its Historical Background* (Cambridge, 1961) p. xi.

8. See G. G. Hough, *A Preface To 'The Faerie Queene'* (London, 1962) p. 6.

9. J. A. Symonds, *Renaissance in Italy*, vol. vii (ed. 1900) pp. 23–4.

10. J. A. Symonds, *Sketches in Italy & Greece* (London, 1874) pp. 204–5.

11. J. A. Symonds, *Sketches & Studies in Italy* (London, 1879) p. 185.

12. J. A. Symonds, *Many Moods* (London, 1878) p. 4.

13. J. A. Symonds, *New & Old* (London, 1880) p. 179.

14. Eg. R. Duppa (1806) and J. S. Harford (1857) – neither of whom had seen the full text of Michelangelo's sonnets, first published in 1863.

15. For frequent references to Sand, see the index to Symonds' *Letters*, ed. H. M. Schueller & R. L. Peters (Detroit, 1967–9). Some of Sand's were among the books he took to Venice in 1862: see H. Brown, *John Addington Symonds*, vol. i (London, 1895) p. 247.

16. See Symonds' review of *The Renaissance* in *The Academy*, iv (1873) 103–5, and Pater's of *The Age of Despots* in *The Academy*, viii (1875) 105–6.

17. Symonds, *Letters*, ed. cit., vol. ii, p. 273.

18. D. Cecil, *Walter Pater, The Scholar-Artist* (Cambridge, 1955) p. 20.

19. W. Pater, *The Renaissance*, Library Edition (London, 1910) pp. 236, 239.

20. W. Pater, *Marius The Epicurean*, Library Edition (London, 1910) vol. ii, p. 184. Other, less significant, evocations of ancient Rome in the fiction of the time include J. H. Newman's *Callista* (1881) and J. W. Graham's *Neaera* (1886).

21. Ibid, vol. i, pp. 53–4.

22. See Vernon Lee, *J.S.S. In Memoriam*, in E. Charteris, *John Sargeant* (London, 1927) pp. 235–55.

23. Vernon Lee, *Gospels of Anarchy* (London, 1928) pp. 306, 320.

24. See the early essay *Ruskinism*, printed in *Belcaro* (London, 1883) and *The Italy of The Elizabethan Dramatists* in *Euphorion*, vol. i (London, 1884) pp. 57–108.

25. Vernon Lee, *Laurus Nobilis* (London, 1909) p. 36.

CHAPTER II

1. Eg. Lord Normanby's *Il Politico* in *The English in Italy* (1825); Charlotte Eaton's *Vittoria Colonna; A Tale of Rome in The Nineteenth Century* (1827); George Croly's *The Italian's Tale* in *Tales of The Great St Bernard* (1829); and the Duc de Levi's *The Carbonaro* (1829).

2. The perverted values of Anglo-Florentine society are again attacked in Lever's *The Dodd Family Abroad* (1852–4). This is one of a series of minor works making fun of the tourist in Italy, including Frances Trollope's *The Robertses on Their Travels* (1846), Richard Doyle's cartoon book *The Foreign Tour of Messrs Brown, Jones & Robinson* (1854) and Anthony Trollope's *Tales of All Countries* (2nd series, 1863) and *Travelling Sketches* (1866).

3. G. S. Godkin, *Life of Victor Emmanuel II*, vol. ii (London, 1879) p. 43.

4. G. Meredith, *Letters*, ed. C. L. Cline, vol. i (Oxford, 1970) p. 343. Letter of 1866.

5. See his *Correspondance From The Seat of War in Italy*, in *Works*, Memorial ed, vol. xxiii (London, 1910) pp. 163–213.

6. T. A. Trollope, *Lenten Journey in Umbria & The Marches* (London, 1862) p. 2, and *Filippo Strozzi* (London, 1860) p. viii.

7. *Foreign Quarterly Review*, xxxiii (Chapman & Hall, London, 1844) 298. For the meeting with Sand see T. A. Trollope *What I Remember*, vol. i (London, 1887) pp. 280–2.

8. T. A. Trollope *What I Remember*, vol. i, pp. 357–8.

9. *North American Review*, cxx (1875) 208–9; repr. in H. James, *Literary Reviews & Essays*, ed. A. Mordell, (New York, 1957) pp. 139–41.

10. All page references to Dickens' works are to the Oxford illustrated Dickens, 21 vols, Oxford, 1947–58.

11. J. Forster, *Life of Dickens*, vol. ii, 10th ed. (London, 1873) pp. 139–41.

12. Letter of Frederic Myers to George Eliot after reading *Middlemarch*, 8 December 1872; see G. S. Haight, *George Eliot* (London, 1968) p. 451.

13. See M. Tosello, *Le fonti italiane della 'Romola' di George Eliot* (Torino, 1956) passim.

14. So does Anne Manning's novel, *The Duchess of Trajetto*, also published in 1863, which champions Savonarola against the Medici, whose fault was that 'they loved Plato better than Christ'. (p. 62) In 1864 Alfred Austin began to write his *Savonarola, A Tragedy* (pub. 1881).

15. Q. D. Leavis, 'A Note on Literary Indebtedness: Dickens, George Eliot, Henry James', *Hudson Review*, viii (1955–6) 423–8. See also F. R. & Q. D. Leavis, *Dickens The Novelist* (London, 1970) pp. 81, 253–5.

CHAPTER 12

1. The first English ed. (1842) was entitled *The Jack o' Lantern*. Quotations are from pp. 1 and vi of the 1888 ed.

2. For frequent minor references to Italy in Cooper's later work, see N. Wright, *The American Novelists in Italy: The Discoverers: Allston to James* (Philadelphia, 1965).

3. H. James, *Hawthorne*, ed. T. Tanner (London, 1967) p. 151; W. D. Howells, *Roman Holidays & Others* (New York, 1908) p. 226.

4. H. James, op. cit., p. 154.

5. N. Hawthorne *Marble Faun*, Centenary Ed. (Ohio, 1968) pp. 411–2.

6. Ibid, p. 355.

7. William Wetmore Story, *Roba di Roma* (London, 1863) vol. i, p. 7.

8. Ibid, vol. i, p. 74.

9. W. D. Howells *Venetian Life* (London, 1866) p. 186.

10. Ibid, p. 162.

11. Ibid, p. 310.

12. Ibid, pp. 98–102.

13. W. D. Howells *Tuscan Cities* (London, 1886) p. 9.

14. Ibid, p. 96.

15. J. L. Woodress, Jr., *Howells & Italy* (Durham, North Carolina, 1952).

16. See H. James, *Literary Reviews & Essays*, ed. A. Mordell (New York, 1957) pp. 198–215.

17. H. James, *Benvolio* (1875), in *Tales*, ed. L. Edel, vol. iii (London, 1962), p. 391.

18. But interestingly, although there is no trace of him in their work, he was highly admired by the Brownings: see E. B. Browning, *Letters*, ed. F. G. Kenyon (London, 1897), index, and *Dearest Isa. Robert Browning's Letters to Isabella Blagden*, ed. E. C. McAleer (Austin, Texas, 1951) p. 78, n. 2.

19. Collected by H. Martineau as *Courrier Anglais* (Paris, 1935–6); see also G. Strickland (ed.), *Selected Journalism From The English Reviews By Stendhal* (London, 1959).

20. Henry James, *Travelling Companions* (1870) in *Tales*, ed. L. Edel, vol. ii (London, 1962) pp. 184–5. Cf. L. Edel, *Henry James. The Untried Years, 1843–1870* (London, 1953) p. 306.

21. N. Wright gives the statistics in *The American Novelists in Italy* (Philadelphia, 1965) p. 217.

22. In *Tales*, ed. L. Edel, vol. iii (London, 1962) p. 37.

23. Ibid, p. 95.

CHAPTER 13

1. See E. Bigland, *Ouida. The Passionate Victorian* (London, 1950) p. 42.

2. Ouida, *Views & Opinions* (London, 1895) p. 274.

3. Ouida, *Pascarel* (London, 1873) vol. ii, p. 133.

4. Ibid, vol. ii, pp. 164, 220; vol. i, p. 241.

5. F. M. Crawford, *Sant' Ilario* (London, 1889) vol. i, pp. 76–7.

6. F. M. Crawford, *Saracinesca* (London, 1887) vol. i, p. 17.

7. He visited Italy at least 25 times: see C. Vita-Finzi, 'Samuel Butler and Italy', *Italian Studies*, xviii (1963) 79. The quotation is from *Alps and Sanctuaries* (ed. 1913) p. 21.

8. *Letters of George Gissing to Members of His Family*, ed. A. & E. Gissing (London, 1927) p. 173. Cf. G. Gissing, *The Private Papers of Henry Ryecroft* (ed. 1906) p. 206.

9. *Letters*, ed. cit., p. 273.

10. Ibid, p. 279.

11. G. Gissing, *By The Ionian Sea* (London, 1901) p. 6.

12. Ibid, p. 61.

13. Ibid, pp. 53, 99.

14. Ibid, p. 32.

15. Ibid, p. 168.

16. Corvo, *Stories Toto Told Me* (London, 1898) p. 65. (volere benè = to love; literally, to wish well.).

17. Ibid, p. 60.

18. Cf. A. J. A. Symons, *The Quest For Corvo* (London, 1934) ed. 1955, p. 244.

19. Corvo, *The Desire and Pursuit of the Whole*, Ed. 1953, p. 255. (Cassell, London).

20. Ibid, p. 299.

21. Quoted in D. Weeks, *Corvo* (London, 1971) p. 358.

22. Published as *A Selection from The Venice Letters*, ed. C. Woolf in *Art & Literature*, v (Lausanne, 1965) pp. 9–63.

23. *Blackwood's*, cxciv (1913) 54–62.

24. N. Douglas, *Siren Land & Fountains in The Sun* (London, 1957) p. 28.

25. Ibid, p. 128.

26. Ibid, p. 196.

CHAPTER 14

1. E. Nehls (ed.), *D. H. Lawrence: A Composite Biography*, vol. i (Madison, Wisconsin, 1957) p. 73.

2. D. H. Lawrence, *Letters*, ed. H. T. Moore, vol. i (London, 1962) p. 180.

3. Ibid, vol. i, p. 147.

4. Ibid, vol. i, p. 222.

5. Unless otherwise stated, all references to Lawrence's work are to the Penguin edition, as the most convenient and reliable to date.

6. D. H. Lawrence, '*Christs in The Tyrol*', *Westminster Gazette*, (22 March 1913), vol. xli, no. 6182, p. 2.

7. Cf *Daughters of The Vicar*, in *The Prussian Officer*.

8. Her name, in fact, was Capelli; the accuracy of Lawrence's portrait of her is suggested by the similarities to the description of the same woman in Tony Cyriax's *Among Italian Peasants* (London, 1919), where she is called Maria Castelli.

9. D. H. Lawrence, *Movements* (ed. Oxford, 1971) pp. 268, 291.

10. *Flowery Tuscany*, in *New Criterion*, 1927; repr. in *Phoenix*, ed. E. D. McDonald (London, 1936) p. 46.

11. F. Lawrence, *Not I, But the Wind* (London, 1935) p. 181.

12. *Autobiographical Sketch*, in *Phoenix 2*, ed. W. Roberts & H. T. Moore (London, 1968) p. 595.

13. R. Bloch, *The Etruscans* (London, 1958) pp. 172–3.

14. The best-known, which Lawrence used, was G. Dennis, *The Cities & Cemeteries of Etruria* (London, 1848).

15. G. A. Mansuelli, *Etruria & Early Rome* (London, 1966) p. 120.

16. D. H. Lawrence, *Making Love to Music*, *Phoenix*, p. 164.

17. D. H. Lawrence, *The Ship of Death VII*; cf. C. Hassall, 'D. H. Lawrence & The Etruscans', *Essays By Divers Hands*, xxxi (1962) pp. 61–78.

Bibliography

In a study covering so many authors a comprehensive bibliography is clearly out of the question. Nor does space permit a list of the very large number of articles which look at one aspect or another of the Italian subject in English and American literature. Many of the sources that have been found most useful are listed in the notes. Other general studies of particular value are:

P. R. Baker, *The Fortunate Pilgrims: Americans in Italy, 1800–1860* (Cambridge, Mass., 1964).

C. P. Brand, *Italy and the English Romantics* (Cambridge, 1965).

V. W. Brooks, *The Dream of Arcadia: American Writers and Artists in Italy, 1760–1915* (London, 1959).

J. R. Hale, *England and the Italian Renaissance, the Growth of Interest in its History and Art* (London, 1954).

C. von Klenze, *The Interpretation of Italy during the Last Two Centuries* (Chicago, 1907).

The bibliography which follows is a selective list of relevant primary texts, listed chronologically as a reminder of how the currents which have been separated out for discussion flowed, in reality, into and out of each other as part of the constant stream of literary writing about Italy. The list will serve as a guide for the reader who wishes to look for himself at the 'Italian' work of any of the authors, periods or genres discussed in this book.

Unless otherwise stated, place of publication is London, or Paris for French titles. Works which remained for many years unpublished are shown in square brackets at the actual or approximate date of their composition, with details of first publication.

1701	J. Addison	*Letter from Italy*
1705		*Remarks on Several Parts of Italy*
1715–25	C. Campbell	*Vitruvius Britannicus*

1729	C. Middleton	*Letter from Rome*
1730	Lyttleton	*Epistle to Mr Pope, from Rome*
1734–6	J. Thomson	*Liberty*
1740	J. Dyer	*The Ruins of Rome*
1743	G. Piranesi	*Vedute di Roma* (Roma)
1745		*Capricci di Carceri* (Roma)
1754	S. Richardson	*The History of Sir Charles Grandison*
1755	E. Clarke	*A Letter to a Friend in Italy*
1756	G. Piranesi	*Le Antichitate Romane* (Roma)
1760	O. Goldsmith	*A Comparative View of Races and Nations*
	G. Keate	*Ancient and Modern Rome*
1763		*The Alps: A Poem*
1764	O. Goldsmith	*The Traveller*
	H. Walpole	*The Castle of Otranto*
	E. Gibbon	*[Gibbon's Journey from Geneva to Rome: his Journal from 20 April to 2 October, 1764*, ed. G. A. Bonnard (London, 1961)]
1765–6	J. Boswell	*[Boswell on the Grand Tour*, ed. F. Brady & F. A. Pottle (London, 1955)]
1766	S. Sharp	*Letters from Italy*
	T. Smollett	*Travels through France and Italy*
1768	G. Baretti	*An Account of the Manners and Customs of Italy*
1770	C. Burney	*Music, Men and Manners in France and Italy*
1771		*The Present State of Music in France and Italy*
1773	P. Brydone	*A Tour through Sicily and Malta, in a Series of Letters to William Beckford*
	Corke and Orrery	*Letters from Italy in the Years 1754 & 1755*
1776–88	E. Gibbon	*The Decline and Fall of the Roman Empire*
1780	W. Beckford	*[Travel Diaries*, ed. G. Chapman (London, 1928)]
1781	J. Moore	*View of Society and Manners in Italy*
1783	W. Godwin	*Italian Letters*
	anon.	*The Arno Miscellany* (Florence)
1785		*The Florence Miscellany* (Florence)
1787	W. Parsons	*A Poetical Tour*
1789	J. Moore	*Zeluco*
	H. L. Piozzi	*Observations and Reflections Made in the Course of a Journey through France, Italy and Germany*
1790	R. Merry	*The Laurel of Liberty*
	A. Radcliffe	*A Sicilian Romance*
1792	E. C. Knight	*Marcus Flaminius*
1794	W. Godwin	*The Adventures of Caleb Williams*
	A. Radcliffe	*The Mysteries of Udolpho*
	J. Courtenay	*The Present State of the Manners, Arts and Politics of France and Italy*
1795	Charlotte Smith	*Montalbert*
	W. Roscoe	*The Life of Lorenzo de' Medici* (Liverpool)
1796	E. Gibbon	*Miscellaneous Works*
	R. Merry	*The Pains of Memory*

1797	A. Radcliffe	*The Italian*
1798	S. Lee	*The Two Emilys* (in *Canterbury Tales*, vol. ii)
1799	W. Godwin	*St Leon*
	A. Ker	*The Heiress di Montaldo*
1801	J. Hinckley	*The History of Rinaldo Rinaldini* (Dublin)
1802	I. Crookenden	*Romantic Tales*
1803	J. de Krüdener	*Valérie*
	M. Young	*Right and Wrong; or, the Kinsmen of Naples*
1805	R. W. Elliston	*The Venetian Outlaw*
	M. G. Lewis	*The Bravo of Venice*
	C. Selden	*Villa Nova*
	W. Roscoe	*The Life and Pontificate of Leo X* (Liverpool)
1806	C. Dacre	*Zofloya; or, the Moor*
1807		*The Libertine*
	C. Maturin	*Fatal Revenge*
	E. Montague	*Legends of a Nunnery*
	Mme de Staël	*Corinne*
1808	B. Thompson	*The Florentines*
1809	M. A. Radcliffe	*Manfrone*
1810	P. B. Shelley	*Zastrozzi*
1811		*St Irvyne*
	A. F. Holstein	*Isidora of Milan*
1812	A. Hatton	*Sicilian Mysteries*
	T. Moore (anon.)	*Spirit of Boccaccio's 'Decameron'*
1814–5	S. Rogers	[*Italian Journal*, ed. J. R. Hale (London, 1956)]
1815	anon.	*Corinne Ressuscitée* (Londres)
	Catherine Smith	*Barozzi; or, the Venetian Sorceress*
1816	F. Hemans	*The Restoration of the Works of Art to Italy* (Oxford)
	L. Hunt	*The Story of Rimini*
	C. Lamb	*Glenarvon*
1817	Byron	*Manfred*
	Stendhal	*Rome, Naples et Florence en 1817* (Paris & London; trans 1818)
1817–8	J. H. Frere	*The Monks and the Giants*
1817–9	W. Gell & J. Gandy	*Pompeiiana*
1818	Byron	*Childe Harold's Pilgrimage, Canto IV*
		Beppo
	W. Sotheby	*Farewell To Italy*
	L. S. Stanhope	*The Nun of Santa Maria di Tindaro*
	P. B. Shelley	*Julian and Madallo*
1819		*The Cenci*
		Lines Written among the Euganean Hills
	A. Hatton	*Cesario Rosalba*
	F. Hemans	*The Maremma*, in *Tales and Historic Scenes, in Verse*
	T. Macaulay	*Pompeii* (Cambridge)
	T. Moore	*Rhymes on the Road*
	W. S. Rose	*The Court and Parliament of Beasts*

1819–24	Byron	*Don Juan*
1820	B. Cornwall	*Sicilian Story*
		Marcian Colonna
	C. Eaton	*Rome in the Nineteenth Century* (Edinburgh)
	W. Herbert	*Pia della Pietra*
	L. Hunt	*Amyntas*
	F. Lathom	*Italian Mysteries*
	J. Keats	*Isabella*
	P. B. Shelley	*Prometheus Unbound*
		Ode to Naples
1821		*Ode to the West Wind*
		Epipsychidion
		Adonais (Pisa)
	Byron	*Marino Faliero*
		The Two Foscari
		The Prophecy of Dante
	J. Chaloner	*Rome; a Poem*
	B. Cornwall	*Mirandola: A Tragedy*
	L. Hunt	*The Nun*
	W. S. Landor	*Poche Osservazioni* (Napoli?)
	J. H. Reynolds	*The Garden of Florence*
		The Ladye of Provence
1822	C. Bury	*Conduct is Fate* (Edinburgh)
	S. Rogers	*Italy*
	W. Roscoe	*Illustrations of the Life of Lorenzo de' Medici*
1822–3	L. Hunt (ed.)	*The Liberal* (Pisa)
1822–9	Stendhal	[*Courrier Anglais*, ed. H. Martineau (Paris, 1935–6)]
1823	B. Cornwall	*The Flood of Thessaly*
	M. Shelley	*Valperga*
1824	P. B. Shelley	*Posthumous Poems*
	W. Irving	*Tales of a Traveller*
		[*Journals and Notebooks*, vol. i, ed. N. Wright (Madison, Wisconsin, 1969)]
	L. E. Landon	*The Improvisatrice*
		Rosalie
1824–9	W. S. Landor	*Imaginary Conversations*
1825	J. H. Bedford	*The Wanderings of Childe Harold*
	L. Hunt	*Bacchus in Tuscany*
	Normanby	*The English in Italy*
		Matilda. A Tale of the Day
1826	E. Barrett	*An Essay on Mind*
	C. Bury	*Alla Giornata*
	W. Hazlitt	*Notes of a Journey through France and Italy*
	A. Jameson	*Diary of an Ennuyée*
1827	Mrs Burdett	*English Fashionables Abroad*
	C. Eaton	*Vittoria Colonna*
	T. Macaulay	*Machiavelli*
1828	Mrs Burdett	*At Home*

	S. Davenport	*Italian Vengeance and English Forbearance*
	L. Hunt	*Lord Byron and some of his Contemporaries*
	W. Sotheby	*Italy, and other Poems*
	E. Wilmot	*Ugolino*
1829	L. E. Landon	*The Venetian Bracelet*
	P. de Levis	*The Carbonaro*
	Stendhal	*Promenades dans Rome*
	G. Croly	*Tales of the Great St Bernard*
1830		*Poetical Works*
	W. Godwin	*Cloudesley*
	L. S. Stanhope	*The Corsair's Bride*
	J. F. Cooper	*The Water Witch*
1831		*The Bravo. A Venetian Story*
	W. S. Landor	*Ippolito di Este*
	G. Sand	*La Prima Donna*
1832	B. Disraeli	*Contarini Fleming*
	W. C. Green	*The Algerines; or, the Twins of Naples*
	A. H. Hallam	*Oration on the Influence of Italian Works of Imagination on the same Class of Composition in England* (Cambridge)
	C. MacFarlane	*The Romance of History: Italy*
1833	C. Bury	*The Three Great Sanctuaries of Tuscany*
	V. Hugo	*Lucrèce Borgia*
	E. C. Knight	*Sir Guy de Lusignan: A Tale of Italy*
	H. W. Longfellow	*Outre-Mer*
	Mrs Sherwood	*The Nun*
	G. Sand	*Lélia*
		Metella
1834		*Lettres d' un Voyageur*
		Le Secrétaire Intime
		Leone Leoni
	L. E. Landon	*Francesca Carrara*
	E. B. Lytton	*The Last Days of Pompeii*
1835		*Rienzi*
	G. Sand	*Mattéa*
	M. Shelley	*Lodore*
	M. Callcott	*Description of the Chapel of the Annunziata dell' Arena*
	H. F. Chorley	*Conti the Discarded*
1835–6	J. Ruskin	*Essay on Literature*
1836		*Velasquez, The Novice*
	A. F. Rio	*Da la Poésie Chrétienne*
1837	anon.	*The Converts*
	Mrs Busk	*Sordello*, in *Plays & Poems*
	B. Disraeli	*Henrietta Temple*
		Venetia
	W. S. Landor	*The Pentameron*
	E. B. Lytton	*Ernest Maltravers*
	G. Sand	*L' Uscoque*

	G. Sand	*Les Maîtres Mosaïstes*
	Mrs Sherwood	*The Monk of Cimiés*
	J. Ruskin	*Leoni: A Legend of Italy*
1837–8		*The Poetry of Architecture*
	W. S. Landor	*High and Low Life in Italy*
1838	J. F. Cooper	*Excursions in Italy*
	E. B. Lytton	*Zicci*
	J. H. Merivale	*Poems*, vol. ii
	J. E. Reade	*Italy: A Poem*
	G. Sand	*L' Orco*
		La Dernière Aldini
1839	anon.	*The Roman Lovers. A Tale*
	Countess of Blessington	*The Idler in Italy*
	A. Domett	*Venice*
	W. S. Landor	*Andrea of Hungary and Giovanna of Naples*
		Giovanna of Naples
	Lord Leigh	*Poems*
	H. Prescott	*Tasso*, in *Poems Written in Newfoundland*
	Stendhal	*La Chartreuse de Parme*
		Chroniques Italiennes
1840	anon.	*Hawkwood. A Romance of Italy*
	R. Browning	*Sordello*
	W. S. Landor	*Fra Rupert*
	J. Waddington	*The Monk and the Married Man*
	J. R. Beste	*The Pope. A Novel*
1841		*Isidora; or, the Adventures of a Neapolitan*
	C. Gore	*Cecil; or, the Adventures of a Coxcomb*
	R. Browning	*Pippa Passes*
1842		*Dramatic Lyrics*
	J. F. Cooper	*The Wing and Wing*
	E. B. Lytton	*Zanoni*
	T. Macaulay	*Lays of Ancient Rome*
	F. Trollope	*A Visit to Italy*
	H. Smith	*Massaniello*
	W. Wordsworth	*Memorials of a Tour in Italy*
1842–4	G. Sand	*Consuelo, suivi de La Comtesse de Rudolstadt*
1843	R. B. Lytton	*Bianca Capella*
	W. S. Landor	*Francesca Petrarca*
	J. Ruskin	*Modern Painters*, vol. i
1844	M. Shelley	*Rambles in Germany and Italy*
1845	H. C. Andersen	*The Improvisatore* (tr. M. Howitt; 1st Danish ed., Copenhagen, 1837)
	J. R. Beste	*The Beggar's Coin; or, Love in Italy*
	Countess of Blessington	*Strathern; or, Life at Home and Abroad*
	A. Jameson	*Memoirs of the Early Italian Painters*
	G. Sand	*Teverino*

	W. Sewell	*Hawkstone*
	R. Browning	*Dramatic Romances and Lyrics*
1846		*Luria*
		A Soul's Tragedy
	N. Hawthorne	*Rappaccini's Daughter*, in *Mosses From an Old Manse*
	C. Dickens	*Pictures From Italy*
	L. Hunt	*Stories From The Italian Poets: With Lives of The Writers*
	A. Jameson	*Memoirs and Essays*
	W. S. Landor	*The Seige of Ancona*
		The Coronation
	E. Robinson	*Caesar Borgia*
	J. Ruskin	*Modern Painters*, vol. II
	E. Lear	*Illustrated Excursions in Italy*
	F. Trollope	*The Robertses on Their Travels*
	G. Sand	*Lucrezia Floriani*
1847		*Le Piccinino*
	Countess of Blessington	*Marmaduke Herbert*
	G. Fullerton	*Grantley Manor*
	E. Harris	*From Oxford To Rome*
	Lord Lindsay	*Sketches of The History of Christian Art*
1848	G. Dennis	*Cities and Cemetries of Etruria*
	J. A. Froude	*The Nemesis of Faith*
	J. Grant	*Adventures of an Aide-de-Camp; Or, A Campaign in Calabria*
	J. G. Grant	*Madonna Pia and Other Poems*
	A. Jameson	*The Poetry of Sacred and Legendary Art*
	C. Lever	*Horace Templeton*
	Mrs Nisbet	*Leonora. A Love Story*
	H. R. Skeffington	*A Testimony. Poems*
1849	J. Ruskin	*The Seven Lamps of Architecture*
1850	A. Jameson	*Legends of The Monastic Orders as Represented in The Fine Arts*
	T. A. Trollope	*Impressions of A Wanderer in Italy, Switzerland, France and Spain*
1851	E. B. Browning	*Casa Guidi Windows*
	W. E. Gladstone	*Two Letters To The Earl of Aberdeen on The State Prosecutions of The Neapolitan Government*
	W. S. Landor	*Beatrice Cenci – Five Scenes*
	Mrs Ogilvy	*Traditions of Tuscany*
1851–2	J. Ruskin	[*Letters From Venice*, ed. J. L. Bradley (Yale, 1955)]
1851–3		*The Stones of Venice*
1852	M. Arnold	*Empedocles on Etna*
	A. Jameson	*Legends of The Madonna as Represented in The Fine Arts*
	M. F. Ossoli	*Memoirs*

	C. Sinclair	*Beatrice*
	C. Lever	*The Daltons*
1852–4		*The Dodd Family Abroad*
1853	G. S. Hillard	*Six Months in Italy*
	G. Ruffini	*Lorenzo Benoni*
1854	anon.	*Angelo. A Romance of Modern Rome*
	R. Doyle	*The Foreign Tour of Messrs Brown, Jones, and Robinson*
	J. Ruskin	*Giotto and His Works at Padua*
	G. Sand	*Adriani*
1854–5	W. M. Thackeray	*The Newcomes*
1855	R. Browning	*Men and Women*
	G. Ruffini	*Dr Antonio* (Edinburgh)
	G. Sand	*Les Maioliques Florentines*
	W. M. Thackeray	*The Rose and The Ring*
	N. Wiseman	*Fabiola; Or, The Church of The Catacombs*
1856	J. R. Beste	*Modern Society in Rome*
	E. B. Browning	*Aurora Leigh*
	A. Manning	*Tasso and Leonora*
	J. H. Newman	*Callista, A Sketch of The Third Century*
	Mrs Ogilvy	*Poems of Ten Years*
	J. Ruskin	*Modern Painters*, vol. iii
	A. C. Swinburne	[*Ode To Mazzini*, pub. 1909]
	T. A. Trollope	*The Girlhood of Catherine of Medici*
	G. Sand	*Histoire de Ma Vie*
1857		*La Daniella*
	C. Dickens	*Little Dorrit*
	T. Doubleday	*The Eve of St Mark's. A Romance of Venice*
	C. G. Hamilton	*The Exiles of Italy*
	G. P. R. James	*Leonora d' Orco*
	C. Lever	*The Fortunes of Glencore*
	J. Ruskin	*A Joy For Ever*
1858		*Cambridge Inagural Address*
	G. Eliot	*Mr Gilfil's Love Story*, in *Scenes of Clerical Life* (Edinburgh)
1859	M. Arnold	*England and The Italian Question*
	H. F. Chorley	*Roccabella: A Tale of A Woman's Life*
	J. Ruskin	*The Italian Question*
	G. Sand	*Elle et Lui*
		Garibaldi
	T. A. Trollope	*Tuscany in 1849 and in 1859*
		A Decade of Italian Women
1860	anon.	*Angelo Sanmartino. A Tale of Lombardy in 1859* (Edinburgh)
	E. B. Browning	*Poems Before Congress*
	J. Burckhardt	*Die Cultur der Renaissance in Italien* (Basel; Eng. tr. 1878)
	N. Hawthorne	*The Marble Faun*
	C. E. Norton	*Notes of Study and Travel in Italy* (Boston)

	M. Roberts	*Mademoiselle Mori: A Tale of Modern Rome*
	G. Ruffini	*Lavinia*
	G. Sand	*Constance Verrier*
	T. A. Trollope	*Filippo Strozzi*
1860–3	A. C. Swinburne	[*Lucretia Borgia*, ed. R. Hughes (London, 1942)]
1861	I. Blagden	*Agnes Tremorne*
	M. Braddon	*Garibaldi and Other Poems*
	P. Fitzgerald	*Roman Candles*
	P. Ireton	*The Broken Troth: a Tale of Village Life in Tuscany*
	C. Lever	*One of them*
	C. Reade	*The Cloister and the Hearth*
	D. G. Rosetti	*The Early Italian Poets, together with Dante's 'Vita Nova'*
	N. Wiseman	*A few Flowers from the Roman Campagna*
	T. Trollope	*Social Aspects of the Italian Revolution*
	T. A. Trollope	*Paul the Pope and Paul the Friar*
		La Beata
1862		*Marietta*
		A Lenten Journey in Umbria and the Marches
	E. B. Browning	*Last Poems*
	A. H. Clough	*Amours de Voyage*
	G. Fullerton	*Rose Leblance*
	J. Ruskin	*Unto this Last*
	H. B. Stowe	*Agnes of Sorrento*
1863	I. Blagden	*The Cost of a Secret*
	G. Eliot	*Romola*
	Mrs Gaskell	*An Italian Institution*
	A. Manning	*The Duchess of Trajetto*
	G. Ruffini	*Vincenzo*
	W. W. Story	*Roba di Roma*
	J. A. Symonds	*The Renaissance* (Oxford)
	A. Trollope	*Tales of all Countries*, 2nd Series
	T. A. Trollope	*Giulio Malatesta*
	G. J. Whyte-Melville	*The Gladiators: a Tale of Roma and Judaea*
1864	W. Bramley-Moore	*The Six Sisters of the Valleys*
	R. Browning	*Dramatis Personae*
	J. A. Crowe & G. B. Cavalcaselle	*A New History of Painting in Italy*
	A. Jameson	*History of our Lord as Exemplified in Works of Art*
	G. Meredith	*Emilia in England* (later called *Sandra Belloni*)
	J. H. Newman	*Apologia Pro Vita Sua*
	C. C. Perkins	*Tuscan Sculptors*
	T. A. Trollope	*Beppo the Conscript*
1864–5	C. Lever	*Cornelius O' Dowd*
1865	A. H. Clough	*Dipsychus*
	A. Manning	*Selvaggio: A Tale of Italian Country Life*
	T. A. Trollope	*A History of the Commonwealth of Florence*

1866	T. A. Trollope	*Gemma*
	W. D. Howells	*Venetian Life*
	G. Meredith	*Correspondence from the Seat of War in Italy*
	Ouida	*Chandos*
	A. Trollope	*Travelling Sketches*
1867	W. D. Howells	*Italian Journeys* (New York)
	G. Meredith	*Vittoria*
	Ouida	*Idalia*
	A. C. Swinburne	*A Song of Italy*
1868		*Siena*
		Notes on Designs of the Old Masters at Florence
	M. Arnold	*Schools and Universities on the Continent*
	C. C. Perkins	*Italian Sculptors*
	C. T. Ramage	*The Nooks and Byways of Italy* (Liverpool)
	W. W. Story	*Graffiti d' Italia*
	T. A. Trollope	*Lenora Casaloni*
1868–9	R. Browning	*The Ring and the Book*
1869	G. Fullerton	*Mrs Gerald's Niece*
	H. King	*Aspromonte*
	M. Twain	*The Innocents Abroad*
1870	B. Disraeli	*Lothair*
	Ouida	*Puck*
	D. G. Rossetti	*Poems*
	T. A. Trollope	*A Siren*
	H. James	*Travelling Companions*
1871	J. A. Crowe &	*History of Painting in*
	G. B. Cavalcaselle	*North Italy*
	N. Hawthorne	*Passages from the French and Italian Notebooks*
	H. James	*At Isella*
	A. C. Swinburne	*Songs before Sunrise*
1871–2	G. Eliot	*Middlemarch*
1871–84	J. Ruskin	*Fors Clavigera*
1872	S. Butler	*Erewhon*
	M. Healy	*A Summer's Romance*
	J. A. Symonds	*An Introduction to the Study of Dante*
		The Renaissance of Modern Europe
		Twenty-Three Sonnets from Michelangelo
1873		*Studies of the Greek Poets*
	A. Austin	*Rome or Death!* (Edinburgh)
	G. Gissing	*Ravenna*
	H. King	*The Disciples*
	Ouida	*Pascarèl*
	W. Pater	*Studies in the History of the Renaissance*
	H. James	*The Madonna of the Future*
1874		*The Last of the Valerii*
		Adina
	W. D. Howells	*A Foregone Conclusion* (Boston)
	D. G. Rossetti	*Dante and his Circle*
	J. A. Symonds	*Sketches in Italy and Greece*

1875	F. Elliot	*The Italians*
	H. James	*Benvolio*
		Roderick Hudson (Boston)
		Transatlantic Sketches (Boston)
	Ouida	*Signa*
	W. W. Story	*Nero*
1875–7	J. Ruskin	*Mornings in Florence*
1875–86	J. A. Symonds	*The Renaissance in Italy*
1876	A. Austin	*The Human Tragedy* (2nd ed.)
	R. Browning	*Pachiarotto*
	G. Eliot	*Daniel Deronda* (Edinburgh)
	R. Monckton Milnes	*Poetical Works*
	J. A. Symonds	*Studies of the Greek Poets, Second Series*
	T. A. Trollope	*The Papal Conclaves. as they were and as they are*
	Ouida	*In a Winter City*
1877		*Ariadne. the Story of a Dream*
	G. Sand	*Nouvelles Lettres d' un Voyageur*
	W. W. Story	*Castle St Angelo and the Evil Eye*
	T. A. Trollope	*Life of Pius the Ninth*
		A Peep Behind the Scenes at Rome
	O. Wilde	*The Tomb of Keats*
	J. Ruskin	*Guide to the Venetian Academy* (Venice)
1877–84		*St Mark's Rest*
1878	J. A. Symonds	*Shelley*
		Many Moods
		The Sonnets of Michelangelo Buonarroti and Tommaso Campanella
	W. D. Howells	*The Lady of the Aroostook* (Boston)
	H. James	*Daisy Miller* (New York)
	Ouida	*Friendship*
	O. Wilde	*Ravenna* (Oxford)
1879	J. A. Symonds	*Sketches and Studies in Italy*
1880	V. Lee	*Tuscan Fairy Tales*
		Studies of the Eighteenth Century in Italy
	Ouida	*Pipistrello*
	J. A. Symonds	*New and Old*
	M. Twain	*A Tramp Abroad*
1880–3	S. Butler	[*The Way of all Flesh*, ed. R. A. Streatfeild (1903)]
1881	A. Austin	*Savonarola. A Tragedy*
	W. D. Howells	*A Fearful Responsibility* (Boston)
	H. James	*Portrait of a Lady*
	J. H. Shorthouse	*John Inglesant. A Romance*
	T. A. & F. E. Trollope	*Homes and Haunts of the Italian Poets*
	O. Wilde	*Poems*
	Ouida	*A Village Commune*
1882		*In Maremma*

	S. Butler	*Alps and Sanctuaries*
	A. C. Carr	*Lucrezia and other Stories*
	J. A. Symonds	*Anima Figura*
1882–3	H. W. Longfellow	*Michelangelo*
	O. Wilde	[*The Duchess of Padua* (pub. 1908)]
1883	F. Alexander	*Story of Ida*
	F. Hueffer	*Italian and other Studies*
	H. James	*Portraits of Places*
	V. Lee	*Belcaro*
		Ottilie
	C. C. Perkins	*Historical Handbook of Italian Sculpture*
	J. A. Symonds	*Italian Byways*
1884	A. C. Carr	*La Fortunina*
	F. M. Crawford	*To Leeward*
		A Roman Singer
	F. Elliot	*The Red Cardinal*
	V. Lee	*The Countess of Albany*
		Miss Brown (Edinburgh)
	J. A. Symonds	*Vagabunduli Libellus*
		Wine, Women and Song
1884–5	F. Alexander	*Roadside Songs of Tuscany*
1885	W. W. Astor	*Valentino* (New York)
	W. D. Howells	*Indian Summer* (Edinburgh)
	W. Pater	*Marius The Epicurean*
	W. W. Story	*Poems*
	A. C. Swinburne	*Marino Faliero*
	R. C. Trench	*Poems*, vol. i (New ed.)
1885–6	J. Ruskin	*Praeterita*
1886	M. Corelli	*Vendetta!*
	J. W. Graham	*Neaera. A Tale of Ancient Rome*
	W. D. Howells	*Tuscan Cities* (Edinburgh)
	H. James	*The Princess Casamassima*
	V. Lee	*Baldwin*
	Ouida	*Don Gesualdo*
	M. Robinson	*An Italian Garden*
	W. W. Story	*Fiammetta. A Summer Idyll*
1887	F. M. Crawford	*Marzio's Crucifix*
		Saracinesca
	W. D. Howells	*Modern Italian Poets. Essays and Versions* (Edinburgh)
	V. Lee	*Juvenilia*
	T. A. Trollope	*What I Remember*
1887–9	F. Alexander	*Christ's Folk in the Apennines*
1888	S. Butler	*Ex Voto*
	H. James	*Louisa Pallant*
		The Aspern Papers
	J. A. Symonds (tr.)	*Life of Benvenuto Cellini*
1889	W. W. Astor	*Sforza* (New York)
	R. Browning	*Asolando*

	F. M. Crawford	*Sant' Ilario*
	W. Pater	*Appreciations*
1890	H. B. Fuller	*The Chevalier of Pensieri-Vani* (Boston)
	G. Gissing	*The Emancipated*
	V. Lee	*Hauntings*
	Ouida	*Ruffino*
	J. A. Symonds	*Essays Speculative and Suggestive*
	(tr.)	*Memoirs of Count Carlo Gozzi*
1891	A. Austin	*Narrative Poems*
	W. W. Story	*Excursions in Art and Letters*
	Ouida	*Santa Barbara*
1892		*The Tower of Taddeo*
	M. Braddon	*The Venetians*
	H. B. Fuller	*The Chatelaine of La Trinité*
	V. Lee	*Vanitas: Polite Stories*
	S. Butler	*The Humour of Homer* (Cambridge)
1893		*On the Trapanese Origin of the Odyssey* (Cambridge)
		L' origine siciliana dell' Odissea (Aci Reale)
	F. M. Crawford	*Pietro Ghisleri*
		Don Orsino
	J. A. Symonds	*Life of Michelangelo Buonarroti*
		In The Key of Blue
		The New Spirit
1893–4	O. Wilde	[*A Florentine Tragedy* (pub. 1908)]
1894	B. Berenson	*The Venetian Painters of the Renaissance* (New York)
	S. Butler	*Ancora sull' origine siciliana dell' Odissea* (Aci Reale)
	G. S. Godkin	*Il Mal Occhio. Or the Evil Eye*
	V. Lee	*Althea*
	Ouida	*The Silver Christ*
	Mrs H. Ward	*Marcella*
1895	F. M. Crawford	*Casa Braccio*
	G. Allen	*The Woman who Did*
	A. Hope	*The Chronicles of Count Antonio*
	V. Lee	*Renaissance Fancies and Studies*
	Ouida	*Views and Opinions*
	W. Pater	*Miscellaneous Studies*
	J. A. Symonds	*Giovanni Boccaccio as Man and Author*
1896	B. Berenson	*The Florentine Painters of The Renaissance* (New York)
	F. M. Crawford	*Taquisara*
	C. Grant	*Stories of Naples and the Camorra*
	H. Crackanthorpe	*Vignettes*
1897	B. Berenson	*The Central Italian Painters of the Renaissance* (New York)
	S. Butler	*The Authoress of the Odyssey*
	V. Lee	*Limbo and Other Essays*

	M. Roberts	*Niccolina Niccolini*
	A. Sergeant	*In Vallombrosa. A Sequence*
	F. M. Crawford	*Corleone: A Tale of Sicily*
1898		*Ave Roma Immortalis*
	Corvo	*Stories Toto Told me*
	A. Gallenga	*Thecla's View*
1899	R. Bagot	*A Roman Mystery*
	M. Hewlett	*Little Novels of Italy*
	W. D. Howells	*The Ragged Lady* (New York)
	V. Lee	*Genius Loci: Notes on Places*
	Ouida	*Strega and other Stories*
1900		*Critical Studies*
	F. M. Crawford	*The Rulers of the South*
	H. Harland	*The Cardinal's Snuff-Box*
	Mrs H. Ward	*Eleanor*
1901	T. H. H. Caine	*The Eternal City*
	M. Carmichael	*The Major-General. A Story of Modern Florence*
	Corvo	*In his own Image*
		Chronicles of the House of Borgia
	N. Douglas	*Nerinda*, in *Unprofessional Tales*
	G. Gissing	*By The Ionian Sea*
	E. Spender	*A Soldier for A Day: A Story of the Itàlian War of Independence*
	F. M. Crawford	*Marietta. A Maid of Venice*
1902		*Cecilia. A Story of Modern Rome*
	R. Bagot	*Donna Diana*
	Corvo	*[Don Renato. An Ideal Content*, ed. C. Woolf (London, 1963)]
	E. G. Gardner	*Desiderio. An Episode of the Renaissance*
	T. Hardy	*Poems of the Past and the Present*
	E. Wharton	*The Valley of Decision*
	H. James	*The Wings of the Dove*
1903		*William Wetmore Story and his Friends*
	F. M. Crawford	*The Heart of Rome*
	E. M. Forster	*Albergo Empedocle*
	G. Gissing	*The Private Papers of Henry Ryecroft*
	E. Spender	*The Law-Breakers*
	V. Lee	*Ariadne in Mantua* (Oxford)
1904		*Hortus Vitae*
		Pope Jocelyn and other Fantastic Tales
	Corvo	*Hadrian The Seventh*
	E. M. Forster	*The Story of a Panic*
	G. Gissing	*Veranilda*
	H. Harland	*My Friend Prospero*
1905	Corvo	*Don Tarquinio. A Kataleptic, Phantasmatic Romance*
	F. M. Crawford	*Southern Italy and Sicily*
		Gleanings from Venetian History
	E. M. Forster	*Where Angels Fear to Tread* (Edinburgh)

	V. Lee	*The Enchanted Woods and other Essays on the Genius of Places*
1906		*The Spirit of Rome*
		Sister Benvenuta and the Christ Child
	F. M. Crawford	*A Lady of Rome*
1908		*Stradella*
	E. M. Forster	*A Room with a View*
	W. D. Howells	*Roman Holidays and others* (New York)
	V. Lee	*Gospels of Anarchy*
		The Sentimental Traveller
1909		*Laurus Nobilis*
	Corvo	[*The Desire and Pursuit of the whole. A Romance of Modern Venice* (pub. New York, 1953)]
	H. James	*Italian Hours*
1910	R. Turner	*Count Florio and Phyllis K*
1911	A. Austin	*Autobiography*
	N. Douglas	*Siren Land*
1912	T. Mann	*Der Tod in Venedig* (Munchen)
1913	Corvo	*An Ossuary of the North Lagoon; on Cascading into the Canal;* and *Venetian Courtesy*, in *Blackwood's*, vols cxciii, cxciv
1914	V. Lee	*The Tower of Mirrors and other Essays on the Spirit of Places*
1915	N. Douglas	*Old Calabria*
	D. H. Lawrence	*The Rainbow*
1916		*Twilight in Italy*
		Amores
1917		*Look! we have Come through!*
	N. Douglas	*South Wind*
1918	H. Adams	*The Education of Henry Adams* (Boston)
	D. H. Lawrence	*New Poems*
1919	Tony Cyriax	*Among Italian Peasants*
1920	E. M. Forster	*The Story of the Siren*
	D. H. Lawrence	*Women in Love* (New York) ·
		The Lost Girl
1921	N. Douglas	*Alone*
	D. H. Lawrence	*Sea and Sardinia* (New York)
		Movements in European History
1922		*Aaron's Rod*
1923		*Birds, Beasts and Flowers*
	(tr.)	*Mastro-Don Gesualdo*
1924	L. Golding	*Sunward*
	P. Lubbock	*Roman Pictures*
	S. Sitwell	*Southern Baroque Art*
1925	O. Sitwell	*Discursions on Travel, Art and Life*
	J. Conrad	*Suspense*
	N. Douglas	*Experiments*
	L. Golding	*Sicilian Noon*
	D. H. Lawrence (tr.)	*Little Novels of Sicily* (New York)

	A. Huxley	*Those Barren Leaves*
	V. Lee	*Golden Keys and Other Essays on The Genius Loci*
1926	D. H. Lawrence	*Sun*
1927	C. Mackenzie	*Vestal Fire*
1928	D. H. Lawrence	*Lady Chatterley's Lover* (Florence)
	(tr.)	*Cavalleria Rusticana and Other Stories*
1929		*Pansies*
	(tr.)	*The Story of Dr Manente* (Florence)
1930	N. Douglas	*Capri: Materials For A Description of The Island* (Florence)
1931		*Summer Islands*
1932	D. H. Lawrence	*Etruscan Places*
		Letters, ed. A. Huxley

Index